2 April 1992

THE WAY MEN THINK

With love on your 11th AA
birthday — for a man who
does, indeed, think.

You bring me joy.

Judy.

THE WAY MEN THINK

Intellect, Intimacy and the Erotic Imagination

Liam Hudson & Bernadine Jacot

YALE UNIVERSITY PRESS

NEW HAVEN & LONDON · 1991

Designed by Robert Baldock

Set in Linotronic Bembo by SX Composing Limited, Essex, England
Printed and bound in Great Britain by Billing and Sons, Ltd., Worcester.

Library of Congress Cataloging-in-Publication Data

Hudson, Liam.
    The way men think: intellect, intimacy and the erotic imagination /
    by Liam Hudson and Bernadine Jacot.
       p.   cm.
    Includes bibliographical references and index.
    ISBN 0-300-04997-8
    1. Men–Psychology.   2. Intellect.   3. Sex (Psychology)
I. Jacot, Bernadine, II. Title.
BF692.5.H83   1992
155.3'32–dc20
                                    91-21918
                                    CIP

CONTENTS

Illustrations by Bernadine Jacot

ACKNOWLEDGEMENTS

The idea of the male 'wound' first occurred to us in the late 1960s, in the course of a study of marriage among academics. For reasons of confidentiality, this was not published, but the present book draws on the material we gathered then, and we want to thank our respondents for what they told us. More recently, the idea has been discussed by members of the research seminar at the Tavistock Clinic; and a number of friends have been kind enough to read earlier versions of what was to become the present text: Bernard Barnett, John Broadbent, Roger Dean, Robert Hale, Peter Hildebrand, Anthony Storr and Michael Wright. Their comments have been invaluable. The responsibility for the faults of what we have finally produced remains, of course, our own.

Acknowledgement is made to Kingsley Amis and Penguin Books for permission to reprint 'A Point of Logic' from *British Poetry Since 1945*, edited by E. Lucie-Smith.

London   L.H.
May 1991   B.J.

This is a book about the imaginative lives of men. Members of both sexes can properly lay claim, of course, to soaring powers of fantasy and invention. We focus on those of men because the male imagination displays a characteristic bias, spin or twist which we believe we can explain.

Briefly, at the very outset of life, male and female children follow the same developmental path. But early in the growth of the foetus, the male diverges physically from the pattern which, until then, both have shared. Similarly, early in childhood, the male *separates psychologically*. For the male, this splitting off creates a source of unease we call the *male 'wound'*. The special interest of this wound, from our own point of view, is that it introduces a permanent element of dislocation into the lives of one sex, but not the other. Once experienced, *the wound generates needs and tensions in the male mind for which there is no direct female equivalent.*

On the question of the wound's origins, our own thoughts sit comfortably with those of other writers who have considered the matter over the last twenty-five years or so. Our interest, though, is in long-term consequences: the influence the wound exerts on the way adult men think, and the explanatory power and range that the idea of the wound proves to possess when applied to the male life span. The existence of the wound, we believe, turns the male of the species into a creature *driven*. We see it as the source of the imaginative energy men characteristically display; and as explaining the forms of imaginative expression the male mind typically adopts. The idea of the wound is particularly helpful, we find, in illuminating men's tendency to conceive of people as though they were inanimate, and of inanimate objects as though they were people. This division within the male mind has in the past been seen by both medically-minded psychoanalysts and sociologically-minded feminists as inherently distorting or stunting.[1] While accepting – in fact, insisting – that the wound creates patterns of cost and benefit, we claim that, in their normal, non-pathological form, these fuel significant parts of our culture, and that incalculable benefits accrue. Rather than a straightforward contrast between the healthy and the warped, what one faces, in other words, are configurations of personal disposition, need and fantasy in which strengths and weaknesses are delicately counterbalanced.

The discussion of male characteristics, the whole topic of sex and gender, is a fraught one. For that reason, we begin with questions of background and context. Chapter 1 looks at the reformers who have moved us, in the course of the last hundred years, from a position of ignorance about maleness and femaleness towards greater intellectual freedom. These remarkable men and women were visionaries; but they were also individuals with private daemons to satisfy. As a result, the picture of human nature they collectively propounded was one which muddles together science and persuasion in deeply insidious ways. Consequently, we have been at pains to launch our own account in terms which are consciously formal and schematic. What we want to offer is a framework within which discriminations about the various aspects of a given person's maleness or femaleness can easily be made. Of the three chapters which make up 'Swings and Roundabouts', Chapter 2 sets out just such a framework. This shows how 'choices' which are in themselves simple can give rise to 'solutions' which are ones of subtlety and nuance. Chapter 3 – the hub of our narrative – describes the wound itself in more detail, spelling out the respects in which it informs the small boy's imaginative life; and Chapter 4 looks at the family context which subsequently shapes and qualifies his imaginative expression.

The middle section of our narrative, 'The Stamping Ground', looks at the consequences of these childhood events in the lives of adult men. Chapters 5 and 6 examine the tendency of men to dominate certain professions, science and technology especially. It is our claim that science and technology are the natural venue for the kind of imagination men possess; and they are so because men (and especially 'male' men) tend to invest the inanimate with passionate emotional significance. Confusions between the categories of *person* and of *thing* are inseparable from this passionate investment; and it is this confusion, in turn, which underlies the subject matter of Chapter 7. There we argue that men's virtual monopoly of sexual behaviour which is criminal or perverse is itself part of the wound's legacy.

We see the wound's influence in the spheres of science and technology as relatively straightforward, and similarly its influence in the
field of sexual perversion. Its impact in the creative arts, though,
must be spelt out with more care. The wound leads certain men not
simply to idealise the women who exert an erotic fascination over
them, but to want to 'petrify' them; that is to say, to make them permanent by turning them into art. Of the two chapters in our final
section, 'The Other Side of the Coin', Chapter 8 gathers together the
theory appropriate to this enterprise – in effect, the rudiments of a
psychology of aesthetics. Chapter 9 looks at the life and work of
three artists and the women who inspired them, and at the startling
paradoxes and reversals with which they found themselves beset.

Our narrative is psychological in character and inspiration, but
also springs from a neighbourly relation with psychoanalysis. It
assumes that each mind has an 'architecture', and that this has an enduring influence on the life led by the individual in question.[2] The
friendliness of this connection in no sense excludes us from others,
however; particularly with biology, and with the sense of the human
organism as a physical apparatus of great delicacy, evolving and
adapting itself according to intelligible rules. Arguments adjacent to
our own have been advanced, too, from within other disciplines –
notably, feminist scholarship.[3] Unfortunately, the knowledge of
specialists in any one field about what is going on in fields belonging
to their neighbours is bound in practice to be inexpert. Among feminists, as among psychoanalysts, biologists, sociologists and philosophers, we are outsiders; we have the wrong tribal 'smell', and our
access to the specialised understandings of those fields is never better
than partial. We do our best to clarify the relation of our own arguments to those of our neighbours by means of footnotes. This should
in no sense be seen as a relegation: our footnotes contain, we feel,
some of our best material. Our borrowings, though, are bound at
times to strike insiders not just as amateurish or light-fingered, but as
positively larcenous. For this impression, we can only apologise in
advance.

In zones as turbulent as those surrounding sex and gender, the
danger of slipping from fact into prejudice or false consciousness is
never far away. There is the danger, too, of being seen to have
slipped even when you have not. In as much as we have insight into
them, our own intentions are even-handed. While our narrative
centres on men and the qualities of mind they display, there is no
assumption of male superiority or inferiority; no hint that men are

either more or less interesting than women, or that the psychology of the male is either more or less fully evolved than that of the female. In particular, there is no implication that the achievements of one sex ought to be valued more highly than those of the other. We see ourselves as contributing, in other words, to the natural history, not the politics, of sex and gender.[4]

There are related issues over which academics are just as eager to shed one another's blood, and it is as well to be clear about these in advance too. We are suggesting neither that the wound is 'innate', nor that it establishes a species of 'grammar' to which all imaginative expression in men conforms. On the contrary, we see the wound as an emergent property of the interaction between forces which are variously biological, psychological and social; and as constituting for that reason a topic about which the various human sciences – biological, psychological and social – are well placed to cooperate.[5] We are equally clear in our minds over the question of difference. Far from being apologetic about differences between the sexes, our argument places these at the centre of our lives, and treats their acknowledgement as a source of imaginative vitality. It is from the play of emotionally charged similarities and differences that the fabric of our own argument grows.

Lastly, there is the question of presentation. In our case, this is more important than it might seem. The conventional format for an argument like ours is a statement of theory, followed by examples which illustrate the theory's implications. Our own policy deviates from this. We are unhappy, in the first place, with the subservient position which the conventional format imposes on evidence about particular individuals and the lives they lead. Such evidence should exist in a state of tension with theory, we believe, and – used without embarrassment, *ad hominem* – should be allowed to answer theory back. Equally, we are reluctant to allow a single case or a handful of congruent cases to exert too persuasive an influence. Accounts of individual lives should be *various*, standing awkwardly not only with regard to theory but with regard to one another. In what follows, we use theory to clarify the movement of the imagination as it seeks to make choices and reconcile contradictions; but at the same time, allow scientific experiments, statistics, clinical case material, biographical and autobiographical vignettes, paintings, sculptures, photographs, poems, fiction, 'faction' and anecdote to rub shoulders with one another on equal terms, each in its own right.[6] At no point is our choice arbitrary or capricious, but if it seems so, this is a price we are willing to pay. For where insight arises, it does so from 'conversations', we would want to claim, not just between theory and evidence, nor simply between bodies of evidence of different kinds, but between the experience embodied in a text and that enjoyed by the reader.[7]

There is the danger that our method of presentation will be seen as fostering an easy-going free-for-all, in which distinctions between truth and falsity are blurred or even abandoned – in science, personal relations, and the arts alike. Our intention is the opposite of this: to show that the exercise of the imagination and questions of truth are necessary to one another, and that, within the life and work of each individual, reconciliations between the two must somehow be reached.

CHAPTER 1

THE GENDER INDUSTRY

THE AIM OF this chapter is to set the scene; not to tell the story of the wound, but to clear the ground and make its telling possible. Much of what we have to say later is formal, and we want to explain why, expecially at the present point in the gender industry's evolution, this formality is appropriate.

Unquestionably, the field is a turbulent one, and it is so for a simple reason: analysis has been invaded by polemic, and vice versa. The scientist who seems to be doing research in a disinterested and even-handed fashion is often using it to promote prejudices about how men and women should behave. Conversely, those whose instincts are political have always found it helpful to disguise their polemic as analysis. The task of disentangling one venture from the other – the scientist's from the reformer's – is complicated by the presence of a third figure, the clinician: the person professionally committed to distinguish the healthy from the morbid or perverse. Sometimes, the roles of scientist, reformer and clinician are played by different individuals; often, though, they compete for the audience's eye within a single mind and within a single sentence. As if these difficulties were not enough, they are overlaid by the academy's cut and thrust: the symbolic war for legitimacy (and funding) waged against one another by members of the various academic disciplines. Far from blustering cynically, many of these warriors passionately believe in their own versions of the truth, and see those who oppose them as deeply morally and personally flawed.

In the resulting turmoil, there are foci of exceptional sensitivity, where issues of fact, justice and clinical judgement are ceaselessly in conflict. This is pre-eminently so in the case of what is *normal* or *natural*. The ensuing battles are fought out in terms of ideas that seem at first sight highly technical, but that prove to be heavily freighted with hidden meaning. Among these, one of the most influential, historically speaking, has been the claim that human beings are in fact bisexual. The eventual truth or falsity of such a claim, it goes without saying, is in no sense dependent on the nature of the private life led by the individual making it. Nevertheless, it is part of the psychologist's task to unpack such ideas, showing why they exert the grip on the imagination they do. What that unpacking reveals, time and again, are individuals in the grip of urgent sexual anxieties – ones that their research and advocacy have helped hold at bay. In psychology, no less than in other walks of life, in other words, the public and private are interwoven. There is nothing inherently shocking or improper in this, but it should make one wary.

THE VISION OF BISEXUALITY

If the folk psychology of our time has a dominant theme, it is that the conventional maleness of males and the conventional femaleness of females are distortions imposed upon us by a repressive culture. The maleness of women and the femaleness of men are assumed to be hidden landscapes, waiting to be rediscovered. If we are to be personally fulfilled, we are encouraged to believe, we must 'get in touch with' those parts of ourselves that the culture has 'conditioned' us to deny. This belief in bisexuality is popularly allied to notions of tolerance: the belief, often passionately held, that the right of an individual to deviate from orthodoxy must be protected, in the sexual sphere as in any other; and, accordingly, that the needs of sexual minorities must be accepted as normal and natural in just the way that those of the majority are. The view of human beings as bisexual is associated, in other words, with an ethic of mutual acceptance and trust. Within this, tolerance turns to censure only if the sexual practices in question are seen as harmful for non-sexual reasons – if they are 'abusive', say, or infringe the rights of children.

Yet when one looks for convincing evidence in support of the bisexual vision, this proves surprisingly hard to find. It is plain that many boys and girls pass through a homosexual phase before settling as adults into a heterosexual pattern; that many adults discover unforeseen facets of their own natures, men finding themselves 'female' in unexpected ways, women finding themselves 'male'; and that some adults of both sexes are more nearly androgynous than others. It is also true that hermaphrodites exist; and that, with appropriate surgery, a tiny minority of people have changed sex. But there is no research showing that, in the erotic sphere of their lives, adults of either sex normally have available to them behavioural repertoires and systems of fantasy radically at variance with the ones already established. It simply is not the case, for example, that most adult male homosexuals can easily be encouraged to desire women. On the contrary, research suggests that the eventual pattern of each individual's erotic nature is determined quite early in life; and that the boundaries in terms of which these patterns are defined are often stubbornly resistant to change.

So while the idea of our bisexuality presents itself to us in the late twentieth century as a fact of life, substantiated in all essentials by scientific research, its true status, in the technical, anthropological sense, seems to be more nearly that of a *myth*. Neither, true nor untrue, it belongs to the class of beliefs that Lévi-Strauss discusses in the context of primitive societies, and that serve, he claims, to resolve the structural tensions and contradictions of those societies in symbolic form. It is the kind of idea that we use in manoeuvring ourselves, individually and collectively, from a position of acute discomfort into one in which our discomfort can be contained or ignored. (It is also the kind of idea from which, in more economically advanced societies, a great deal of money can be made. There exists a fully elaborated commerical apparatus, that of 'unisex', waiting to help our processes of self-discovery on their way.)

In the lives of the great pioneers, these discomforts seem often to have been specifically sexual. Marie Stopes, who courageously advocated birth control to a world desperately in need of it, suffered an unconsummated first marriage and a second little better; and her admirable good sense about birth control was offset by prejudices about the rights of the underprivileged to breed. It was she who said that 'there is no more immorality in the enjoyment of sexual intercourse, than in the enjoyment of mince pies (unless the pies are stolen)'. But she also believed that all of 'low-grade intelligence ought to be sterilized'.[1] Henry Havelock Ellis, too, was a great liberaliser. He has been claimed as one of the modern age's first real enthusiasts for sex; but it seems he was largely impotent, and that he was in his own terms a 'undinist'. That is to say, he found sexual excitement in being urinated upon; and perhaps could find it in no other way.[2] In such instances, the relation of private anxiety to public advocacy is crude. Much more subtly illuminative is the biography of Freud himself.

FREUD AND SEXUAL THEORY

In 1897, the turning point of his life, Freud was forty-one.[3] Apparently content with his wife Martha, he renounced sexual intercourse with her, his later comments about marriage strongly suggesting sexual boredom and even physical disgust:

> satisfying sexual intercourse in marriage takes place only for a few
> years; and we must subtract from this, of course, the intervals of
> abstention necessitated by regard for the wife's health. After these
> three, four or five years, the marriage becomes a failure in so far as
> it has promised the satisfaction of sexual needs. For all the devices
> hitherto invented for preventing conception impair sexual enjoy-
> ment, hurt the finer susceptibilities of both partners and even
> actually cause illness.... The spiritual disillusionment and bodily
> deprivation to which most marriages are thus doomed puts both
> partners back in the state they were in before their marriage, ex-
> cept for being the poorer by the loss of an illusion...[4]

The year before, Freud's father had died, and arguably it was this that had released Freud, as it had earlier released Darwin, to undertake his mature work. For, in 1897, he embarked on the self-analysis from which his theory of the unconscious sprang. He was to launch on the world a theory in which sexual energies were the centrally placed ones, and he was to do this with passionate conviction. His dominant preoccupation, though, remained one of control. 'We liberate sexuality through our treatment', he wrote, 'not in order that man may from now on be dominated by sexuality, but in order to make a suppression possible – a rejection of the instincts under the guidance of a higher agency.'[5]

The force of Freud's eventual conviction in sexual explanations was none the less startling. Jung first met him in 1907, when Freud was a little over fifty. 'There was no mistaking the fact that Freud was emotionally involved in his sexual theory to an extraordinary degree,' he later recalled. 'Anything that could not be directly interpreted as sexuality he referred to as "psychosexuality".' When Jung protested that, followed to its logical conclusion, this attitude reduced culture to a 'farce, the morbid consequence of repressed sexuality', Freud had assented. It was 'a curse of fate', Freud said, 'against which we are powerless to contend'. Three years later, the impression of excessive commitment was even stronger. 'My dear

Jung,' Freud had urged his colleague, 'promise me never to abandon the sexual theory. That is the most essential thing of all. You see, we must make a dogma of it, an unshakeable bulwark.' When Jung asked what the bulwark was against, Freud had replied: 'Against the black tide of mud... of occultism.'[6]

Many years earlier, in 1887, Freud had met an ear, nose and throat specialist, Wilhelm Fliess. Subsequently, they struck up an intimate friendship. The years between 1897 and 1900 were to be Freud's darkest, and during them the bond with Fliess was all-important. 'Your praise is nectar and ambrosia to me,' he wrote to Fliess.[7] He also wrote of the 'perhaps feminine' side of his nature which his friendship with Fliess satisfied; and, repeatedly, of the fervour with which he looked forward to their next meeting and of his longing to be united with Fliess.

Looking back, it is easy to depict Fliess as a dangerous crackpot, and to castigate Freud for his credulousness in taking to heart Fliess's beliefs. In 1895, through gross carelessness, Fliess had nearly killed one of Freud's patients, Emma Eckstein, in the course of operating on her nose. He left a half-metre strip of iodoform gauze in a sinus cavity; it became infected, and when it was removed, she nearly died of haemorrhage.[8] A month later, there was still so much bleeding that the ligation of the carotid artery was considered. 'Gloomy times,' wrote Freud to Fliess, 'unbelievably gloomy.' Meanwhile, Fliess was proving a prickly colleague. He demanded a formal retraction at the least hint of criticism from Freud, and was in a position, later, to insist on the deletion of any material from Freud's *The Interpretation of Dreams* that he found professionally compromising. Yet, subsequently, instead of shying away from his friend as anyone of good sense would, Freud more than once submitted his own nose to Fliess's knife, in the hope that the operation would cure him of arrhythmia. 'The Kepler of Biology' he was to call Fliess. His critical faculties, it seems, were completely numbed.

But these were also the years in which Freud did his most original work. He moved by means of his self-analysis from his earlier scientific preoccupations to *The Interpretation of Dreams*; and, in fact, there were good reasons why Freud should have chosen Fliess as his soul's mate. For Fliess was a forceful proponent of several influential theories in which sex played a key part. He believed in the principle of bisexuality; in biorhythms; in infantile sexuality; and in the theory that sexuality is closely linked to the sense of smell – and hence that emotional disorders of a sexual origin could be cured by operating on the turbinal bone of the nose. As Sulloway shows in *Freud, Biologist of the Mind*, certain of these ideas had respectable scientific pedigrees. Fliess's numerical system of human cycles was by no means as bizarre as subsequent critics were to make it seem. The same can be said of his theories about sex. In 1871, in *The Descent of Man*, Darwin had claimed that human beings were descended from lowly species like the ascidians, many of which 'have their sexes united in the same individual'. In some species the sexes were separate, but even among these 'the males never possess special organs for finding, securing, or charming the females, or for fighting with other males'.[9] Activity in such creatures was dependent on the cycles of the moon; and their sexual energies, the German evolutionary theorist and philosopher Ernst Haeckel had argued soon afterwards, must be triggered by chemotropisms – that is to say, by the primitive equivalent of the sense of smell.

When Fliess put these ideas to Freud in the 1890s, Freud's mind would already have been attuned to them. As a medical student, he had taken a course in evolutionary biology given by Carl Claus, who was engaged at that time in research on crustacea. Certain of these creatures, Claus had discovered, began their lives as males and ended them as females. Freud would have been struck by his professor's discovery; and, in turn, must have made a good impression on Claus. For it was through his professor's good offices that Freud went on to do research in Claus's new marine biology laboratory at Trieste; and it was there, under Claus's supervision, that he did his first published research, on the male sex organs of the eel. Freud's second important piece of research, one he was to treasure for the rest of his life, was on the spinal nerves of a primitive creature, the petromyzon. Not only is the petromyzon itself bisexual; it is a close relative of the ascidians which Darwin saw as man's distant ancestors.

Also important to men like Darwin, Haeckel, Claus, Fliess and Freud was the evidence of human embryology; the fact, particularly, that rudimentary internal ducts for both male and female reproductive systems are initially present in foetuses of both sexes, the inappropraite ones subsequently becoming vestigial under the influence of hormones like testosterone. It was plain, too, that hermaphrodites existed, albeit with the status of freaks; and that, occasionally, women showed every sign of turning into men, and vice versa. Krafft-Ebing had reported the spontaneous transformation at the age of thirty of a woman who grew a full beard, and de-

veloped hair on her abdomen and chest. There were signs of a progressive masculinisation of her genitals, she became aggressive and
her voice deepened.

In other words, Fliess's theory of bisexuality was an elaboration of
ideas then widely current; and while there ensued a rift between
Freud and Fliess which was to become permanent, the idea of bisexuality played an important part in Freud's subsequent theorising. It
also evolved. Modern psychoanalytic theory as a result sees bisexuality both as instinctual and as arising from the child's identification to
differing degrees with both parents. On the strength of these identifications, the child's awareness is assumed to be sexualised, a wide
range of behaviour and experience, at first sight non-sexual, being
treated as characteristic of one sex or the other. What is passive, intuitive and receptive is assumed to be inherently feminine; what is assertive, analytic and penetrative to be inherently male. These are
issues taken up again in Chapters 2 and 3.

ALFRED KINSEY AND THE POLICY OF COUNTING

The persuasive functions of research in the human sphere are strikingly evident in the life of another great pioneer, Alfred Kinsey.
Although their work could scarcely have been more dissimilar, one
sees in Kinsey's biography, as in Freud's, the same cross-currents of
rational argument and hidden impulse; and evidence, too, as it happens, of heart-felt attraction to a member of his own sex on the part
of a stably married, middle-aged man.[10]

Like Freud, Kinsey began life as a scientist. Though born nearly
forty years apart, the two men stand in many ways as paradigms of
the two cultures from which so much of modern pychology has
sprung. Both first-born sons, both with adoring mothers, both 'outsiders', one was the product of middle-class Jewish culture, the other
of the puritanical wing of the Protestant Church.

Kinsey's background was humble. His father had reached only the
eighth grade at night school, and his mother was less than fully literate. The household was strictly sabbatarian, and even the delivery of
milk on Sunday was forbidden. Despite his father's insistence that he
become an engineer, and the quarrels between them that resulted,
Kinsey developed a passion for natural history. Though suffering
curvature of the spine serious enough to keep him out of the army,

Kinsey was wholeheartedly committed to the outdoor life, and became one of America's first Eagle Scouts. He was unusually shy, it seems, and lacking in interest in the opposite sex; and later, as a college student, he remained devoutly religious. One day, when a fellow student confessed to him his guilt over masturbation, the two young men knelt in the dormitory together at Kinsey's suggestion, and prayed that his friend be given the strength of will to abstain.

Kinsey married the first young woman he dated – their honeymoon a camping trip – and in quick succession they produced four children. His academic gifts and determination led him from high school to Bowdoin College, from Bowdoin to Harvard, and from Harvard to a teaching post at Indiana University. There he established himself as an expert on the gall wasp, an insect the size of a small ant, the eggs of which, laid deep inside a tree's tissues, produce abnormal swellings or galls. An obsessive man, as taxonomists seem characteristically to be, Kinsey was to collect and classify some four million of these creatures in the course of his career; and, in his mid-thirties, he produced a major work about them, *The Gall Wasp Genus Cynips: A Study in the Origin of Species*. This was followed six years later by a second volume; together, these were received as serious contributions to natural history and genetic theory.

The appeal of the gall wasp eventually waned. Kinsey made his last field trip to collect them when he was forty-five. The previous summer, the university had placed him in charge of a new course on marriage; presumably on the grounds that such courses were the province of the biologist, but also, perhaps, because Kinsey had expressed an interest. Run on a non–credit basis, it was accompanied by individual consultations, the material of which was 'to be considered confidential', and 'not to be available to the disciplinary deans'. It was these private consultations that tilted open the lid of Pandora's box. Soon, Kinsey's field trips were in pursuit not of gall wasps but orgasms. Where once he had imposed his classificatory will on the parasites of oak trees, he now imposed it on events in bedrooms. First, he travelled to Chicago to gather information about homosexuality, divorce and big city prostitution. Later, he journeyed more widely. 'What I remember most', his collaborator Wardell Pomeroy says, 'from thousands of hours of interviewing, is the driving, driving, driving under the lash of Kinsey's determination to get more and more histories.' Kinsey always wanted 'just one more'.[11]

Kinsey's approach to each interview was one of inflexible conviction. 'He was determined to get sex information from people',

Pomeroy recalls, 'and he intended to get it no matter what obstacle might intervene.' Kinsey was also committed to strict standards of confidentiality, and, perhaps for this reason, found his informants forthcoming. Most seem to have found it intrinsically rewarding to make the hidden explicit; and some took the opportunity to unburden themselves of a lifetime's guilty secrets. But secret and previously hidden the information was, and his access to it placed Kinsey in a position of unrivalled power; something, Pomeroy believes, he enjoyed. On the Indiana campus alone, Pomeroy suggests, there were at least twenty professors with homosexual histories unknown to anyone other than Kinsey.

Kinsey's tone is in fact nowhere more level than it is in his treatment of the male homosexual. At a time when it was normal to damn homosexuality as unnatural and treat it as a crime, Kinsey spoke of it as just another facet of human variousness. If 37 per cent of American adults admit to some homosexual experience or other in the course of their lives, what rationale can there be, he patiently inquired, for laws against homosexuality – or, for that matter, against any other deviation from the sexual norm that is not illegal for quite separate reasons?

It was an essential feature of Kinsey's method that he should concern himself with 'outlets', a choice of format that removed sex at once from the realm of moral censure. If a man reported having an average of fifteen outlets a month, how these were achieved was, within Kinsey's scheme, a matter of purely technical interest. As a scientist, and more specifically as a taxonomist, his role was simply to categorise and count. In reality, of course, as Pomeroy makes obvious, Kinsey and his collaborators enjoyed the *frisson* of talking purely objectively about outlandish sexual practices. He recalls a journey he and Kinsey made to the south-west to take the history of a 'quiet, soft-spoken, self-effacing' 63-year-old, a 'college graduate who held a responsible government job'. This man had kept careful records of his sex life, and claimed to have had sexual relations with 600 pre-adolescent boys, 200 pre-adolescent girls, countless adults of both sexes, and animals of many species. He had set out a family tree going back to his grandparents, and of the 33 people in that tree he claimed to have had sexual relations with 17. It had been his grandmother who had introduced him to heterosexual intercourse, and his father who had introduced him to homosexuality. At one point in their lengthy interview, this man claimed to be able to masturbate to ejaculation in ten seconds 'from a flaccid start'. When his visitors expressed disbelief, he calmly demonstrated himself right and them wrong.

The notion that their informant might be systematically delusional or psychopathic does not seem to have crossed the investigators' minds. Nor is there any sign of anxiety on their part that he might have traumatised some of the pre-adolescents with whom he had sexual contact. Nor, if even a hundredth part of his claims were true, that he could have infected pre-adolescents of both sexes, post-adolescents of both sexes, certain relatives, and any number of animals of other species, with a wide variety of venereal diseases. The only indubitable fact Kinsey and Pomeroy had was that their informant could masturbate more quickly than they could. Yet they were content to take what he said at face value and to treat it as evidence, merely, of human exuberance and variety.

Kinsey's achievement, though, was not quite the disinterested feat of rationality it was made to seem. For – like Freud, like Havelock Ellis, like almost all the rest of us – he, too, had personal uneasinesses to accommodate. In his forties, it seems that he was deeply attached to a young colleague, Ralph Voris, who quite soon thereafter died. It is a feature of the research method Kinsey evolved that it would have absolved him from any guilt he might have felt about his love for Voris, and that it would have done so automatically, without argument. It is of interest, too, that – as with Freud – the preoccupation with sex as a field of inquiry became overriding for Kinsey only in middle age. Indeed, in Freud's case, it was only his late forties and early fifties, in the decade after the publication of *The Interpretation of Dreams*, that he began to use sexual explanations in ways that critics like Jung saw as obsessing and over-inclusive.[12]

'NORMALITY'

While both were deeply committed to the values of science, Kinsey and Freud pulled their audience in opposite directions, and did so nowhere more forcefully than over the question of 'normality'. Implicitly, Kinsey celebrated variety and was never censorious, itself an important moral position and a characteristically modern one. Freud in contrast explored sexuality with a view to controlling it. As a result, the standard of normality he offered the world – 'genitality' – was very exacting indeed. In Erik Erikson's well-known reformulation of Freud's vision, the utopia of genitality must include:

1 mutuality of orgasm
2 with a loved partner
3 of the other sex
4 with whom one is able and willing to share a mutual trust
5 and with whom one is able and willing to regulate the cycles of
   (a) work
   (b) procreation
   (c) recreation
6 so as to secure to the offspring, too, all the stages of a satisfactory development.[13]

There is no allowance here for partners of the same sex, partners who
are not loved, a variety of partners, or partners who are anonymous.
There are few of us, perhaps, who meet such a standard; but that, as
Freud would have pointed out, is not the issue. Genitality exists not
as a description of what we actually do in our cravenness and frailty,
but of the ideal towards which, in the interests of our own and subsequent generations, we ought to aim. It is a standard that lends our
intimate lives a significant (and significantly heterosexual) sense of
direction. To Kinsey, any such standard was arbitrary. To outward
appearance medical, and drawing on notions of health as opposed to
morbidity, what Freud's notion of genitality actually articulates, he
would have wanted to argue, are the conventional, middle-aged virtues. Far from softening prejudices towards sexual minorities and
alleviating the suffering members of those minorities experience, it
exacerbates both.

   In the decades since Kinsey produced his volumes of sexual statistics and Erikson reformulated the psychoanalytic Nirvana of genitality, we have become wary both of prescriptions and of prescribers'
claims to objectivity. The implicit challenge of orthodox psychoanalysis remains with us, even so. Some forms of intimate self-expression still seem more desirable – for lack of better terms, more
normal, healthy or natural – than others. Yet more seem bizarre or
sick. The distinction between moral and clinical judgement in psychology and psychiatry does not go away, in other words, because it
is difficult to articulate. (Is it right, for instance, to rape? Or to have
sexual intercourse with your own children? We are almost all agreed
that the answer is 'no'. But in reaching this judgement many of us remain unsure whether these acts are intrinsically wrong, or wrong for
other reasons: that they are violent assaults on the person, say, or infringe the rights of minors. It is wrong, then, to have intercourse

with sheep? Or with dead bodies? Or to have orgasms with your spouse while imagining acts of humiliation or cruelty? 'Yes', we want to say; and 'yes', even though, in the first case, the act may give pleasure to both parties; in the second, there is no one 'there' to object; and in the third nothing cruel 'really' happens. 'Philosopher's examples', the libertarian may protest, meaning that these instances are extreme or trivial. Not so, replies the orthodox psychoanalyst. What is more, if the libertarian admits that any one of these acts is inherently wrong, he is on a slippery slope. Where and why does he draw the line?)

MEAD-PLUS-MARX

By the 1950s, paperback psychology took the idea of our bisexual natures for granted, using it to suggest that we could each lead richer lives if we were more androgynous, allowing the opposite sides of our nature fuller expression. These views were seen as sanctioned by the theory of the relation between bisexuality, repression and the unconscious popularly attributed to Freud: the belief that the individual's dominant sex represses the mental representation of the subordinate sex – with the result that the nucleus of the unconscious in the male is 'female', and that in the female 'male'. Although Freud was to repudiate it, the influence of this simple formulation remained considerable.[14] Such claims were seen to be all of a piece with a more broadly rational and progressive attitude to life: one that endorsed birth control, sex outside marriage, the abolition of censorship and capital punishment, the acceptance of homosexuality as natural, the relaxation of parental discipline, the abandonment of prescriptive methods of education – a broad array of beliefs and admonitions that centred on the right of the individual to be rid of authoritarian nagging and censure.

The idea of human bisexuality fused in turn with a different but complementary notion then taking shape in the minds of sociologists and anthropologists. Far from being reflections of the innate, social scientists were now beginning to insist, the categories 'male' and 'female' are themselves wholly culturally determined. They are categories foisted upon us by the cultures into which we happen to be born. Especially influential in this respect were the anthropological writings of Margaret Mead. In *Sex and Temperament*, published as early as 1935, she had already expressed herself with memorable clarity. Human nature was, she claimed, 'almost unbelievably malle-able'. As a consequence, 'we may say that many, if not all, of the per-sonality traits which we have called masculine or feminine are as lightly linked to sex as are the clothing, the manners, and the form of head-dress that a society at a given period assigns to either sex.'[15]

Following Mead's lead, textbooks of the 1960s made play with the contrasts between three primitive peoples, the Arapesh, the Mundu-gumor and the Tchambuli.[16] The Arapesh, it was claimed, were a people among whom both men and women act as we would expect women to act. The Mundugumor were a people among whom both men and women act as we would expect men to act. And the Tchambuli were a people among whom our own expectations are re-versed, the men acting as women and the women as men. The per-suasive force of such examples was considerable, and few were in a position to discover that the evidence about primitive tribes pointed in a quite different direction.[17] In fact, it indicated that while there are any number of economically primitive cultures in which it is the women, not the men, who carry heavy burdens, there is not one in which the women wage war while the men look after the home. More than that: the symbolically significant activity of fashioning weapons seems in every primitive culture known to anthropology to be largely or exclusively a male preserve. Far from the maleness or femaleness of an activity being biologically arbitrary, in other words, the ethnographic evidence suggests that the use of these categories is in fact biologically rooted very directly indeed: first, in a social domi-nation of women by men based on differences in physical strength; and, second, in two sex-linked preoccupations – of men with violence and of women with nurture.

Such embarrassments notwithstanding, the belief that maleness and femaleness are wholly culturally determined gathered weight; and, in due course, merged with another, even more radical one. Loosely speaking, this was Marxist in origin. It amounted to the claim that, in more economically advanced cultures if not in more primitive ones, sex roles could be re-engineered. Pertinent distinctions – the fact that sexual difference does not entail sexual inequality, and that sexual inequality does not entail sexual oppression – were sub-merged within a belief which was at once an assertion and a banner: women need remain different from men only as long as they are bemused by the conventional and self-serving rationales that men themselves have created.[18]

This new brand of social science – 'Mead-plus-Marx' – was to exert a magnetic attraction on the minds of students on both sides of the Atlantic; and, rivalled only by behaviourism in psychology, it became the academy's great success story in the post-war years of prosperity and expansion. The appeal was not just to heart and mind, but to the sense of style. Like behaviourism, what Mead-plus-Marx offered its adherents was a belief that was exhilarating in its simplicity, and as modern in its own sphere as Le Corbusier's architecture. It was also a belief backed by a brilliantly successful argumentative technique. Rather than standing apart from the reformers' assault on convention, anthropologists and sociologists often enlisted as its shock-troops. In interdisciplinary seminars and colloquia, their impact was formidable. Doubters, especially those who appeal to 'the facts', were assumed to be both denying self-evident truths, and revealing attitudes that were morally repugnant. The resulting onslaught was one few conventionally educated academics were equipped to withstand. It was heated, and it exploited a double ambiguity: simultaneously factual and moral, it occurred within a framework which denied that either facts or morals exist.

Subsequently, this attack on the biological foundations of sex and gender became more radical still; and, in the hands of poststructuralists, it now focused on the idea of the person, even on that of the body itself. Within this new frame of reference, men and women cease to be mammals with stable and in some cases genetically determined, hormonally mediated characteristics. Their bodies cease to be envelopes of flesh and blood. Both are now the sites of inherently unstable, irreducibly ambiguous games of signification. The aim is to 'decenter' our culture's 'phallogocentrism'. Bodily categories are to be 'denaturalized' and 'resignified', and allowed to proliferate subversively 'beyond the binary frame'.[19]

But if the style is new, the purposes are familiar. In part, the intention is genuinely scholarly, a question of grasping the truth amid appearances. In part, it is that of removing the last hint of opprobrium from practices or states of being – homosexual ones, for example – seen in the past as abnormal or unnatural. In part, it is to prosecute the wars of legitimacy which social scientists wage unrelentingly against the supposed authority of the natural sciences. For, strange though this may seem, many able philosophers and sociologists now believe that scientific explanations can never be more than stories, and that notions of scientific 'fact' and 'discovery' are merely aids which scientists use in heightening the dramatic effect of their own theatrical performance.[20]

The dominant tone of such deconstructive analysis is permissive. It subverts assumed authority, celebrates variety, and legitimates the needs of previously stigmatised minorities. It seem likely, nevertheless, that the field is one in which further revisions and reversals of persuasive intention are in store. Twenty-five years hence, current beliefs about sexual liberation may well seem as muddled and hypocritical as the sexual beliefs of the nineteenth century seem today. The pendulum may swing back towards old values. Perhaps for political reasons, perhaps for aesthetic or moral ones, apparently outdated notions like those of virginity and innocence could once again inspire respect. Alternatively, under the threat of sexually transmitted diseases likes AIDS, we could move to a welfare morality which focuses exclusively on the uses to which our bodies are put. A third possibility harks back to the strictures of radical critics like Herbert Marcuse.[21] In its currently popular form, the doctrine of sexual liberation insists on individuals' rights as consumers of pleasure and on the arbitrariness of their 'turn-ons'.[22] Although this view is assumed to be a release from puritanism, it might turn out to be the reverse of this: an expression of the Manichean tendency in a new guise. It could be yet another expression of our fearfulness in the face of real pleasure; a defence against the sustained gratification that only erotic intimacy can provide. There is always the chance that it will be around the notion of intimacy that a new standard gels.

STEPPING BACK

There is no reason, of course, why a theory should not meet its advocates' private requirements and at the same time be true; nor why ulterior motives cannot bring about genuinely humanitarian social change. In the chapters that follow we shall have reason to be grateful both for the information Kinsey garnered and the insights for which Freud strove. Nevertheless, what one sees in their extraordinary feats of application is not simply the triumph of reason over ignorance and superstition, but the mind helping make the raw edges of personal experience smooth. Kinsey, from a background of intense puritanism, used his taxonomic discipline as a vehicle within which to protect himself from the possibility of moral censure. Freud not only drew on his private experience in formulating his theory of libidinal energies, but used his impassioned commitment to that theory as a means of keeping himself on an even keel.

The consequence is an atmosphere of simmering excitement but also of potentially intractable confusion. Even for the most dispassionate of inquirers - those who are eager for the truth, who are weary of symbolic warfare, who are willing to leave issues of reform to others, and who do their best to keep their private anxieties and *idées fixes* on a short leash – the going is difficult. Rather than there being a stable basis of fact and theory from which to tackle the perplexities of sex and gender, that basis is itself unstable and at times perplexing. In as much as they are evidence of passion's ability to shape and channel formal thought, inquiries like Freud's and Kinsey's form part of the knot to be disentangled.[23]

Our own policy, accordingly, is to tread warily: to rehearse the arguments and evidence as best we can, and to keep any recommendations we might otherwise be tempted to make to ourselves. We do this in the belief that, in explanatory terms, psychologists can realistically hope to 'get somewhere'; that there are truths about human experience which we can expect to establish. We do it in the belief too that, especially after periods of serious upheaval, the truth may reveal itself most readily to those who, like painters in front of the canvas, step back. Far from being arcane or deeply technical, significant features of that truth – like the male wound – may be staring us in the face. Their formal arrangements may speak for themselves.

Rather than pressing ourselves on our subject matter with ever greater force and ingenuity, performing feats of will at its expense, we can retreat a stride, and in doing so, allow what we already know (or can quite easily find out) to shine through. As Keller says, one can 'risk the suspension of boundaries between subject and object without jeopardy to science' precisely because science is not necessarily premised on that division. As in painting, 'cultivated attentiveness' plays its part too.[24]

SWINGS AND ROUNDABOUTS

CHAPTER 2

SIMPLE CHOICES,
COMPLEX SOLUTIONS

A NY SPECIFIC PROPOSAL about sex and gender – like ours about the male wound – needs a framework. This must be clear, of course, but it must also be sufficiently flexible to accommodate the variety, and often instability, of the desires people experience and the behaviour they display. As Roger Brown says, the deepest thinkers seem always to have understood the need for 'a general theory of sexual orientation in which paths are traced for all existent outcomes' – and not just of orientation, we would add, but of our sexual nature more generally.[1] Starting and ending with anecdotes, this chapter sets out the scheme we find most satisfactory. In it, the biological, the psychological and the social components of sex and gender interlock, and do so in a way which allows the scheme as a whole to function dynamically, as a system. It enables fine distinctions to be drawn, but at the same time allows connections to shine through. Order emerges from it instead of being coercively imposed; and space is created within it for the male wound, which the next chapter describes.

The scheme we offer is simple, non-committal and open-ended. For the purposes of analysis, no person or practice is excluded; and no clinical or moral judgement is implied. Its aims are:

- To create a setting within which the various facets of maleness and femaleness can be separated from one another and their different significances grasped;
- To show how these facets combine, in each of us, to form part of a distinctive personality; and
- To highlight a motivational principle often overlooked – that, once in being, such a system acts ceaselessly to resolve its own dissonances and, however precariously, to achieve equilibrium.

As our argument unfolds, the bearing of this principle on the imaginative energies of the male mind should quite quickly become clear.

HARRY

A tall, raw-boned man in his mid-thirties, 'Harry' is still active as a rugby player, and has a well-earned reputation for ferocity. He says, as if it were a feature of his experience that puzzles him, that on Saturday evenings in the rugby playing season, he drinks a good deal and sometimes arrives home in the early hours without his trousers. Notoriously, in rugby clubs up and down the land, grown men totter drunkenly on to table tops, drop their trousers, and reveal their private parts to the assembled company. To that extent, his comments about himself are less than startling. A further revelation *is* unexpected, though. He is a teacher. In fact, he says, he teaches jewellery.

Harry's personality, plainly, is a system within which countervailing forces are at work. It combines 'male' and 'female' elements, and does so in unconventional ways. His muscular physique, austerely abrasive manner and the sense he conveys of violence held barely in check: all this is in keeping with the mores of rugby football. So too is getting drunk enough to act 'out of character'. In these respects, Harry is a hard man in a hard world: an inhabitant of a culture in which the roles of the two sexes remain sharply segregated, and in which the status accorded to the feminine is subservient. His son attends a junior school where, until recently, the asphalt playground was divided like a zoo paddock into male and female zones by iron railings, through which representatives of the two halves of humanity habitually communicated with one another by spitting. It is a society that views softness or effeminacy in men with revulsion.

Obviously, the tendency of certain sportsmen to shed their trousers in public when drunk can be construed as evidence of latent homosexuality. There are resemblances too, though, between such episodes and the dominance and submission behaviour of apes. Arguably, what they signify is not so much latent homosexuality as unresolved conflicts about aggression. Either way, a chink in Harry's formidable masculinity has clearly opened.

It opens further when we consider Harry's choice of profession. It is not just that jewellery-making requires extreme manual dexterity and technical finesse, as those who have tried to repair even the simplest piece of jewellery will have discovered. It demands the exercise of judgement that is sensuous, and the reconciliation of that sensuousness with extremes of technical control. Moreover, this elusive reconciliation is typically sought in the context of women's bodies. Some men wear jewellery, and jewellery has many functions, among them those of social observance and ostentation, but one of its prime purposes remains that of accentuating the attractiveness of women. It establishes them as precious.

It is here that the tensions implicit in Harry's nature begin to make themselves felt. Plainly, maleness and femaleness are not simple, unitary properties. As has already been argued in *Bodies of Knowledge*, four basic layers or levels of sex and gender are in play:[2]

- Biology
- Gender identity
- Object choice
- Presentation of self.

It is from these four facets of maleness or femaleness that the personality of each individual is composed – and sometimes recomposed.

ANATOMY AND PHYSIOLOGY

No woman on earth shares Harry's physique. Few, one imagines, would wish to. Height, six feet three or four. Weight, in the region of 220 pounds. Lean and hard-muscled rather than beefy; generously endowed with facial and bodily hair; a voice that stirs easily into a deep-throated roar. No woman on earth, either, has external genitals like Harry's or, for that matter, his son's. In turn, no man menstruates, or has the internal reproductive apparatus that would enable him to sustain a foetus.

These differences between men and women in reproductive anatomy and physiology are categorical. Reproductive behaviour is regulated, of course, by 'male' and 'female' sex hormones; and the secretion of these hormones is controlled by the pituitary gland, at the base of the brain. The functioning of the pituitary is controlled in turn by the hypothalamus, a part of the brain itself. Consequently, as Tanner says, 'endocrine maleness resides in the hypothalamus and not in the testis or the pituitary'.[3] Just as the male genitalia are differentiated from the female, in other words, so part of the male brain is differentiated from part of the female brain. The changes in question concern the hypothalamus's cell structure, and once established, it seems, are irreversible.

Other physical differences between the two sexes are less clear-cut. Some we are intuitively aware of; others are so marginal to our experience that we scarcely know they are there. Most of us are intuitively alert, for instance, to the fact that adult women tend, relatively speaking, to be broad in the hip and narrow in the shoulder, whereas the tendency among adult men is the reverse. This difference arises during adolescence. The tissues of the shoulder in both sexes are sensitive to the influence of male sex hormones; the tissues of the pelvis in both sexes to that of female sex hormones. In adolescence, the male body is flooded with male hormones; the female body with female ones. Hence, it is the shoulders of boys and the hips of girls which tend to broaden.

Altogether less apparent is a difference mentioned by Tanner, concerning our hands. Though we look at them many times a day, every day of our lives, there is an oddity about our *fingers* that few of us spontaneously notice. In most of us, the fourth finger on each hand is longer than the index finger. However this difference, Tanner says, is sex-linked. It is usually more marked on the left hand of a woman; on the right hand of a man.

These sex-linked differences in physique and dozens of others like them exist on the average and to varying degrees. In the case of the distinction between hip width and shoulder width, Tanner's data suggest, some 10 per cent of men conform to the 'female' pattern; some 10 per cent of women conform to the 'male' one. Such anatomical differences probably in turn explain why it is that, on average, men can run faster, jump higher or throw further than women, yet a minority of women are in such respects more athletic than most men.

Differences between men's and women's bodies are significant, of course, to the extent that we perceive them to be so. We can ignore them, or, alternatively, treat them as charged with intense meaning. Yet again, we can use them as the site of elaborate social and aesthetic games. At the moment, one of the more intriguing of these centres on the difference just mentioned of shoulder and hip. It is currently fashionable among affluent women in Western cultures to have bodies – and, especially, hips – 'like boys'. This urge to be boy-like is by no means restricted to the frivolous, and can be found among the doctrinally exacting too. Recently, this preoccupation has been geared to a fashion which uses padding massively to emphasise the apparent width of women's shoulders. The result is as visually exciting as it is biologically perverse.[4]

Deserving more careful thought, perhaps, is yet another difference that shows every sign of having a physiological basis – this time a question of function rather than physique, and a recurring theme of sex research for half a century at least. Kinsey's evidence is in this respect typical. He showed that, purely in terms of their sexual outlets or energies, the two sexes follow dissimilar paths. Males show every sign of reaching a peak of sexual energy in their early teens, with the onset of puberty. Thereafter, these energies tend on average to decline. The deficit is usually readily perceptible by a man's thirties or forties, and by his fifties and sixties is a fact of life that can easily seem a disability. The female pattern is quite different. The evidence varies in detail, but the impression is that of a plateau of sexual energy reached in late adolescence or early adulthood, and which extends, little altered, into a woman's forties or fifties, and often beyond.

Here, as elsewhere, there exists vast scope for individual variety. Kinsey's survey reveals an appreciable proportion of women who had several orgasms each time they had intercourse; in some cases three or four, in a few as many as a dozen. But also a woman who had her first orgasm having been married to the same man for twenty-eight years. Among Kinsey's males, there is the 'scholarly lawyer' who claimed to have had an average of thirty-three orgasms a week for thirty years; and the male prostitute in his late thirties, still reportedly capable of '6 to 8 ejaculations' as the occasion demanded. Yet Kinsey also found a man, still of an appropriate age and apparently of sound health, who had ejaculated only once in three decades.

Despite the remarkable variousness of human sexual capacity, there is no mistaking the difference of trend. While for women sexual energy is a relatively stable feature of adult experience, for men it is a capability in decline. Where, for young women, sexual energy is often roughly congruent with the demands of a culture in which sex is linked to love and intimacy, for young men this usually is not so. On the contrary: in the male, sexual energy characteristically reaches its peak long before any enduring heterosexual intimacy can take shape; and thereafter, for a while at least, it threatens to disrupt such intimacies once they form.

'INSTINCTS'

There is no reason that we know of for doubting that anatomical and physiological differences between the two sexes are genetically entrained. It is at least arguable that the sexual fascinations men and women experience also have an instinctual foundation. In all mammals, evolutionary experts claim, the primary function of the male is to inseminate; that of the female to harbour the growing foetus. There may well exist in the human male, consequently, a genetically mediated urge to compete with male rivals for the right to inseminate the greatest possible number of available females. In women, too, there may be complementary urges: to be inseminated by the dominant male in the 'troop' to which she belongs; and to have babies and to cherish them. All this may be part of our 'biogrammar'.

Such evolutionary arguments can also be used to explain homosexuality. Self-evidently, a genetic advantage accrues to a species equipped automatically to make heterosexual choices; but, arguably at least, there also accrues an advantage to the species that equips the young of both sexes to respond sexually rather than aggressively to violent attentions from older members of the same sex. At the risk (in the young male's case) of homosexual rape, the young survive and in their own turn can breed. Submissively homosexual patterns of response, as a result, may be 'wired in'. This line of explanation, on the other hand, is one that says nothing about homosexual patterns which are aggressive.

Analogous arguments can be used, too, in making sense of an intriguing finding from recent sex research: not only that men are on average more promiscuous than women, but that homosexual men are on average more promiscuous than heterosexual men, whereas among women there is no equivalent difference, the average number of sexual partners being modest for heterosexual and homosexual alike.[5] Other than for purely commercial purposes, it seems, few women seek brief, anonymous sex in the way that some men do. It is perfectly plausible, again, that their respective biogrammars explain why this is so. The suggestion is that while the promiscuous pattern is natural to all men, it is masked in heterosexual men by the moderating effects exerted on them by the women they desire. (An alternative explanation of these data, of course, is that the groups in question differ in their motives. Promiscuous men, it can equally be argued, are activated by hostility – the promiscuously homosexual especially; while women, the homosexual and heterosexual alike, are moved by the need to recreate primary bonds.)

For the time being at least, what one makes of explanatory ventures like these is very much a matter of personal taste. What is objectionable about the use of evolutionary arguments in such contexts, in any case, is not the idea that men and women have instincts. As mammals, it would odd if we did not. It is the assumption that these must act as imperatives or commands, overriding whatever else it is that our culture requires of us. The action of genetically mediated instincts on a creature which possesses a massively elaborated central nervous system and which lives in a complex symbolic culture will usually be indirect or, to use the animal behaviourist's term, 'under-determining'. They colour our behaviour rather than governing it. The role of instincts in human beings is to establish the patterns of behaviour which are easily learnt and come spontaneously to hand: the acquisition of language, for example, and the formats of sex and gender. It is these patterns which are the raw material on which the institutions of a particular culture set to work – and chief among those institutions, as we argue in Chapter 4, is the family.[6]

GENDER IDENTITY

The biological layer of our maleness or femaleness is closely linked to a second, our gender identity – the sense we have of belonging either to the male half of the human race or the female half. This is firmly established, research suggests, by the age of eighteen months. Studies of hermaphroditic children, those whose genital apparatus is anatomically ambiguous, indicates that, after this age, the sense of belonging among the males or the females is difficult if not impossible to change. Until quite recently, these identifications were assumed to be automatic and internally consistent, and for that reason were largely ignored. In practice, though, they sometimes turn out to be patchy or confused. A man may experience himself as unambiguously male on the football pitch, yet as genderless, even 'female', when making love. A woman may experience herself as genderless, even 'male', while selling life insurance, but as unambiguously female when she baths her child. Our framework must make space, in other words, for people whose sense of their own maleness or femaleness is intermittent or subject to local reversals. Also for those in whom fragments of maleness and femaleness coexist, mosaic-like, but who lack any overriding sense of commitment to one sex or the other. Even for the strangest cases of all, the transsexuals: the 'man' who perceives himself as locked inside a woman's body, the 'woman' who perceives herself as locked inside a man's body, and both of whom see their bodies as categorically alien.[7]

Some of the determinants of gender identity are the obvious ones: children's discovery, sooner or later, that their genital anatomy places them either with the males in their lives or with the females; their names, usually either male or female; and their parents' expectations, male infants usually being treated as belonging to one category, females to another. Other determinants of the adult's gender identity are more subtle, as we shall argue later.

OBJECT CHOICE

Our 'object choice' is the person on whom we find our erotic passions focused. It refers to that person not just as a unique individual, but as a representative of a group or type: 'our type'. The same sex as ourselves or the opposite sex. Similar to ourselves in personality and social background or different. And so on until the specification of our heart's desire is complete. (The phrase 'object choice' is well-established, but unfortunate. It is not objects that are at issue but people; not consciously deliberated choices but unconsciously regulated fascinations.)

The perpetuation of the species depends, needless to say, on the existence of a norm: that we will each find ourselves drawn to members of the opposite sex. But an appreciable minority do not adhere to this pattern, making instead the homosexual object choice which in reproductive terms is maladaptive, unnatural. Despite decades of intense curiosity on the subject, explanations of this phenomenon remain largely speculative. The options have recently been reviewed by Brown, but he emerges from his scrutiny more or less empty-handed. The search for hormonal differences between adult homosexuals and heterosexuals has been fruitless; while psychodynamic arguments about excessive closeness to the parent of the opposite sex remain, in his view, largely conjectural.[8]

A line of inquiry which does strike Brown and others as hopeful is one concerning hormone levels in the foetus. There are cases in which, at a crucial period in the female foetus's development, it is immersed in excessive quantities of male sex hormone. In these instances of 'foetal androgenisation', girls grow up as tomboys, and are more likely than other girls to be either homosexual or bisexual.[9] The evidence suggests, in fact, that excessive levels of male and female sex hormones at critical periods in the foetus's development could have effects in both sexes which are subtly differentiated, the four levels of sex and gender discussed here being influenced separately. For the time being, though, despite the air of expectancy surrounding this area of research, the influence of our hormones on our erotic orientation, whether heterosexual or homosexual, remains a puzzle unresolved.

Rather than weighing the pros and cons of explanatory stories like these, there is in any case a much more pressing task closer to hand. For we must be clear that the traditional distinction between homosexuality and heterosexuality is not what it seems. It scrambles together patterns of sexual need which are, in fact, quite different. A man who sees himself as a man and who desires other men is making a choice of like-with-like. He is sexually attracted to people who belong to the same category as himself. A man who sees himself as a woman and desires other men is making a choice that, in an important sense, is one of like-with-unlike. That is to say, he is sexually attracted to people whom he sees in a significant respect as categorically *un*like himself.

The same holds, of course, for heterosexual relations; and for both men and women. A man who sees himself as a man and is drawn to women is making a choice of like-with-unlike, the conventional pattern. But if he sees himself as a woman and is attracted to women, there is a significant respect in which he is a not heterosexual but a 'lesbian'.

The necessary distinctions do not stop there. The man who sees himself as a man and is attracted to other men may be drawn to men whom he sees as like himself, masculine. Alternatively, he may be drawn to other men whom he sees as unlike himself, effeminate. There is all the difference in the world between the male 'lesbian' who is drawn to women who are powerful and by whom he hopes to be dominated, and the male 'lesbian' who desires women who are even more feminine than he perceives himself to be. In practice, the success or failure of a particular erotic venture will often depend on precisely such distinctions as these.

Just as there exist 'mosaics' in gender identity, so these complex

patterns exist, too, in our object choice. Individuals may discover
themselves to be both heterosexual and homosexual, either con-
currently or by turns. They may be attracted to similar personal
qualities in both male and female partners; a gentleness in both, say,
which leaves them free to dominate. Or the pattern of their attraction
may be gender-specific. A man may find that he has fatal weaknesses
for both the 'female' man and the 'male' woman. In bed with either
he may well be playing the same game of dominance and submission; but he may use the change of sex in his partner as his cue to
switch from one of the game's roles to the other – dominant, say,
with the 'female' men, submissive with the 'male' women.

In *Sex and Gender*, Stoller describes a housewife in her mid-thirties
with two pre-adolescent sons, whose sexual experience demonstrates
how specific these transformations can be.[10] This woman had grown
up wanting fervently to be a boy. Since early adolescence she had had
homosexual relationships, and her private sexual fantasies were
'male': 'When I want to stimulate myself sexually I imagine myself as
a man with a woman in various sexual situations.' 'When I'm having
sexual relations with a woman', she said, 'I can feel completely masculine, as long as she doesn't touch me in the pubic area. No matter
what sexual activity I'm engaged in with a woman I always have an
orgasm when she has one, and this can occur without my genitals
having been touched. During my sexual relationship with a woman I
actually feel as though I have a penis. I feel totally masculine and
superior to the female I'm with. When I experience an orgasm I feel
that I ejaculate.'

She was energetically bisexual, however; and her experience of
pleasure was quite different in the heterosexual case from the homosexual one. 'I never felt masculine', she said, 'while having sexual relations with a man.' 'I can have sexual relations with a woman, have
one orgasm and be completely satisfied. When I have intercourse
with a man I have to have several orgasms before I can relax and feel
satisfied.' As Stoller remarks in another context, women often seem
to move easily from one erotic format to another. For men, such
manoeuvres seem in comparison harder to execute.

PRESENTATION OF SELF

The fourth level of the scheme deals with our presentation of self as
social beings. In almost all cultures, there exist powerful expectations
about how males and females should behave.

In our own culture, at least until recently, the male is expected to be socially aggressive and entrepreneurial; the female to be nurturing, reactive. The cultures of the football club or building site remain 'male' in a sense that those of the jeweller, ballet dancer or nurse are not. These linkages between gender and public life are by no means immutable, or course, but they are well entrenched; and they constitute the background against which we each establish habitable identities of our own. Our maleness or femaleness is tied, then, both to our posture *vis-à-vis* the world around us, and to the venues in which we choose to operate, both as we earn our livings and in our leisure.

It is important, again, that our analysis should not be clumsy. The attack of the enlightened on the hide-bound has centred on the falseness both of 'machismo' in men and of the stance of the 'little woman' – all gentleness and intuition, headaches and womanly wiles. These are defences against anxiety, their critics plausibly insist, and are stunting, pathogenic. Both patterns, it is true, often do ring hollow. On the other hand, forthright expressions of masculinity or feminity are not necessarily false; and in some, like Harry, they are interestingly divided. Within each job or profession, too, new pathways continually open up and many prove to be gender-linked; some clearly 'male' or 'female', others more androgynous. Jewellery is a case in point. A jeweller like Harry can gravitate towards the descipline's more obviously technical wing, specialising in the use of precious metals and in the cutting, polishing and setting of precious stones. Alternatively, he can move towards those parts of jewellery that are closest to the world of fashion, where the preoccupations of the expert are sensual and sometimes erotic. In either case, he can choose to work with the natural grain of the culture in which he finds himself, or across it. If he needs it, he still has ample room within which to express ambivalence. He can take technically-minded students who are learning jewellery as a trade skill, and expose them to the febrile excitements of fashion. Alternatively, he can rub the noses of students fascinated by fashion in the technologies of metalworking and stone polishing.

In the same way, initiates discover that there are fiercely technical and more intuitively judgemental ways of being a historian. There is room inside many disciplines, in other words, to pick and choose between avenues that are of different stereotypical significance. Ernest Hemingway is in this sense revealing: a genuinely tough and courageous man who, in real life, appeared to give a slightly ham performance of a man who is tough and courageous. The special interest of Hemingway in the present context is not that he was yet another sensitive spirit masquerading as a saloon bar tough, eager to display his brawn and to patronise 'womenies'. It is that, when translated into his work as a novelist, his preoccupation with gritty masculinity led to a genuine cleansing of the prose in which the modern novel is written. His sentence structure was economical in just the way he wished his own character to be. 'For Hemingway', Richard Ellmann observes,

> writing was a kind of suppression with only partial release. He behaved in life as in his art, going without food to save money, then engaging in some gush of expense, but all the time keeping a money heap in reserve. His capacity for retention extended to keeping his early notebooks in bank vaults for many years, for future exploitation. Even his method of composing a paragraph in circles around key words suggests a peristaltic movement. Though he wanted to be known as swashbuckling, his strength came from self-concealment. His well-known competitiveness was as much as anything an attempt to protect his winter stores.[11]

STEREOTYPES

Not only are a large number of professions and spare-time pursuits sex- and gender-linked; the framework of stereotypical perception within which we each perceive and make sense of them is itself structured in terms of gender.

The cultural stereotype, we want to argue, is an element of the mind's furniture which has seriously been misunderstood. Far from being arbitrary constraints imposed on our thought by unwitting parents or self-serving advertisers (or, more sinisterly, by capitalism or the military-industrial complex), it is increasingly clear that the stereotypes of the arts, science and technology, although the grossest of over-simplifications, are frames of thought or schemata which have a solid psychological foundation in the child's early development.

A good deal of research on the perception of the arts and sciences was done in the 1960s, a proportion of it by ourselves.[12] In detail, its findings need updating; but its message was unequivocal. The typical physical scientist, the physicist, say, is someone we all picture within a constellation of values that is overwhelmingly 'male'. The typical

arts specialist, the novelist, is someone we perceive within a constellation of values that is androgynous or positively 'female'. This is
as true of the British as it is of Americans; of young teenagers whose
academic experience is as yet unspecialised as it is of students for
whom the process of academic specialisation is already seriously
under way.

The typical scientist is seen as dull, hard and cold; as highly intelligent but unimaginative; as dependable, hard-working and valuable; as rough rather than smooth; and – needless to say – as manly
rather than feminine. The typical artist, in contrast, is seen as exciting, soft and warm; as highly imaginative but as less than outstandingly intelligent; as undependable, lazy and lacking in value; as
smooth rather than rough; and as genderless.[13]

In the present context, this evidence about stereotypes has three
lessons to teach. They concern:

- The division between the pleasure-seeking and puritanical components of our collective system of values;
- The emergence of stereotypes at different developmental stages;
  and
- The willingness of individuals to join groups which they perceive in an unfavourable light.

The division such research demonstrates between the pleasure-seeking and puritanical is sharp. The scientist, the quintessentially 'male'
figure, is seen as valuable but as largely devoid of personal glamour
or attraction. The male artist, the androgynous figure, is seen as
personally attractive but as lacking in value. Despite our apparent en-
lightenment, in other words, we agree with the Victorians in seeing
moral worth as associated in men with the control of impulse. In
their eyes, virility equalled self-control; effeminacy equalled licence.
Virility, it was believed, was endangered by loss of semen, sexual excess leading to degenerative illness and insanity. It is not the 'strong
athletic boy', wrote William Acton, the Victorian gynaecologist,
'who thus early shows marks of sexual desires, but your puny
exotic', the one whose intellectual education has been fostered at the
expense of his physique.[14] The typical scientist emerges from the research on stereotypical perception, then, as in the Victorian sense
virile: the male whose mind is disciplined and whose capacities for
pleasure and erotic adventure are curtailed. It can hardly be an accident, consequently, that the value around which many everyday
judgements in the scientific community in fact turn should be one so

richly expressive of bourgeois propriety: that of scientific *respectabil-ity*.

The second remarkable fact about these stereotypes is that, de-velopmentally speaking, they crystallise at different ages. We have found that the idea of the dull but worthy scientist exists, ready-made, in the minds of intelligent British eleven-year-olds who have no first-hand experience of science or scientists; and that it alters scarcely at all, throughout adolescence.[15] The same holds for the images of the mathematician and engineer. Also for that of the lawyer. This tendency is lop-sided, however. Among eleven-year-olds, there exists no comparable consensus about the arts or human-ities. The collective vision of the exciting but unreliable artist takes shape only more gradually; and it is not until the age of seventeen or eighteen that this image is as clearly etched in the collective aware-ness of intelligent teenagers as that of the scientist.

The physical scientist, the mathematician, the engineer and the lawyer all embody the principle of impersonal authority or control. The image of the artist, in contrast, embodies that of excitement and personal attraction. The impression is strong that the first group of stereotypes reflect the preoccupations of what psychoanalysts have called the 'latency period': the years between the ages of five and eleven, when we acquire the impersonal skills of reading, writing and arithmetic, and when the conscience is notoriously fierce. The stereotype of the artist, in contrast, shows every sign of reflecting the concerns of adolescence, when the dominant concerns are inter-personal, erotic. We shall argue in the next chapter, in fact, that, in outline at least, the semantic structures defining the scientific and artistic ways of life exist in the minds of almost all males from the age of two or three.[16]

The final curiosity of these stereotypes is that young men who choose to become scientists do so with the apparently unfavourable image of the dull-but-worthy scientist fully in view. Likewise, with specialists in the arts and humanities and the image of the raffish-but-attractive artist. For, give or take 'halo effects', the stereotypes of the arts and sciences are ones that both young arts and science specialists demonstrably share.[17] Doubtless, we each see ourselves as set apart from the people among whom we choose to work; but the im-plication must be that the culture of physical science and technology is not merely 'male', but one populated with men (and the occasional woman) who are reconciled to what they perceive as their own dull-ness and lack of personal magnetism. The arts and humanities are made up of people, many of them women and relatively androgynous men, for whom the issues of personal attraction, style and charisma remain very much alive. At the same time, they have turned their backs on the thought of working lives that are, in the down-to-earth sense, worthwhile.

SEX AND GENDER AS A DYNAMIC SYSTEM

At each level of the scheme as we have presented it, the individual faces a binary choice between 'male' and 'female' options. In combination, these choices constitute the configuration of sex and gender characteristic of the man or woman in question. In barest outline, the scheme permits sixteen different outcomes – among them, the two patterns our culture accepts as its norms: the man who perceives himself as a man, desires women, and presents himself in a masculine light; and the woman who sees herself as a woman, desires men, and presents herself as feminine. In between, there are fourteen more, each subtly differentiated. There is the woman, for instance, who perceives herself as a man, desires other women, and presents herself as masculine; and the man who perceives himself as a man, desires women, but presents himself to the world as effeminate. Each is a distinctive resolution to the conundrums that sexual identity and desire pose.

But as we have already suggested, life is rarely neat. At each level, what seems at first glance a single choice can turn out to be a cluster or nest of choices. We do not necessarily present ourselves to the world straightforwardly, as either 'male' or 'female'. Instead, many of us create public *personae* which combine the two: not just mosaics but mosaics within mosaics.[18] The total number of distinctively different outcomes the scheme permits is therefore indefinitely large. The upper limit depends in practice on the determination and ingenuity with which we each fashion configurations for ourselves, persisting until a point of perceived equilibrium is reached. This venture may turn out to depend on the precise course the individual steers through the prevailing fashions in clothing and adornment: the decision, say, on the part of a woman to wear a trouser suit to work in a lawyer's office, or of a man to wear an ear-ring. It may equally depend on professed interests and attitudes – towards body-contact sports, perhaps – or on mannerism and gesture. The minutest inflection of 'camp' may find its way into a presentation of self which is otherwise conventional; or it may momentarily be absent at points where the spectator confidently expects it.

There is a sense in which the more intricate and delicately poised of these solutions are akin to works of art: deployments of personality in which potent dissonances are skilfully controlled and contained, and in which the effect of balance is achieved by means of scarcely perceptible nuance. As in art, each choice is context-bound. For a woman to wear trousers to work in a given legal department may be just permissibly daring at one moment in the evolution of fashion; but three months later, commonplace. For a man to wear a skirt in the same department would usually be preposterous – unless the department happened to be in Scotland and the skirt was a kilt. Wearing it could then become an act of virile affirmation and conformity.

The combinatory patterns of sex and gender are inexhaustible. They flow, logically, from the action on one another of separate but related facets of maleness and femaleness, which, taken together, constitute a system. In isolation, each facet centres on a binary distinction: 'male' versus 'female'. But when these distinctions are combined and allowed to interact, outcomes differentiate themselves from one another boundlessly. While fuelled by biological drives, particularly (but by no means exclusively) sexual ones, the system in practice operates homeostatically, seeking to play off ambiguities and dissonances against one another, reducing the tensions these generate to within tolerable limits. In terms of motivational principle, in other words, *it is a system that seeks among emotionally charged similarities and differences for a sense of equilibrium.* In sex and gender, as in modern mathematics, intricacy derives from the combination of elements, which, in themselves, could scarcely be more simple.

Many solutions will be stable. Although they may contain powerful elements of ambiguity, they will usually alter, once established, only under considerable external pressure – a stably heterosexual man becoming homosexual in fantasy and action, say, only if deprived of female company for years on end. Equally, however, such stability may be to varying extents illusory. A precarious choice made at one level can beget precarious choices at other levels; and, in the process, latent pathways may be created which the individual subsequently discovers and explores. The resulting shifts from one configuration of desire to another may take place suddenly, and apparently of their own accord.[19]

An extreme example of such a reversal is the unfortunate 'Eric'.

He has already been described in *Bodies of Knowledge*. Like Harry, he was a teacher. When interviewed, he was in his thirties, a timid, physically fragile creature who had grown up in the shadow of older sisters. As a teenager, he was taken in hand by a young woman of unusually forceful character. They married and became parents. As he subsequently described them, their intimacies were conventional, but her sexual appetite far outran his. She exhausted him sexually, and then embarked on a series of affairs, often with his work-mates, which she conducted under his nose. On at least one occasion, he said, she unzipped his fly and took out his penis while male colleagues were in the room with them; an event that he experienced as a humiliation. Isolated, Eric took to reading and looking at pornography; particularly, photographs of boys. An openly affectionate man, he had fallen into the habit of fondling not only his own son but the son of neighbours. Without in the least realising what was about to happen, he found one day that he had enacted with this boy (and, subsequently, with others) every carnal fantasy that two male bodies permit. Listening to him speak, it was as if his pornographic reading and gazing had established in his imagination a repertoire of gross and forbidden acts. In him, as a result, two erotic repertoires – two solutions – existed side by side: the first heterosexual, physically inhibited, emotionally committing; the second homosexual, physically uninhibited, blame-free. Far from his homosexual exploits being the discovery of his true need, buried for so long beneath his convention-bound heterosexuality, they were simply things he had done with his body; or, more strictly, things which he found his body did. The discovery of the second solution did not displace the first, or show it to be false. Rather, they served, between them, as expressions of a profoundly fissured nature – one which had led him to a cell in a maximum security prison.

In retrospect, Eric showed no trace of guilt. The boys were willing accomplices, he said, and one turned out to be a male prostitute and amateur blackmailer. On the other hand, he shed hot tears, still, over his wife, who had left him for a more forceful rival, a leader of the esoteric religious community to which she belonged. She had taunted him for his lack of virility, both in private and in front of his colleagues. Repeatedly, she had been unfaithful to him; and now he was incarcerated, she had abandoned him. But he showed every sign of being bound to her in his imagination, and there was the real risk that, when his sentence was complete, he would repeat his error – searching out a powerful, sexually demanding woman to fall in love with; and then, when this relationship foundered, falling back on pornography and sexual episodes with boys.

Admittedly exceptional, Eric's experience also points a more universally applicable moral. Our four-tier scheme serves as a rudimentary sketch of a system within which unresolved tensions lead to sudden plunges and their attendant rushes of blood. In fact, unforeseen – and, in the technical sense, 'catastrophic' – lurches from one configuration to another are features we would expect many solutions in the field of sex and gender to display.[20] Less dramatically, the tensions implicit in this system can give rise to erotic projects, often pursued exclusively in the mind's eye, radically at odds with the acknowledged, everyday self. More generally, we will assume that imaginative activity (and especially eroticised imaginative activity) exists in response to internal divisions and fissures, and constitutes an effort to bring the dissonances caused by these fissures under control. More generally still, we will assume that, in the arts and sciences alike, there is no creative work without internal fissuring and the dissonances to which fissuring gives rise.

CHAPTER 3

THE MALE 'WOUND'

A S WE HAVE so far described it, our scheme assumes that the kinds of internal fissuring that characterise Harry's personality and Eric's are just as likely to occur in a woman as a man. We now introduce to the scheme a kind of fissure that is specifically male. From it there flow, we believe, the frames of mind and patterns of action typical of men. In this chapter we describe the source of this fissure; in the next, the family context in which it takes shape. The rest of the book is taken up with its implications.

STEP BY STEP, OUR PATHS DIVERGE

To begin with, in the earliest stages of the foetus's growth, only its chromosomes enable us to distinguish female from male. Although they will later develop either into testes or into ovaries, the male and female embryos' gonads are at this stage alike. The male's gonads grow more quickly than the female's, though; and, within a few weeks of conception, the male's are recognisable as testes. In another week or so, specialised cells make their appearance in the male's testes and, triggered by secretions from the placenta, these begin in turn to secrete the sex hormone testosterone. This causes the male's external genitalia to take shape as a penis and scrotum. From other specialised cells in the male's testes, there is also secreted a second hormone. This serves to atrophy the structures that, in the female, will later develop into the fallopian tubes. But it is the action of testosterone, it seems, that is crucial. Without it, the external genitalia of both sexes take the female form.

For the vast majority of mortals, this is the parting of the ways. Thereafter, we are each destined to live inside a body recognised as male or recognised as female. To the extent that our bodies are our fates, this is the point at which these are sealed.

Although there have been dissenting voices, the orthodox view is that the female pattern is the basic one, and that the male pattern is a systematic, genetically programmed variation upon it, triggered by the action of the relevant sex hormones. This is certainly the view taken by Tanner. 'The female', he says, 'is the "basic" sex into which embryos develop if not stimulated to do otherwise.'[1] It is also the attitude expressed by Stoller:

> The biologic rules governing sexual behavior in mammals are simple. In all, including man, the 'resting state' of tissue – brain and peripheral – is female. We can now demonstrate without exception, in all experiments performed on animals, that if androgens in the proper amount and biochemical form are withheld during critical periods in fetal life, anatomy and behavior typical of that species' males do not occur, regardless of genetic sex. And if androgens in the proper amount and form are introduced during critical periods in fetal life, anatomy and behavior typical of that species' males do occur, regardless of genetic sex. We cannot experiment on humans, but no natural experiments (for example, chromosomal disorders) are reported that contradict the general mammalian rule.[2]

For boys, but not for girls, a further surge of testosterone occurs in the six months after birth. Little work has yet been done on the psychological implications of this second surge, but it is a period in which important structures are taking shape in the brain, and in which differential effects on male and female could well arise. Evidence is still sketchy, but there are indications that visual perception in four-, five- and six-month-old girls is superior to that of boys, because, it has been suggested, testosterone inhibits the development of the appropriate cortical tissues in boys.[3]

Our own argument begins with another such parting of the ways. This occurs in infancy, in the two or three years after birth rather than in the months before it; and instead of being anatomical and physiological, it is psychological – a question, that is to say, of individuals' perceptions of who they are and how they relate to the people who constitute their intimate world. Although impossible to locate neatly in time, this shift undoubtedly occurs; and it, too, moves the male away from a pattern which, until then, both sexes have shared. We are by no means the first to notice that this is so. We do seem to be the first, though, to realise how powerfully two-edged the implications of this developmental change are bound to be, and how comprehensively it undermines certain simple-minded beliefs about the paths men and women are subsequently at liberty to follow.[4]

The theoretical background is familiar and is at heart straight-forward. As infants, both male and female usually draw primitive comfort and security from their mother or mother-substitute. It is on this intimate, symbiotic relationship with a caring and supportive maternal presence that the subsequent normality of an infant's development depends. As Greenacre says, the foetus 'moves about, kicks, turns around, reacts to some external stimuli by increased motion. It swallows, and traces of its own hair are found in the meconium. It excretes urine and sometimes passes stool.' Grunberger likens the uterus, accordingly, to 'a heavenly, radiant source of bliss and a chamberpot'.[5] It is this pre-natal experience of wholly unqualified physical intimacy which is sustained in the symbiotic intimacy between mother and child. Where this bond is lacking, the individual's subsequent competence as an adult is disturbed – for chimpanzees no less than for human beings, as the Harlows' 'terry towelling mother' experiments show. In chimpanzees, mating and maternal behaviour are disrupted; in humans, it seems to be the capacity to form intimate relationships which is most seriously impaired.[6] It is also in the context of this symbiotic bond with the mother, though, that the infant will first experience pain and frustration: milk that is not instantly forthcoming, griping pains in the stomach, the urge to explore thwarted. The mother, to put the same point in another way, becomes the butt not only of the infant's warmest pleasures but also of its fear and rage.

As well as establishing a position for itself *vis-à-vis* the emotionally charged features of its world, the infant must also establish a sense of its maleness or femaleness: its gender identity. For the little girl, it is easy to see what is at stake. She remains identified with her mother; the source of all her most potent emotions, positive and negative, pleasurable and painful. As a result, she perceives herself as the same sort of being as her mother, through and through. If, as she probably does, she learns to perceive both her mother and herself as an amalgam of the pleasure-provoking and the pain-provoking, the 'good' and the 'bad', her sense of herself is to that extent internally fissured. Nevertheless, she remains all of a piece with the creature, her mother, on whom her sense of reality depends. When the little girl moves on to establish for herself an appropriate 'object' on whom to focus her desires, she again has her mother available to her as model. She can follow the line of her mother's gaze towards her father and towards other males. The object of her desire is thus a creature inherently unfamiliar to her, even alien, but one whom she addresses from a psychologically coherent foundation.

The male infant's task is dissimilar. As the psychoanalyst Ralph Greenson seems to have been the first to point out, if the little boy is to identify with his father, he must first separate himself imaginatively from his mother – until then, the source of all comfort and security.[7] Greenson describes this as 'a special vicissitude'. 'I am referring to the fact', he says, 'that the male child, in order to attain a healthy sense of maleness, must replace the primary object of his identification, the mother, and must identify instead with the father.' It is this additional step, he believes, that accounts for the special problems from which the adult male suffers and from which the adult female is exempt.

DIS-IDENTIFICATION AND COUNTER-IDENTIFICATION

This first step, the one that the little boy takes in order to free himself from his symbiotic connection to his mother, Greenson refers to as *dis-identification*. The subsequent step, independent of the first, and which enables him positively to identify with his father, Greenson calls *counter-identification*. The first establishes the boy's separateness; the second, his maleness. *It is these two developmental processes in combination which we call the male wound.*[8]

With the benefit of hindsight, it is possible to see Greenson's account of the consequences of dis-identification and counter-identification as too limited, but there is no doubting the shrewdness of the insight itself. In order to align himself with his father, the little boy first creates within himself a dislocation; and in as much as he imitates his father's object choice – his desire for women – he must do so with this dislocation as its prior condition.

Initially, while symbiotically connected to their mother, both son and daughter perceive their father as 'other'. But then, as the male gender identity crystallises, the son sees that 'other' (his father) as 'same', and what was 'same' (his mother) as 'other'. That is to say, *the son experiences a reversal – one of similarity-in-difference and difference-in-similarity – which his sister does not*. The elements of this reversal carry a powerful emotional charge; and its form, we are going to argue, is one which will echo and reverberate throughout the male's subsequent experience. If we are right, it is in the light of this reversal that each of the male's later ventures will be cast, his choice of work and imaginative expression no less than the character of his sexual desire.

No one yet knows what causes the male infant to divert his attention from his mother, to dis-identify. It seems likely that, in some way as yet unestablished, he is biologically influenced to do so. For reasons eventually traceable to the intrauterine environment, say, he may be more restless than his sisters, less tolerant of frustration, less attuned to the eye contact on which intimate traffic with his mother depends.[9] Male and female infants, in other words, may be biologically programmed to respond differently to a given maternal regime.

An alternative line of explanation, on which there are several variants, is more transactional. It holds, again for reasons that may be largely biological in origin, that most mothers from the very outset treat their male infants in one way, their female infants in another. There is evidence that mothers, while their babies are still new-born, are more likely to initiate interactions with their daughters than with their sons; and that in these interactions, it is the infant's physical movement which plays a central part in the case of the sons, whereas in the case of daughters it is mutuality of vocalisation and gaze.[10] As Hinde and Stevenson-Hinde have stressed, quite small sex differences in biological propensity on the infant's part will in any case be quickly magnified by the mother, whose perception is bound to be influenced by cultural stereotypes of maleness and femaleness, and who is bound, too, to see her son as 'other' in a way that her daughter is not.[11]

The child whom the mother sees as 'other', it is important to grasp, does actually differ in material ways from his sisters. While boys become larger and stronger than girls, girls mature more rapidly. Half way through pregnancy, the development of the skeleton is already three weeks more advanced in girls than in boys. At birth the difference in maturation corresponds to 4–6 weeks of normal growth, and by the time puberty is reached, to two years. This sex difference is common to many mammals and nearly all primates, and while the impact on the body is less than entirely uniform, the 'girls earlier' rule has few exceptions. Although both sexes acquire their milk teeth at the same time – one of those few exceptions – the permanent teeth erupt earlier in girls, and the canines by as much as eleven months.[12] We know too that by the sixth or seventh month, girls are beginning to display greater powers of physical co-ordination than boys; and, more specifically, that they are more likely than boys to gain a measure of control over their urinary function.[13] Girls are also quicker to acquire a control over language. At any given stage, their vocabulary is larger than that of boys and they are more articulate. Such differences are bound to be ones that are perceived, at least in part, as ones of *responsiveness*; of repaying the nurture the mother provides. However subliminally, the small boy will accordingly be perceived as the more intransigent partner in the parent/child relationship, the small girl as the more rewarding (or biddable) one.

An adjacent train of thought expands on this differential perception on the mother's part. Long before her son is in a position to sit up – which he usually does at the age of 8 or 9 months – and to discover what his own genital apparatus looks like, his mother will be alert to this difference between his anatomy and her own. She may not simply see him as 'other', that is to say; she may become erotically invested in his 'otherness'. It could be this erotic preoccupation, sometimes physically expressed, which hastens her son's dis-identification. It does so, it might be argued, because he fears engulfment by his mother; because he is sensitive not just to his mother's erotic investment in him but also to her guilty ambivalence about that investment; or, as classical Freudian theory suggests, because he intuits that his mother's body differs anatomically from his own, and that this discovery creates in him intolerable anxiety.[14]

We do not know which of these explanatory avenues will prove the most satisfactory. Whatever the predisposing circumstances turn out to be, it is clear that Greenson's insight permits three quite different patterns:

- The conventional one, in which the biological male dis-identifies with his mother and counter-identifies with his father;
- The biological male who neither dis-identifies nor counter-identifies; and
- The biological male who dis-identifies but fails to counter-identify.

Of these patterns, it is the first, we are arguing, that yields the 'male' male – the man who sees himself as male and acts as a male. The second leads to effeminacy, even in extreme cases to transsexuality –

in adulthood, the man who, for all purposes of gender identity, is in substantially the same position as his sister, except that he will some-how have had to accommodate the fact that his own reproductive anatomy and secondary sexual characteristics are unlike his mother's and sister's, and like his father's and brother's. The third yields the male who in adulthood experiences a sense of androgyny or gender-lessness.

Granted that no one knows how biology, psychology and culture interact in causing the wound, it would be an error to advance detailed qualifications. Nevertheless, it is easy to see how the effects of dis-identification and counter-identification might arise at later ages than the one we envisage – in adolescence, say, rather than at two or three. Appropriate scenarios can be conjured up. In one, a mother brings up her son alone. When her son is in his early teens, she marries and son and stepfather subsequently establish a close bond. In such cases, the son's sense of himself as male could be real enough, but it may be less deeply rooted, less apparently instinctual, than it otherwise might. He may seem to belong to the first of the patterns just outlined, but in truth more nearly belongs to the second or third.

As one reflects on Greenson's distinction, it becomes clear, too, that other outcomes are possible. These are of special interest in that they help make explicit certain of the assumptions on which the theory of identification rests. Particularly, one can envisage:

- The male child who counter-identifies with his father without first having dis-identified with his mother.

At first sight implausible, such a pattern might arise in a household where the personalities of mother and father are somewhat similar, where both are emotionally distant in their dealings with their son, and where the responsibilities for his nurture are shared. The net effect, from the son's point of view, would be a personality in which the 'male' and 'female' are weakly etched and poorly differentiated. It is also a pattern, though, that could take a more extreme form. In this – as in Harry's personality – both 'male' and 'female' character-istics are pronounced, coexisting on the strength of segregations and dissociations that, to the outside eye, are bound to seem arbitrary.

Such outcomes aside, one can also picture:

- The male child who dis-identifies with his mother, but counter-identifies with another woman.

The context for the emergence of such a pattern might be the community in which the care of children is the responsibility of women collectively. Likewise:

- The male child who dis–identifies with his mother, but counter–identifies, subsequently, not with a person but with an emotionally charged idea or symbol: the Fatherland, the Hero (Napoleon), the Leader (Stalin), the Genius (Beethoven or Freud).

Households in which the father is weak or absent form a likely setting for this configuration, likewise cultures where massive coercive pressures are brought to bear on children in the service of a civic ideal.[15] As social psychologists point out, identifications with figures outside the family in any case become increasingly significant as a child grows older, developing both a social identity and the potential for extravagant commitments and loyalties.[16]

The fifth and sixth of these patterns also raise an important issue of interpretation. The common–sense assumption is that the father or father-substitute must be present for counter–identification to occur. Such evidence as we have tends to bear this out, as the next chapter shows. Another train of thought is less literal. It assumes that the maleness at issue is abstract: a property not of individuals but of the disciplines inherent in child-raising and in the child's acquisition of impersonal symbolic skills. Either parent can be seen both as a source of physical and psychological comfort and as the embodiment of authority. On this argument, the male child counter–identifies not with his father, but with those aspects of his parents he intuitively perceives as impersonal (and in that sense 'male'). The role of the father, on this view, is essentially confirmatory. He consolidates developmental changes that can take place of their own accord within the confines of the mother/son relationship.[17]

Without doubt, identity and identification are awkward notions, the modelling at issue concerning not just what one does but who one is; not just behavioural patterns and propensities, but states of being. These are precisely the sorts of question with which philosophers, and especially Anglo-Saxon philosophers, have traditionally had difficulty. (In Exodus 3, God appears to Moses in a burning bush and says to him, 'I AM THAT I AM'. Moses's correct response, the Oxford philosophers of our youth would insist, was 'You are that you are *what*?) Practically speaking, there is a distinction between the person's social identity – as a Catholic, or a member of the working class, or a Liverpool fan – and the identifications implicit in the mother/infant relationship, the first being the province of the social psychologist, the second that of the developmental psychologist and psychoanalyst.[18] In the latter, fundamental questions are at issue; ones about what it is that passes between any two people who are emotionally significant to one another. For our intimate relationships commit us not just to propinquity and rational dialogue, but to the non-rational; to a hazardous two-way traffic in unacknowledged desires and fears.[19]

THE COSTS

One commentator's reassuring conclusion is that 'identity is a concept no one has defined with precision, but it seeems we can move ahead anyway, because everyone roughly understands what is meant'.[20] Our own policy, certainly, rather than compounding difficulties of theory already dense, is to concentrate on consequences rather than causes.

In as much as he seems himself as male and acts as a male, the boy is cut off from the primitive comfort his mother could otherwise provide. It must follow, then – for lack of a better metaphor – that most males differ from most females in terms of what they have 'inside' them. Inside most males but not inside most females there must be a species of existential gulf. This, as Greenson and others have pointed out, will act to the male's disadvantage.[21] The male's position is by no means entirely bleak, even so. It consists, in fact, of a pattern of strengths and shortcomings; and it is these we want to explore.

On the debit side, there are two shortcomings to which the adult male is particularly vulnerable:

- Personal insensitivity, and
- Misogyny

The small boy, Greenson's insight enables us to predict, will find it more difficult than his sister to reciprocate affection, and his capacity for empathy will be impaired. He will tend to see those aspects of the world that are unmistakably emotional in black and white terms, either as heaven-on-earth or as unspeakably distasteful. He will be slow, too, to make sense of emotions that conflict; to detect the many shades of grey that separate black from white, and to realise that greys are often blacks and whites intricately mixed. Whatever his strengths elsewhere, in the field of intimate relations the 'male' male is bound to be at a disadvantage; even something of a cripple. His ability to experience a relationship as 'intersubjective' – as a meeting of experiential worlds – will be curtailed.

In stepping clear of the warm, symbiotic presence of his mother, the small boy may also leave unresolved a sense of loss and resentment; and perhaps, too, the fear of punishment or revenge. A consequence is that there will often exist in the male mind subterrranean currents of violently negative sentiment; and that while these will in some cases work themselves out in symbolic form, remote from their source, in others they will focus directly on the female sex and on the female body. We would predict, then, that beneath the surface of his attitudes to the opposite sex the adult male will often betray potently misogynous attitudes and fantasies. Women may well be idealised, and the idea of sexual access to them idealised too. But, at the same time, there may circulate – perhaps just within the range of awareness, perhaps beyond it – the vision of women as pollutors, beheaders and castrators; creatures to be feared, and in whom, despite appearances, sinister powers reside.

These misogynous preoccupations are expressed stereotypically in Don Juan; the sexual athlete who perceives women as desirable objects, and who ravishes them, but who must make good his escape before the potentially engulfing dangers of sexual intimacy can wreak their havoc. They were also expressed with formidable accuracy during the Renaissance, in the northern, incipiently Protestant, tradition of painting and sculpting the female nude. Where the Italian tradition of Titian and Veronese depicted the nude in idealised terms, the draughtsmen and carvers working north of the Alps explored in minute detail precisely those ambivalences and reversals to which heterosexual desire renders the male subject. Naked rather than nude, the 'bulb-like' women and 'root-like' men of this northern art, as Kenneth Clark remarks, seem dragged from the protective darkness of the previous thousand years.[22] The alternative convention of the nude thus created is based on different bodily proportions from those established by the Greeks – broader in the hip, narrower in the shoulder, longer, more pear-like in the abdomen. It also dwells on puckers and wrinkles, not on the judicious arrangement of smoothed surfaces and coherent volumes.

Perhaps the definitive statement of this extraordinary vein of invention and discovery is Conrad Meit's carving of Judith and Holofernes. Small and made of alabaster, Meit's *Judith* was produced in

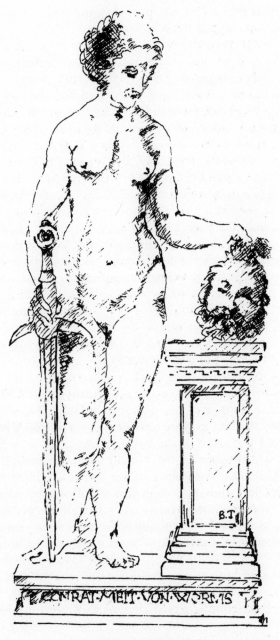

Judith and Holofernes

the first quarter of the sixteenth century. One commentator speaks of her serene command of space, but finds her eroticism 'almost repulsive'. Another sees her as 'probably the most satisfying' expression of the Renaissance the north ever saw.[23]

At first sight, especially to the eye trained in classical proportions, Judith is grotesque: head and hips too big, rib-cage and breasts too small; the distance from breast to navel twice what we expect it to be. Unathletic, her stomach protrudes and her flesh threatens to sag; a body not only able to bear children but one which has already done so. In her right hand, close to her naked pelvis, she props a massive sword, the handle held abstractedly, very much as if it were an erect penis which was not particularly her concern. In her left hand, held away from her, separated from the sword handle by her lower abdomen and clearly carved vaginal cleft, is Holofernes' bearded head. It is severed; and, holding it by its hair, she is balancing it casually on a plinth. The male has been dismantled, head in one of Judith's hands, sword in the other. As many commentators have noticed, Judith, far from being the grotesque she initially seems, proves on closer inspection to embody an unusually insistent sexual allure. Consequently, the conjunction of sword handle, vagina and severed head could scarcely be more eloquent. Here is the intimation that the male psyche, unlike the female one, is the kind of apparatus which comes apart. Its competences are real – the beard is manly, the sword convincingly massive – but it is subject to collapse when in proximity to the naked female body. It is in physical intimacy with the opposite sex, we are being told, and, more specifically, in sexual intercourse, that such dismantlings of the male psyche take place.[24]

Misogyny, then, is not a feature of the male mind which is simply a byproduct of a narrow-minded upbringing or of sexist biases in education. It is built into the male psyche. Stemming from fears which are a direct consequence of the wound, it lingers in a hinterland where notions of separation and engulfment, erotic excitement and dismay mingle. These fears, obviously, can express themselves in a variety of ways. In a generalised horror of women. In a specific revulsion from sexual intercourse with them, even though their presence is otherwise seen as pleasurable and a reassurance. Or in panic once sexual intercourse with them has been enjoyed. If they are not to be expressed destructively, these are sentiments which must somehow be contained or translated as they were by Meit.

THE BENEFITS

There are, however, more positive consequences in store. Three interest us particularly. These concern:

- The idea of agency – the individual's freedom, that is to say, to act on the world in the light of his own needs and intentions;
- The wound as a constantly replenishing source of psychic energy;
- The notion of abstract passions.

If his search for an alternative focus of identification is successful, the little boy has established for himself, as Greenson points out, a measure of separation. Even more tellingly, he has learnt a primitive lesson which he will not otherwise learn: that of *agency*.[25] Where, in sustaining her gender identity with her mother, the female infant must somehow accommodate whatever frustration is inherent in the relation between them, the male infant discovers that you can reject a source of frustration, and, simultaneously, find a stance independent of it. This discovery will be made at the cost of anxiety, no doubt, and of anxiety's attendant suppressions and repressions; but it is a valuable one, even so. The more 'male' the male, the greater the imaginative gulf separating him from his sources of primitive comfort; and the greater that gulf, we would predict, the greater his underlying existential insecurity is bound to be. He is perfectly poised, nevertheless, to heal his wound at one symbolic remove; to use the anxiety his separation provokes in him to create systems of ideas which can stand in the place of lost intimacy, and within which he can strive for coherence and harmony.[26]

Also, being rooted in a primitive separation, the male's energies are in principle inexhaustible. They will last as long as his wound lasts. With them at his command, he can go on for a lifetime searching for order in chaos. Alternatively, he can disrupt the forms of order that already exist – either for the pleasure of disrupting them, or with a view to replacing them with a form of order that is superior and identifiably his own. On this argument, the wound is not just an introduction to the experience of agency. It is an *energy source*, fuelling symbolically significant action – typically in fields distant from mothers and fathers, sex and gender. The defining characteristic of such activity is that it is pursued with passion; not for extraneous reasons like profit or status, but as an end in itself. As Anthony Storr has pointed out, conventional psychoanalytic theories tend to define good mental health by equating it with the ability to sustain rich human relationships.[27] But in the 'male' male at least, the connections between creativeness, human relationships and mental health are not simple. The biographical evidence – and we shall rehearse what we hope are representative fragments of it later – suggests that the richest relationship many sane and highly creative men establish is with systems of ideas or with pieces of machinery.

From the moment an imagined space opens up between the small boy and his mother, we are suggesting, he is in principle primed to execute within it at least three separate but related sorts of manoeuvre. As he matures, he can pursue abstract ideas, which are, in a sense, surrogates for his mother, in that they bear a complex symbolic relation to her.[28] He can think about matters, personal or inanimate, in ways that rehearse and celebrate the distance from his mother he has created – he can think, that is to say, in ways that appear objective and dispassionate. And, the possibility of most immediate bearing on our own argument, he can pursue ideas quite unrelated to his mother with the kind of passion he had previously felt towards her. (Notice, we are not saying that the thought processes of the 'male' male are distinctively objective. What we are saying is that he has a driven need to use his intelligence on impersonal problems; and that in doing so he can display remorseless powers of application.)[29]

Psychologists' efforts to come to terms with such phenomena have in the past had about them an air of contrivance. They usually suggest either that a biological energy – sex, aggression – has somehow been diverted or 'sublimated' into a new channel; or that the motive underlying abstract thought cannot be what it seems: that, after all, it must boil down to ambition, say, or territoriality, or envy, or the desire for access to attractive members of the opposite sex. These explanatory enterprises, it has long been realised, sit uncomfortably with the facts as we know them: the small boy paying rapt attention to his collection of postage stamps; Isaac Newton absorbed to the exclusion of all other considerations by the laws of gravity. In contrast, the idea of the male wound offers a plausible account of just such absorption: that it springs from a dissociative movement of the mind in which the inanimate – things, systems of ideas – acquires the intense emotional significance previously lodged in people, and in which people, stripped of that significance, are treated as though they were things.

It is the wound's capacity to engender fascination with the impersonal that immediately concerns us. For in doing so, it helps makes sense of what, in evolutionary terms, is our species' most conspicuous characteristic: *our capacity for abstract passion*. It explains our ability not merely to think analytically, nor even to think analytically with passionate intensity, but to think analytically and with passionate intensity about topics that have no detectable bearing on our ordinary biological appetites or needs. For the 'male' male – and, in explanatory terms, this is crucial point – *such passions will be the more enduringly gratifying the more completely divorced from human relationships they are*. The more abstract their context, the more his enterprises take on a quality that is simultaneously impassioned and aesthetically pure. Nor is there any requirement that the operations the male performs within a framework of objectifying thought will themselves be disinterested in tone and inspiration. On the contrary, what is proposed is that the male can express within this framework – safely and at a distance – any of the impulses an intimate relationship might otherwise have inspired.

At the heart of our account of the psychology of the male imagination, then, is a two-part claim. That, in combination, dis-identification and counter-identification create in the 'male' male a sense of agency, allied to a constantly replenishing source of imaginative energy. And that these same processes draw him towards the inanimate – the world of things, mechanisms, abstract ideas and systems within which he operates with the commitment and fervour we might otherwise have expected him to display towards people.[30]

THE INTELLECTUAL AND THE PERSONAL

A significant consequence of dis- and counter-identification, we assume, is the existence of complex patterns of linkage and splitting between the nature of a man's work and that of his private life.[31] Often, these linkages and segregations are highly specific. In a study of eminent men in British universities, for example, we found that the humanities, biology and physical science each had their own patterns of marriage, fertility and divorce. Many eminent men in the humanities had remained single, as many as four out of every ten distinguished classical scholars recording themselves as childless. In contrast, nearly all the eminent biological and physical scientists had followed a more conventional pattern, and were married with children.[32]

We also found that rates of divorce varied strikingly from group to group, being six times as high, for instance, among eminent physicists as among eminent chemists. The most marked difference of all, though, occurred among the biologists. Those who had risen to eminence through the roles they had played in the fusion of old-fashioned biology with mathematics and the physical sciences – who had helped establish the modern discipline of genetics, for example – were some twenty-five times more likely to divorce than the biologists of the next decade who had implemented these pioneers' discoveries. It seems, in other words, that upheavals in the intellectual and personal spheres echo one another, serious matrimonial disturbance being most common among men in whom intellectual boundaries have been breached. In terms of Kuhn's distinction between 'revolutionary' and 'normal' science, divorce seems a close concomitant of the first, and to bear only an incidental relation to the second.[33]

The scheme outlined in Chapter 2 also alerts us to the possibility that the male's dis-identification and counter-identification can be partial or precarious. Where this happens, the abiding preoccupations of the individual in question will deviate significantly from the 'male' norm. Some of the most subtle of these deviations arise in science, and, more specifically, in biology. An experimental scientist can approach living subject-matter reductively, with a view to explaining it in terms of mathematics, physics or chemistry. He can work on living forms as a taxonomist; distinguishing, cataloguing, counting. He can explore the living as Darwin did on HMS *Beagle*, hoping to gain access to its hidden laws. He can explore the living as some ecologists do, with a view to conserving and celebrating its variety. Most interesting of all in the present context, he can use biology as a platform from which to attack the human, showing that the distinctive features of our experience – our capacity for love and access to the transcendental – are in principle indistinguishable from those enjoyed by baboon or hamster.

In summary, the male is at liberty to relate the objectifying to the personal in a variety of ways. He can:

- Segregate his experience: on the one side of an invisible dividing line, rapt attention to the impersonal; on the other, the personal acknowledged but left to wither.

Alternatively, he can attempt to knit the personal and impersonal together. If a sustained attempt at integration is made, he may use the impersonal to:

- Attack the personal, and subjugate it; or
- Recreate it in symbolic terms.

The policy the individual adopts will be influenced, we are going to suggest in Chapter 4, by the position he occupied within his family as he grew up, and on the nature of the relations with his mother and father he enjoyed – not just his separation from one and his identification with the other, but the terms on which feelings of warmth and hostility within the family were expressed. Of the three options just listed, the first corresponds, in terms of roughest approximation, to the dominant preoccupations of *science and technology*. The second corresponds to the dominant preoccupations of the more fiercely reductive forms of *biology and psychology*. The third corresponds to the dominant preoccupations of the *creative arts*. Between them, in briefest outline, they encapsulate much of the rest of what we have to say.

Even where the long-term effects of dis-identification and counter-identification appear completely secure, hints of instability may none the less linger. If they do, the task of shoring up the relevant barricades will continue throughout life. Each venture into the realm of the abstract thus becomes an affirmation of the internal arrangements the wound originally set in place. As distant echoes, each venture may bring with it too the anxieties that thoughts of collapsing defences and the prospect of re-engulfment provoke. Abstract thought thus becomes a venue for the expression not only of pleasures once associated with symbiotic intimacy, but also of the hostility (and in extreme cases, the panic) engendered by the thought that the symbiotically intimate will not stay in its allotted place. Like 'the black tide of mud' that once threated Freud, and against which his sexual theory was a bulwark, thoughts of excessive intimacy may menace even the most resolutely formal of thinkers, and - like Freud's vision of 'occultism' – need repeatedly to be banished with each piece of work undertaken. Threatened access to such thoughts and fantasies may account not only for the combative atmosphere of so much science, but also for its tendency towards internecine rancour, differences in the preferred method of shoring up defences appearing as dangerous as the incoming tide itself. More tellingly still, it may be the intuitively perceived encroachment of the excessively intimate which serves many (conceivably, all) abstract thinkers as their imaginative trigger, launching each of them on yet another venture into the realm of formal thought.

THE WOUND'S NATURE

Later, we are going to illustrate the qualities of the male imagination in more detail. Before we move on, it is important to be clear about the kinds of claim we are making on the wound's behalf, there being the risk that these will seem grandiose and over-inclusive.

Our assertions are not ones about biology as destiny any more than they are about the effects of prejudice in a sexist society. As we have outlined it, the wound is a psychological phenomenon; an emergent property of the conjunction of a body with an alert and re-flexive intelligence. It takes shape in response to biological realities, that is to say, but, once in being, has an autonomous life, propelling individuals imaginatively along different paths, facilitating heart-felt performance here, stifling it there.[34]

Of the wound we are saying that:

- It is a centrally-placed feature of the 'male' male's mental archi-tecture;
- It is an energy source – a source of unresolved (and in principle unresolvable) tensions;
- It exerts a formative influence on the imaginative needs the male subsequently experiences;
- It imparts to the expression of those needs a characteristic bias or spin;
- Its action is evidenced by a loose-knit group of tell-tale signs;
- Its influence is of the kind that, in the short term, can often be overridden, but that tends stubbornly to reassert itself over the longer run; and
- Its forms of expression in the adult are protean.

To date, the tendency in psychology has been to propose relatively rigid sequences of developmental phases, and to see such sequences as marked by critical periods, during which learning most naturally and spontaneously occurs. It is also widely assumed, as we ourselves tend to, that the early years are the formative ones; and that it is the qualities acquired early in life that are the warp and weft of the adult personality. To change the metaphor, it is these qualities that seem *ingrained*. To change it again, they become, in the language of the engineer, part of the individual's 'spec'.

We must be cautious, though. The focus of our own research has been on the academic choices of adolescents, on the career paths of adults, and on the relation of adults' careers to their private lives. Research of this kind teaches an important lesson. It is variousness that characterises biographical evidence. Whatever the eventual role or accomplishment, there is always, or almost always, more than one antecedent biographical pattern. In the development of adult traits and talents, in other words, one is dealing, as so often in psychology, and as we were in the previous chapter, not with one-to-one linkages, but with the action on one another of a variety of causes within a network or lattice, and with the path or trajectory that a series of choices within that lattice creates. So, although the evidence about adults may sometimes yield clear-cut differences between 'male' men and genderless or effeminate men, and between men as a whole and women as a whole, such differences are not the only form of evidence compatible with our theory of the wound. Differences of detail and nuance have a bearing on it too. Where stark differences do arise, these indicate not that the relevant options and linkages are themselves stark, but that, for one reason or another, the groups in question have steered consistently different routes though a complex lattice.

A feature of such lattice patterns is that a single point of departure is connected to widely diverse destinations, while closely adjacent destinations can be reached by a wide variety of routes.[35] We each carry our past with us, what is more. A man who follows a career like Truman Capote's will practise the art of the novelist in one way; a man who follows a career like Ernest Hemingway's will practise the same art in another. It is within a model of the mind in which sequences of choices interact and interdepend that our notion of the wound is deployed.

PREDICTIONS AND CONJECTURES

If the theory discussed so far is substantially correct, we would expect that the wound's effects:

- Will be stable over broad stretches of the lifespan, not evanescent byproducts of the individual's culture or the social roles he happens to occupy;
- Will express themselves in observable, quantifiable terms

among samples of men, and between samples of men and women, as well as in the lives of individuals; and

- Will be resistant to changes in patterns of child-raising and family life.

We would expect, too, that:

- In the lives both of individuals and of groups, the wound's effects will often be characterised by apparently arbitrary inconsistencies and segregations.

The existence of the wound leads us to expect that character traits like misogyny or personal insensitivity will express themselves spontaneously among men whose gender identity is clearly 'male'. But we are dealing with a system within which migrations and dissociations are the norm. So misogyny could turn out to express itself in different ways, discipline by discipline: in womanising among poets, say, in celibacy among classical scholars, in high rates of divorce among radically innovative biologists, and in forthrightly sexist prejudice among engineers. Its expression could also alter within a discipline, decade by decade, as the nature of that discipline and recruitment to it changes. So while expecting a quality like misogyny to express itself in both the intellectual and the sexual spheres of an individual's life, we remain alert to the possibility that its expression can become localised, specialised. A man may be treacherous in his work, treacherous in his sex life, or treacherous in both alike. Over the years, his mendacious tendencies may spread from his working life to his sex life, or vice versa. They may also migrate. A previously blameless working life may be invaded by the tendency to lie and finagle at just the point when his private life, previously distorted by hostile impulses, at last achieves a more decorous balance.[36]

Despite these propensities for translation and migration, we expect the evidence to reveal, both in its aggregate forms and in detail and nuance, the persistence of certain themes. We would expect the wound to be associated with:

- Segregations of the personal from the impersonal;
- A preoccupation with issues of intellectual control; and
- The conjunction of that control with partisan and aggressive sentiment.

More specifically, we would expect to find the wound associated with:

- Characteristic patterns of cost (misogyny, personal insensitivity) and benefit (agency, imaginative energy, abstract passion);
- Characteristic patterns of career choice; and
- Orderly relations between the first of these patterns and the second.

In terms of style, the 'male' cast of mind will:

- Be intolerant of 'messy' arguments – i.e., ones that lack formal structure and are, variously, intuitive, empathetic, indeterminate; and
- Emphasise the virtues of dispassion and objectivity (although what is displayed will usually be the exercise of intelligence in the service of enterprises which are partisan and combative, and in that sense impassioned and non-objective).

The existence of the wound also creates expectations of the evidence that are less clear-cut, and that have the status more of conjectures. Particularly, it leads us to expect the existence of 'male' formats of thought. These will differ, of course, from field to field, but, in essence, their features are those of the wound itself.[37] The 'male' mind should typically show a taste for:

- Arguments cast in terms of dualities and dialectical oppositions (like male/female, conscious/unconscious, mind/body, theory/evidence) and their reconciliations;
- Arguments that depend on the maintenance of conceptual boundaries and segregations (like that between natural sciences and the social ones), and on colonising forays across such boundaries;
- Arguments (e.g., about classification) that depend on a deep preoccupation with similarities and differences;
- Arguments that are reductive, especially ones that explain the subtly experiential in terms of the prosaic and literal; and
- Arguments centring on ideas – often highly technical – the truth of which is perceived as luminous.

There are also grounds for suspecting, as we have already said, that even the most stable solutions to the dilemmas of dis- and counter-identification contain hints of precariousness; and that, as a consequence, the work of maintaining the wound's dissociations is never quite done. As we shall see, even in the most austerely abstract of 'male' thought, traces of the wound's intimately human origin are often detectable, and are perhaps never finally expunged.

CHAPTER 4

THE FAMILY NEXUS

THERE IS STILL ample scope for disagreement among psychologists, biologists and social scientists about the extent to which the new-born male infant is already programmed as he enters the world. Almost everyone concedes, nevertheless, that the influence of parents is formative. It is the domestic family unit – the 'family nexus' – that determines whether the effects of the wound are going to be so extreme as to appear a self-caricature; or, conversely, that they will be obscured to the point where they can seem vestigial.

In the 1950s and 1960s, a number of ingenious studies were undertaken to gauge the influence of child-raising practices on the personality of the growing child; and, in turn, the influence on child-raising practices of the parents' culture. Certain of these studies became quite famous, and although in the end inconclusive, the research effort of which they were part sensitised psychologists to certain points of principle. In one study of that period, Sears and his colleagues interviewed American mothers who had five-year-old children in kindergarten. They found *orderly relations between the mother's policy in disciplining her child and her child's temperament*. It was the mothers who were controlling but who punished mildly who had unaggressive children, the sons especially; and those who were permissive but who punished harshly whose children were aggressive. As the authors themselves insisted, it was not clear whether mothers punished harshly because they had aggressive children or vice versa. Still less was it clear whether it was desirable for five-year-olds to be aggressive or calm; but the existence of linkages between the child-raising practices of the parent and the temperament of the children was firmly established, and have since been explored in greater detail. In a second study, Kagan and Moss discovered both *a 'sleeper' effect* and a tendency of *the same child-raising pattern to influence boys in one direction, girls in another*. Following an American sample longitudinally, they found that it was the mothers' behaviour towards their children in the first three years of life, rather than their behaviour towards them subsequently, which was most powerfully predictive of those children's behaviour when they themselves became adult. Kagan and Moss also found that a protective attitude on the mother's part towards her children was predictive of 'involvement in intellectual mastery' when their children became adults – but only in the case of boys. It was the critical mothers whose daughters later tended to shine intellectually.[1]

It became clear too that, far from varying randomly from one culture to another, *the basic objectives of child-raising remain roughly constant.* By one means or another, each culture aims to establish the male's maleness, it being the route rather than the destination that varies. Whiting and his colleagues examined ethnographic evidence about economically primitive societies, for example, and demonstrated that societies which have sleeping arrangements in which the mother and baby share the same bed for at least a year to the exclusion of the father, and in which taboos restrict the sexual behaviour of the mother for at least a year after giving birth, are much more likely than others to have male initiation ceremonies at puberty. The eventual maleness of males is the culture's concern, in other words, whether achieved by the processes of dis-identification and counter-identification as we might expect to find them in our own culture, or ritually and categorically at the beginning of adolescence.[2]

Layer by layer, psychological and social, the family environment is structured in terms of sex and gender. In our own culture, it is the nuclear family – mother and father, living together with their children as a stable unit – that provides the context within which the male wound takes its typical form. But, in the prosperous West, the conventions governing family life have begun to slacken. Women no longer feel forced to marry the fathers of their children; and both sexes are beginning to free themselves from the belief that nurture is women's work. There are couples among whom the conventional roles are reversed, the father caring for the children and the wife bringing home the wages. Other domestic recombinations and permutations have been attempted besides. Girls and boys brought up by their fathers living alone. By lesbians living together. By male homosexuals living together. In communes where child-raising is shared by all and sundry. Even by pedophiles.

For the time being, the consequences of these natural experiments can only be guessed at. On the strength of the distinctions drawn in the last chapter, we would predict that certain factors will deepen the wound and potentiate its effects; others minimise both. At least six considerations should have a bearing:

- The mother's gender identity – whether 'female', more androgynous or positively 'male';
- The mother's parental style – whether encouraging separation in her son or fostering symbiotic union;
- The son's character – whether wilful and intolerant of frustration or compliant;
- The continuous presence in the household of an adult male with whom the mother is sexually intimate, or the absence of such a figure;
- That male figure's gender identity – 'male', androgynous or 'female'; and
- A climate in the household which favours the stereotypical differentiation of the sexes or tells against it.

As Stoller says, 'masculinity in males starts as a movement away from the painless but potentially dangerous... mother/infant symbiosis.' If he is to be masculine, the boy 'must first find the urge within his biological inheritance' to separate and individuate, and be blessed too with a mother who encourages this. If she cannot allow him to separate, 'she will prolong and therefore augment his primary state of feminity'. If, on the other hand, 'she beats at him too harshly to forego all she considers feminine, she may produce the frozen, brutal, phallic character that results when the possibilities of even momentary return to her are foreclosed'.[3] The mother who fosters symbiotic intimacy; the father who is absent; the son who is compliant: this should produce a wound so shallow as scarcely to be perceptible. The mother who encourages separation from the outset, but is herself 'feminine'; the father who is deeply 'wounded' yet accessible to his son; the son who is intolerant of maternal frustration: this is a pattern, we predict, likely to produce a wound in the son the effects of which are enduring and unmistakable.

In discussing the evidence that follows, we look first at what happens to a boy when the influence of his mother on his early experience is overwhelmingly strong. Then we look at the reverse of this: at instances where the mother's influence breaks down – because she dies while her son is still an infant, or finds him impossible to love. Finally, we summarise the influences parents have on the development of their child's imagination, pointing to a serious awkwardness which we illustrate with a further example. Continuously present is the idea of costs and benefits counterbalancing one another; of gains on the swings compensating for losses on the roundabouts, and vice versa.

SINGLE PARENTS AND MATRIARCHS

If a young mother, through choice or force of circumstance, brings up her son alone, the impact on her son will depend, we are claiming, on two factors at least: on how intimately invasive of her son the mother is, and on the terms on which her son can become attached to men. The mother may feel shy of her son, keeping him at a distance from her and, both consciously and unconsciously, fostering his separation. Alternatively, she may dress him up continually, fondle him in intimate ways, flirt with him, and sleep with him in her arms. Stoller describes mothers, those of future transsexuals, who create relationships with their sons so intimately symbiotic that the son's body seems an extension of the mother's and his mind a compartment of hers.[4] The single parent mother may have a retinue of lovers or none. She may live in a setting where her son has continuous access to male relatives and male neighbours, or in social isolation. And just as individuals can find themselves committed to unorthodox domestic arrangements, so too can whole communities. A mother can be a single parent in a society that treats stably married heterosexual couples as the norm; alternatively, she can live in a matriarchal community, itself at variance with the dominant culture surrounding it.

In 1965, before the riots and the emergence of the Black Panthers, we spent ten days in the Woodlawn ghetto of Chicago (for English people, a privilege we owed to a friend then using the University of Chicago as a base from which to foster black parents' commitment to their children's schooling). Unemployment had been endemic among the males of Woodlawn for as long as anyone could remember; and, in practice, responsibility as a consequence lay in the hands of women. Those we spoke to led lives in which husbands played no detectable part. It did not follow, of course, that there were no males on whom these women's sons could model themselves. In this particular matriarchy, the small boy has such models galore. What he lacks is a stable male presence within the home. There is no one man in whose direction his mother's attention continually turns; no adult couple committed to one another, and with whose enduring sexual intimacy he has to come to terms.

THE ABSENT FATHER

The young male who imitates foot-loose and disaffected men can be expected to grow up foot-loose and disaffected; their projects become his project. The real damage, however, is more insidiously over-determined. For while such young men have adult males to imitate, they have none with whom to identify; a pattern which characteristically results, the theory of the wound predicts, in a defective sense of agency. It is just this frame of mind which, in ghettos like Woodlawn, makes it so difficult for black males to break the cycle in which a sense of rootlessness leads to unemployment and delinquency, and unemployment and delinquency heighten a sense of rootlessness.[5]

Communities like Woodlawn have other effects besides. By no means necessarily harmful, these are of special psychological interest in that they shed an unexpected light on the male wound and its consequences.

The art of interpreting the results of intelligence tests given to children in environments like Woodlawn is a difficult one. A theme recurs in such research, even so; and it has cropped up in work in the West Indies too. Both in North American black ghettos and in the West Indies, where mothers are fully as dominant as they are in Woodlawn, boys have been reported as showing an unexpected pattern of mental ability. One might well predict, on the strength of poor schooling or truancy or sheer indifference, that black boys from such backgrounds would be somewhat weaker at reasoning in terms of words than they are at reasoning in terms of patterns. Yet research has often shown the reverse of this. These boys perform adequately on verbal tasks, but are unexpectedly weak on non-verbal ones – just the tasks on which young males usually perform well.[6]

The evidenced is patchy and inconclusive, though, and the topic would scarcely be worth pursuing had not similar-sounding results arisen in quite different sorts of 'absent father' study. In an unusually ingenious piece of research, Lyn Carlsmith looked at sons who later became students at Harvard.[7] She concentrated on a sample whose fathers had been away serving in the armed forces during the first three years of their sons' lives, but had then returned. By the time they entered Harvard as students, these men's sons were high in verbal skills, but lacked the particular strength in non-verbal reasoning that such a sample might usually have been expected to display. Their pattern of their abilities, in fact, was one more usually found in samples of highly academically accomplished young women.

On the basis of other studies – among them, work one of us was then doing at Cambridge University – it was clear that a non-verbal bias of intelligence was characteristic of young men specialising in disciplines like mathematics, physics and engineering; and that a marked verbal bias was usual among those in the humanities.[8] Physical science and technology were not just dominated numerically by men, in other words, but by men with a particular intellectual bias; and a bias which was linked in turn to patterns of upbringing. Taken together, this research had two clear implications:

- That, even in the early years, the presence of the father in the home has a significant influence on his son's subsequent development; and
- That this influence reaches well beyond the realm of personal relations, and into that of formal thought.

LITTLE BOY IN A FROCK

Of course, history has played more bizarre tricks upon small boys than those facing the males of Woodlawn or the Caribbean. The victim of one of these was a boy born in Prague just over a hundred years ago; and it is instructive to look at what became of him.

The boy's father had been an army officer.[9] He had served with distinction in the Austrian campaign against Italy fifteen years earlier, but had been forced to resign his commission through ill health. A disappointed man, he worked as a railway official. Contemptuous of civilian life, his consolation was the thought that his son might one day take up the military career he had abandoned. Described as nervous and as a philistine, the father was a source of irritation to his son, but also of security. The boy's mother, in contrast, is described as imaginative and as possessing great vitality, but also as silly, snobbish, and with a tendency towards 'pure, nearly childish hedonism'. Later in life, this buoyancy evaporated. 'In her womanly way', a close but sharply critical commentator was to observe, she 'merely holds forth with inane emphasis'.[10] In her personal relationships she seemed never properly to 'meet' the other person; never quite to be *there*. As he grew older, his mother's vacuous expansiveness was something her son came to dread.

There had been an older sister, but she had died in infancy. The boy's mother consoled herself by bringing up her son as though he were a little girl. A century ago, it was by no means unusual to put small boys in dresses and to train their hair into ringlets. But she also called him by a girl's name, and until he was five, he played with dolls, his only contact with boys of his own age being on his birthday. Unfortunately, too, when he was nine, his parents' marriage, never a happy one, foundered. They separated, his mother going to live in Vienna and his father staying on in Prague. Perhaps because they could not afford to send him to a *gymnasium*, perhaps to satisfy his father's military ambitions for his son, the little boy was dispatched for five years to board in military academies, where all expenses were paid by the state. There he learnt little, made no friends, was intensely miserable, and was eventually removed on grounds of continual ill-health. After a further year spent boarding at a commercial academy in Linz, he returned in his mid-teens to live with his father in Prague.

What did this contradictory and inadvertently cruel upbringing produce? The little boy turned into a young man committed to write. Obsessively concerned with intimate relationships, he was so at one remove, driven to turn them into sentences on the page, pages in a book.

Despite a frail physique – chin receding, neck thin, shoulders narrow and sloping – and those formative years spent wearing frocks and playing with dolls, his object choice was heterosexual. Drawn to powerful women, he was to exert a considerable attraction over them in return. In his mid-twenties, he married a sculptor, a pupil of the concupiscent Rodin. Together they had a daughter, but being poor and ambitious, decided to live separately and meet whenever they could. Leaving their daughter in the care of her maternal grandparents, the two drifted apart, but were to remain on friendly terms.

Before his marriage, he had studied at the universities of Munich and Berlin; and it was in Berlin, at the age of twenty-one, that he had fallen in love with an older woman, a formidable creature by any standards, and whose androgyny created a counterpoint to his own. The woman he fell for, and whom he pursued and won with a barrage of letters and poems, was married and in her mid-thirties, the sixth child and only daughter of a former general in the Russian Imperial Army. Their passionate affair was followed by a friendship lasting for the rest of his life. Long before she and the young man met, the philosopher Nietzsche had been in love with her; and many years later, the men over whom she cast her spell were to include Freud. 'I have never known a more gifted or more understanding creature,' Nietzsche said of her, when she was scarcely out of her teens. She was, he claimed, 'prepared like none other for that part of my philosophy that has hardly yet been uttered'.[11] Many years later, Freud was to give her roses and escort her home. When she failed to turn up for one of his lectures, he admitted that he 'stared as if spellbound' at the vacant chair reserved for her. Twenty years later still, then in her seventies, Freud was to tell her of her 'superiority over all of us – in accord with the heights from which you descended to us'. In his obituary of her, he was to describe her as a person 'beyond human frailty'.[12]

She became well known as a novelist and essayist; and, in later life, was a privileged member of Freud's inner circle and practised as a psychoanalyst. On the other hand, there was a darker side to her. Whether or not Freud found himself exposed to it is unclear, but others certainly were, and counted the cost. She was a *femme fatale* who, despite the mesmerising power of the attraction she exerted over cerebral men, seems to have had something amiss with her sexually – the attraction she exerted presumably being so powerful for just this reason. In her mid-twenties, she had married a much older man, a scholar of Near Eastern languages, but the marriage was not consummated. Later, she was to claim that she saw devotion to any one man as physically repugnant, 'a spiritual slavery'. 'A woman has no other choice', she wrote, 'than to be unfaithful or to be only half herself.'[13] She was a mistress, then, but also a rejector; and in her rejection of them, is said to have contributed to the death of two remarkable men: the philosopher Paul Rée, killed in a climbing accident, and the psychoanalyst Victor Tausk – 'brother animal', she called him – who committed suicide.[14]

This disquieting woman was Lou Andreas-Salomé; and of the men she drew to her, it was the young man – the poet Rainer Maria Rilke – who was arguably the most gifted of all. Certainly, it was he who made on her the deepest impression. When well into her fifties, she was to write: 'One day there was Rainer standing at the garden gate in the twilight, and before we said a word we clasped each other's hands over the fence. The whole time he spent here made me so very happy! Not just as a reunion, but because it was so very much a reunion with *him*...'[15]

In his life, as in his poetry, Rilke combined passionate attraction with an abstemious holding back. He was driven, he would claim, by two related but opposed preoccupations: the idea of a perfect lover, and also that of the 'early departed' – those who die in childhood, before they have had the opportunity to love. Both had their origin, he said, in his own loneliness as a child. He was profoundly moved in later life by the news of the death of a beautiful adolescent girl, Wera Knoop, who became the inspiration of his *Sonnets to Orpheus* – a girl, incidentally, whom he had met only once or twice, several years before. He was haunted, too, by the death in childhood of his cousin Egon; the ruff he wore, his slender neck, and his beautiful brown eyes, disfigured by a squint. Lou spoke of 'the prodigously expansive way' her lover 'surrenders himself inwardly to things'. She also noticed, though, that while delicately constituted and while he gave of himself unrestrainedly, he was durable. His battles centred not on her or any other living person, but in his own work. (As she also remarked, somewhat disapprovingly, Rilke's pleasure in sexual intercourse was impaired by an 'essentially noxious hostility to the body'; hers, no doubt, no less than his own.)[16]

At the time, the poet was in early middle age and was blocked; and it was a reasonable guess that he might permanently remain so. Although, throughout his career, he had written on occasions with great fluency, these episodes had become increasingly intermittent. It is clear that he suffered long periods of depression. As he matured, the character of his work changed too, ceasing to be a matter of lyrical expression, and becoming one of workmanlike 'making', with results increasingly dense and gnomic.[17] It worried Lou that the separate elements of his personality might knit themselves together, but do so in such a way that he could not write at all. History was to prove her right and wrong. As she correctly sensed, a conflict was unfolding, and Rilke was to remain blocked for nearly another decade. But when 'utterance and release' finally came, it did so definitively: in the form of the bulk of the *Duino Elegies* and all fifty-five *Sonnets to Orpheus*, more than 1,200 lines of poetry written in eighteen days, largely without correction.[18]

In as much as his parents represented the nineteenth-century ideals of maleness and femaleness in stereotypical form – one the thwarted man of action, the other the creature of fancy leaps and phrases – it is tempting to see Rilke as effecting a retreat to a point equidistant from both, and to explain his creativeness in terms of his position in gender's midground. We know that he experienced androgynous, hermaphroditic yearnings, and saw these as expressed in his work. It is tempting to extrapolate from this and to equate all forms of creativeness with androgyny. A glance at the lives of other writers demonstrates, though, that this would be a serious mistake. There are great writers – Marcel Proust, for instance – who have haunted gender's midground;[19] but there are others like Ernest Hemingway who were not merely forthrightly masculine, but whose masculinity seemed so stereotyped as to be parodic.[20] Arguably, Hemingway as much as Rilke was a creature internally divided in terms of gender; and arguably too, both found a way of reconciling their internal divisions in work. But it would be a mistake to press the argument further than that.

COOLER CLIMES

If absent fathers and consciously feminising mothers obscure the wound's effects, we would expect maternal coldness or absence to accentuate them. Though it is circumstantial, some of the most interesting evidence in this context concerns the personal relations of successful scientists. In monographs published in the early 1950s, the psychologist Anne Roe described her work with American scientists of eminence. Conveniently for our own purposes, she drew contrasts within her data between physicial scientists, biologists, and human scientists – that is to say, psychologists and anthropologists.[21]

Early in life, Roe found, her eminent physical and biological scientists divorced themselves from personal relations, and in many instances experienced considerable isolation. There was a general picture of shyness, and of a lack of overt interest in the opposite sex. As adults, her scientists showed considerable independence from their own parents, for the most part without guilt – a pattern also observable among successful business executives. Her evidence demonstrated, she insisted, that extremely useful and deeply gratifying lives could be led without the kinds of intimacy that psychologists considered essential. Many of her biological and physical scientists took little interest in personal relations, and were happy that this was so. Among her psychologists and anthropologists there was evidence, on the other hand, of enduring conflict. A number of these, although outwardly independent, still harboured resentment and rebellion towards parents, even though these were in some instances long dead. As she pointed out, this preoccupation with personal relationships, allied to the sense of personal superiority harboured by many of her psychologists and anthropologists, may well have had a biasing effect on prevailing theories of the mature personality. In the light of such theories, the personalities of her physical and biological scientists were bound to seem 'compensatory'. But there was no evidence that this was so; nor, for that matter, as she pointed out with warmth, was it self-evident that compensatory mechanisms were necessarily undesirable.

Others' studies told a similar story, about the physical scientist especially. Summarising a number, David McClelland concluded a decade later that the successful physical scientist tends characteristically:[22]

- To be male,
- To come from a 'radical Protestant' (i.e. puritanical) background without himself being religious,
- To avoid personal relations,
- To work with great single-mindedness,
- To avoid complex emotions,
- To like music and dislike painting and poetry,
- To be intensely masculine,
- To develop a strong interest in analysis, in the structure of things, early in life – often by five and usually no later than ten.

Since Roe collected her samples and McClelland published his review, the mood of the physical sciences has changed, becoming more urbane and more fanciful.[23] There has developed a lightness of touch far removed from the solemnity of 'schoolmaster' scientists like Ernest Rutherford, and the painfully clumsy humour of the Cavendish Laboratory in his heyday. It is easy to be misled by this change of style, though. The 'schoolmaster' scientists were capable of brilliant intuition, and were so in what many psychologists would regard as a human void; while those who have succeeded them still keep the warmly intimate at a safe distance.

THE FLIGHT FROM WOMEN

Research like Roe's offers no direct evidence about the kinds of mothering abstract thinkers in fact receive. It was this topic that was broached, in the mid-sixties, by Stern.[24] He looked at the lives of Descartes, Schopenhauer, Tolstoy, Kierkegaard, Goethe and Sartre, and found in all six evidence of the same tendency: a retreat from human intimacy into formality and abstraction. 'The six are an ill-assorted lot', he admits, but they are like 'a chain gang, chafing against the same iron.' In each he detects the same 'Manichean streak'; a revulsion from the pleasures of the flesh. The most accessible of the cases Stern cites are those of the two great philosophers: the seventeenth-century Frenchman René Descartes, and the early nineteenth-century German, Arthur Schopenhauer.

Descartes was born into a family of the minor French aristocracy, his father an influential civil servant and his mother the daughter of a lawyer. His mother died in child-birth when René was little more than a year old; and from the age of eight he was cared for by the Jesuits. Sickly both as a child and as an adult, he grew up to have platonic relations with several of the formidable women of the day: the Duchess of Aiguillon, Anne-Marie de Schurmann, Princess Elizabeth and Queen Christina of Sweden. He is also said to have retained a life-long attachment to his wet-nurse. The only woman with whom he is thought to have had an affair, Helena Jans, was probably a domestic servant.

As a mathematician and scientist, Descartes did work of a fundamental nature in geometry and made major contributions to the study of optics. As a philosopher, he articulated the doctrine of dualism, which establishes an absolute distinction between mind and matter. The natural world, he claimed, and in particular the human body, is like a huge piece of clockwork: a totally determinate apparatus. The life of the mind is parallel to it, but separate from it. It was on the strength of this assertion that Descartes has since been celebrated as the founding father not only of modern philosophy but of the scientific method.[25]

Schopenhauer's childhood experience was equally damaging, perhaps, but quite different. His forebears were Hanseatic merchants of vast prosperity and influence. When Peter the Great and the Empress Catherine came to stay in his house, Arthur's great-grandfather is said to have inspected their room before they arrived, and, finding it

damp, ordered that the floor be covered in brandy and set alight. The
room was filled with a pleasant aroma, and the floor was left bone
dry. It is said, too, that Frederick the Great once spent two hours in
private conversation with Arthur's father, trying unsuccessfully to
persuade him to leave Danzig and settle in Prussia.

In fact, the Prussians invaded Danzig when Arthur was five, and
the family fled to Hamburg. Their wealth was largely unimpaired,
however, and they travelled widely. As a result, Arthur became cos-
mopolitan: fluent in English and French as well as German, and at
home, too, with English and French culture. When he was seventeen, Schopenhauer's life was suddenly transformed by the death of
his father, apparently in an accident but perhaps by suicide. Schopenhauer was released from the prospect of a lifetime in the family business, and could devote himself to his studies. His mother Johanna,
nearly twenty years her husband's junior, was released too. She became a figure of renown in her own right: the German counterpart of
Madame de Staël and George Sand, and a significant presence in the
literary life of her time. One of her poems was set to music by
Schubert, and she embarked on a career of international standing as a
romantic novelist. Years later, long after Schopenhauer's great work
as a philosopher had been published, he was still known, to his intense chagrin, as 'Johanna Schopenhauer's son'.

Johanna's reputation is that of an exceptionally cold-hearted and
rejecting mother, although, at this distance, it is impossible to be
sure that she has not been maligned. A contemporary certainly
described her in unflattering terms: 'A rich widow, she makes a profession of being erudite. A writer. She talks a great deal and very
well; is sensible; but has no heart or soul. Self-satisfied and eager for
applause, smug.'[26] Bryan Magee describes her as 'one of those brit-
tle, socially oriented personalities who are almost totally devoid of
true feeling'.[27]

Schopenhauer spent his early years on the family's remote country
estate with his mother, but never in harmony with her. Later, he was
to say that his happiest years as a child were those spent away from
her; and after his father's death, the antipathy between them grew
more intense. When, as a student, it seemed that he might come to
live with her in Weimar, she wrote to him: 'It is needful to my happi-
ness to know that you are happy, but not to be a witness of it. I have
always told you it is difficult to live with you; and the better I get to
know you, the more I feel this difficulty increase, at least for me. I
will not hide it from you: as long as you are what you are, I would

rather make any sacrifice than consent to live with you.'[28] Subsequently, she was to form an intimate friendship with a young man of roughly Arthur's age. Son and mother were soon estranged, and never met again.

An anecdote captures something of Johanna's style – or, more strictly, her son's reconstruction of it. When Arthur completed his first philosophical work, he presented his mother with a copy. It was called *On the Fourfold Root of the Principle of Sufficient Reason*. His mother's response was to make a sarcastic remark about its title; it sounded, she said, like something written for pharmacists. He is said to have replied, hotly, that his book would still be available when the rubbish she was writing was long forgotten; and she is said to have replied, sweetly, that she was sure that he was right – that the entire first printing of his book would still be available.

Magee depicts Schopenhauer as 'a prodigous conversationalist – zestful, wide-ranging, well-informed and witty'. He expressed himself forcefully on the page, too. Subsequently regarded as one of the great masters of modern German prose, his style combines 'lucidity with musicality, sharp-edged precision with haunting metaphor, torrential energy with logical rigour'. 'Above all, there is a man speaking: a whole man, a whole life, a whole way of seeing the world are embodied before us on those pages, in those sentences. No writer is more 'there', more with you, almost tangibly and audibly present when you read him.' His style expresses a *joie de vivre* which is 'almost gargantuan'. Throughout his life, though, his style remained at odds with the content of what he wrote, which was typically 'corrosive, sarcastic, derisive, pessimistic, sometimes almost despairing'.[29]

Schopenhauer was a 'one-book' philosopher, his masterpiece *The World as Will and Representation*, being written when he was in his twenties, and published in 1818 when he was thirty. His view of it was by no means modest: 'Subject to the limitation of human knowledge', he said, 'my philosophy is the real solution of the enigma of the world.' At the time of its publication, though, it went largely unnoticed; and, meanwhile, rivals like Hegel, whom Schopenhauer regarded as charlatans and time-servers, flourished. It was not until his old age that he could watch his own fame grow.

Like Descartes', Schopenhauer's philosophy can be seen as centring on a simple dualism or dichotomy; but where Descartes' was primarily one of method, the dualism in Schopenhauer we would now regard as psychological. The worlds Schopenhauer opposes are those of brute nature or 'Will', and those of pure reflection, the 'Idea'. Rather than being harmonious but separate, as in Descartes' philosophy, Schopenhauer's twin worlds are in conflict. It is the forces of nature that are life-giving. The urges of procreation and self-preservation have a status within his philosophy equivalent to that of the force of gravity, and it is the genital organs and the sexual acts they perform that are the Will's true focus. But it is the life of the mind that, from the vantage point of the human perceiver, is real. Hence there is a war inside each individual's head between the realm of blind impulse and that of ideas and ideals. As in certain Eastern religions, about which Schopenhauer was knowledgeable, the Will must be subjugated if the Idea is to find expression – a battle, in his view, that man is bound to engage in, but is doomed to lose.

Where Descartes is treated as the founder of modern philosophy and the scientific method, Schopenhauer's philosophy of Will has sometimes been portrayed (for instance, by Bertrand Russell) as the poisonous seed later to burgeon as Fascism. This is doubly unfair. Descartes might just as well be blamed for the mindless proliferation of modern technology, and, more specifically, for inhibiting the development of those areas in medicine where mind and body interact; while Schopenhauer was precursor of the twentieth century's characteristic way of thinking about itself: psychoanalysis. Freud's distinction between 'primary' and 'secondary' processes – in his own view, mistakenly perhaps, the most important theoretical contribution he ever made – echoes Schopenhauer's distinction between Will and Idea quite closely; and so too does his insistence on sex as the psyche's driving force. Freud even inherited from Schopenhauer his pessimism about the chances of the instinctual and the reflective ever reaching a satisfactory accommodation.[30]

Magee likens Schopenhauer to Beethoven:

Each was of barely medium height, stocky and muscular, with a huge head and short neck set in bull shoulders. Both were bustlingly energetic and alarmingly vehement, irascible, truculent, suspicious. Both were marked out above all by (apart from genius) a disconcerting independence and forcefulness of personality which was accompanied by a propensity to declare home truths roundly regardless of circumstances, fashion or persons. Both were profoundly musical yet deaf from early manhood. (Schopenhauer's deafness was less extreme than Beethoven's, but always troublesome.) Both had a powerful heterosexual drive yet never

married: they lived as solitaries, subsisting on a thin and intermittent sexual diet of shallow, casual relationships, probably with
recourse to prostitutes in their younger days and servant girls later.
Both longed for acceptance and love, yet fiercely drove everyone
away from them, persistently living in a self-created isolation
which they bitterly resented and for which they misanthropically
blamed mankind.[31]

There were points of difference too, of course. In person, Beethoven
was slovenly, Schopenhauer dapper and well ordered; Beethoven
was humourless, Schopenhauer 'blisteringly funny'. And where
Beethoven's political sympathies were those of a radical, Schopenhauer became a counter-revolutionary. In the course of a political
riot, he is said to have invited soldiers into his house so that they
could shoot at the mob from his windows, and subsequently set up a
fund to support the widows of the soldiers who had been killed. In
later life especially, Schopenhauer also became, almost to the point of
self-parody, misogynous. Women he describes as 'short-legged,
long-torsoed, narrow-shouldered, broad-hipped, teat-bedecked
creatures'. 'Only the male intellect befogged by its sexual urge', he
claimed, could regard them as beautiful.[32]

INTIMACY AND THE GROWTH OF THE IMAGINATION

Notoriously, biography is a perilous enterprise, the past continually
rewriting itself in the light of the present's needs.[33] Lives like those of
Rilke, Schopenhauer and Descartes organise themselves, even so,
around certain recurrent themes. In particular, it seems that extreme
movements of imaginative energy, away from the realm of flesh-
and-blood and towards that of abstraction, occur in conjunction with
early deprivation or loss. Consequently, as Anthony Storr[34] has
pointed out, many of the world's great thinkers – not just Descartes
and Schopenhauer, but Newton, Locke, Pascal, Spinoza, Kant, Lieb-
niz, Nietzsche, Kierkegaard and Wittgenstein – have not reared families or formed close personal ties. Some had transient affairs with
other men or women; others like Newton, remained celibate. None
of them married, and most of them lived the greater part of their
lives alone.

The evidence we have described in this chapter does have a sense
of internal coherence, in other words, and it suggests three general-

isations:

- To greater or lesser degree, upbringings leave the individual in a state of internal dislocation or fissure;
- The resulting ambivalences and dissonances can often be contained (and temporarily resolved) by the displacement of imaginative energy into activity which is symbolic; and
- Such displaced energy is likely to be of passionate intensity where the underlying dislocation and fissuring is profound.

As we have portrayed it, the context in which the imagination is orginally shaped is personal: the infant's idea-of-the-mother and idea-of-the-father, each highly emotionally charged. The extent to which formal thought can become completely segregated from the personal is still unclear, as we have already said. The symbiotically intimate could threaten to make incursions only in dreams and fantasied recollections, not in everyday actuality, yet still serve the abstract thinker as his trigger. Whether or not this happens, there plainly exists a spectrum of imaginative enterprises, ranging in their focus from the exclusively human to the exclusively impersonal. There are:

- Adults for whom the imagination finds its most gratifying expression in an intimate (and, more specifically, intimately sexual) relationship. If the relationship fails, sexual intimacy becomes a battle ground, centrally placed and obsessing. In as much as it succeeds, such intimacy is self-fulfilling, *an end in itself*;
- Others for whom intimate sexual relationships are vital, but as a *context* - the one in which their gifts blossom, whether as architect, say, or dancer, or entrepreneur;
- Those – Rilke, for instance – for whom the imagination finds expression in the *idea* of sexual intimacy, not in its actuality, and for whom this idea becomes the subject of whatever work they do;
- Those like Schopenhauer (and also Freud) for whom the psychic energies let loose in sexual intimacy must somehow be understood and *brought under intellectual control*; and
- Those like Descartes for whom the imagination, while remaining intuitive and impassioned, can only flourish in settings which are *abstract*.

AN ASSOCIATED DILEMMA

The suggestion is that, in the last three of these fertile patterns, thought in the public realm is fuelled as a matter of course by the displacement of passion which in its origins is private. This is in no sense to impugn that thought's value, or to insinuate that it can be explained away in psychological terms. On the contrary: we are simply accounting for the fact that such thought is so conspicuously the expression of driven force. It is a formulation, nevertheless, that poses a serious awkwardness; and, before moving on, it is important that its presence should be acknowledged. For the moment in our exposition has been reached when the notion of costs and benefits counterbalancing one another, which until now has given a comforting impression of even-handedness, shows its teeth. The biographical evidence strongly suggests that the less harmonious the individuals' upbringing and consequent internal arrangements, the more displacable passion they will have at their command. Conversely, the implication is that *the more harmonious the individuals' upbringing, the less passion they will have to displace.* Where exceptional displacements of imaginative energy arise, that is to say, they do so on the strength of upbringings which no sane man or woman could countenance. The dilemma, then, is a practical one. Parents and teachers want to foster creative energies in children, but cannot reasonably exert upon them the kinds of pressure from which serious feats of originality actually spring.

The relevant psychological literature – about 'creativity' – was largely a product of the 1960s; and in retrospect it has an oddly anodyne, Panglossian air. It often assumes that creativeness is our natural heritage, and that we can all achieve good mental health, harmonious personal relations and imaginative vitality by an simple expedient: the removal of the inhibitions and conformities which repressive upbringing and education bring about. Carl Rogers could claim 'that the human organism is, at its deepest level, trustworthy; that man's basic nature is not something to be feared, but to be released in responsible self-expression; that small groups (in therapy or in classrooms) can responsibly and sensitively build constructive interpersonal relationships and choose wise individual and group goals; that all of the foregoing will be achieved if a facilitative person assists by creating a climate of realness, understanding, and caring'.[35] We have found no echo of such affirmative sentiments in the biographies of men and women who have actually been creative; and it certainly has none in our own immediate experience of creative people. In characterising the exceptionally original men and women we have met in the last thirty years, the adjective which comes most readily to mind is '*driven*'. It is only against a background of their often prodigious powers of application that the playful or divergent elements of their thinking make sense.[36]

The costs and benefits implicit in this driven state are ones the life of the great Victorian art critic John Ruskin demonstrates with gloomy clarity. Ruskin, his biographer Rosenberg tells us, 'passed his childhood in serene but unrelenting solitude, lightened only by the ingenuities of his own observation. He examined the patches of color on the floor, counted the bricks in the walls of the neighbouring houses, and, with rapturous and riveted attention, watched from the nursery window as the watercarts were filled from a dripping iron post at the pavement edge'.[37] The only son of a prosperous sherry importer and his puritanical Scottish wife, Ruskin's education was received from his mother. It was based, as many Victorian children's were, on the Bible. The upbringing he received may seem to our eyes inhuman, but it was in fact rooted in an excessive solicitude. There grew up between Ruskin and his parents so intense a respect that he was to consult them subsequently on every major decision in his life, and, while his father was alive, published nothing of which his father did not approve.

As an adolescent and adult, Ruskin's imagination was highly charged, its very vigour seeming to throw his insanity into question. As Rosenberg says, he was 'eye-driven, even photoerotic'. The visual world leapt to life before his eyes, and he had the gift of translating this visual excitement into prose. With the 'accuracy of a solitary fanatic', he recorded in his diaries every 'thought, image, and emotion which crossed his consciousness', his medium a prose informed by the 'sudden clarity of first sight'. It is not diffuseness, but 'an almost licentious amassing of detail' that characterises the purple passages in *Modern Painters*. He was a man who looked at the material world with a 'preternatural vivacity and clarity, and believed that what he saw was divine'.[38] 'The greatest thing a human soul ever does in this world', Ruskin once said, 'is to *see* something, and tell what it *saw* in a plain way. . . . To see clearly is poetry, prophecy, and religion, – all in one'.[39] 'Life without Industry is sin', he also proclaimed, 'and Industry without Art, brutality.'[40]

Ruskin began to write in earnest at the age of seven, and was in the course of his life to publish more than forty books, and several hundred lectures and articles. His influence was immense. He shaped the sensibilities of a generation in questions of painting and architecture; and, through his writing, altered the lives of men as disparate as William Morris, Marcel Proust, Clement Attlee and Mahatma Gandhi. Nevertheless, his personal life ended in disillusionment and mental ruin. His marriage to Effie Gray was unconsummated, and he subsequently conceived an unrequited passion for a young girl, Rose La Touche. Seized by terrifying visions of snakes, he ended his days insane. Ruskin's imaginative life was one in which the benefits were great, but in which the costs could scarcely have been more cruel.

THE STAMPING GROUND

CHAPTER 5

MALE STRENGTHS

Freud once remarked that the proper aim of man was *Lieben und Arbeiten*, to love and to work.[1] The world is full of 'objects', he believed, that the man (and, presumably, woman) who has quelled the polymorphously perverse contents of his unconscious is at liberty to pursue. He has sexual intercourse wholeheartedly with someone whom he unreservedly desires, and works in ways he finds genuinely gratifying. It is just this, in fact, which the Freudian vision of genitality implies.

It cannot be that simple, however. On entering the worlds of love and work, as the evidence of Freud's own biography demonstrates, the male enters a system within which costs and benefits are counterpoised, and precarious balances must be struck. From the moment the wound is established, all relationships a male forms, whether with systems of ideas or with other people, are conditioned by it. If the wound limits and distorts the male's capacity to sustain a sexual intimacy, it empowers him in his work. In his working life, what is more, the goals he seeks exist within a culture itself structured in terms of the wound. As the feminists have noticed, our institutions are ones that reserve special applause for public performances – in science, for instance – in which the needs created by the wound are assuaged.

In this chapter and the next, our emphasis is on the benefits that flow from the wound. While the personal costs can be high, the intellectual advantages are often commensurately great. For the wound leads the male mind to pursue enterprises in the inanimate world with intense – and, at root, intensely personal – passion. The implication is that the world of emotionally charged but abstract symbols is the 'male' man's natural milieu. Science and technology, far from requiring an extension or distortion of imaginative processes that are properly personal, provide the 'male' imagination with venues within which it can be deployed in its most fluent and spontaneous forms. If, for whatever reason, a 'male' man gets to grips with the intimate personal, as he may well if he becomes a novelist or psychologist, he will do so with this world of emotionally charged abstraction as his foundation.

In this chapter, we begin by looking at the 'stamping ground' itself: at those areas – both in their work and in their leisure – where men (and especially 'male' men) congregate, and where male fascinations find spontaneous expression. Next, we consider the ways in which his institutions can serve the adult male as his 'exoskeleton'; a secure structure within which the irrational elements of his thought are contained. We then examine migrations across the boundaries with which 'male' areas of work are surrounded. Finally – taking a longish sideways glance – we look at the evidence, sketchy but intriguing, that there are not just male, female and androgynous minds, but male, female and androgynous brains; and consequently that intellectual expressions of maleness may prove to have a biological root.

THE ACADEMIC SPECTRUM

While numerical equality between men and women has become a realisable vision in many aspects of public life, others remain dominated for no very obvious reason by men: engineering and the physical sciences – and, at the level of popular culture, the world of technologically sophisticated equipment or 'kit'.

In terms of rough approximation, there are probably as many successful women novelists at work in the affluent West as there are men. But, despite serious efforts to recruit them, practising female mechanical or civil engineers are still a rarity, outnumbered hundreds of times to one. One in every fourteen practising architects in Britain is a woman; but, of that minority, most at present shun the engineering and quantity surveying sides of the profession.[2] To attend a conference of professionals concerned in one way or another with the construction industry is, as a result, to take part in an occasion peopled almost entirely by men. At the first meeting of the Building Industry Council for heads of university courses, held at the Institution of Civil Engineers in Westminster on 24 May 1989, the speakers were all men, and the audience of two hundred or so was almost entirely male, most of the few women present being in sup-

portive roles like conference organiser and personal assistant. One of
the two government ministers to address the meeting noted the poor
female representation in the constituent professions of the building
industry; a stubborn irony in a nation led at that time by a woman
trained as a physical scientist.[3]

Broadly, there exists a spectrum from mathematics, physics and
the technologies at one extreme to the arts and humanities at the
other. The one is numerically dominated by men. The other sees the
two sexes mixing on an equal footing, the atmosphere being largely
gender-free, and, in terms of student numbers, women often out-
numbering men. Somewhere in the midground, there are disciplines
like psychology that, when examined closely, prove to have an internal structure that is sex- and gender-linked; the self-consciously
scientific parts of psychology being dominated by 'male' men, while
the humane parts are the province of women and of men who are
more androgynous.[4] Also in the midground, there are the professions like law and medicine, where women have recently begun to
colonise territory traditionally seen as male. Even here, though, sex
differences persist. While men now outnumber women in the membership of the Royal College of Obstetrics and Gynaecology by only
two to one, practising female surgeons remain almost as rare as practising women engineers.[5] Doubtless, many such differences arise
from conventional prejudice, but to assume that they all do so is un-
reasonable. Massive and quite explicit institutional barriers were
placed in the way of Jewish scientists in America after the Second
World War, but this did not prevent a remarkable proportion of
them winning Nobel Prizes.[6]

Not only are science and technology numerically dominated by
men who are 'male', they are also dominated, it seems, by men who
are heterosexual. As George Steiner has remarked, 'homosexuals
have contributed formidably to the arts, to literature, to philosophy.
There are noon-times in the history of civilization, in Periclean
Athens, in the city-states of the Italian Renaissance, in Elizabethan
England and the *fin-de-siècle*, in which the role and style of the homosexual seems almost dominant. But in so far as we have evidence –
this *caveat* is all-important – homosexuals have played only a very
minor part, if any part at all, in the evolution of the natural and exact
sciences.'[7] He was writing in the context of a significant exception to
this rule, Alan Turing. A fellow of King's by the age of twenty-two,
Turing was an engineer who became a mathematical logician, and
was arguably the first to conceive of the computer as an instrument

that could not only calculate but think; not just obey but learn. As such, he was the spiritual uncle of the networks now used by theoretical biologists to explain the brain's ability to think and dream.[8]

Should there prove to be an affinity between a homosexual object choice in men and a career in the arts and humanities, and a hostility between that object choice and a career in hard science or technology, we might have a vital clue, as Steiner says, to 'the dynamics of reciprocity between eros and intellect'.

OLD CAMERAS, SAY...

Sex differences are a feature not only of working life, but of the spontaneous expressions of curiosity and need adults display when not at work. The hi-fi buff, fascinated by the technical specification of his equipment, yet who uses it to play only pop records or none at all: he is almost always male. Likewise the sports car enthusiast, the steam roller enthusiast and the model railway enthusiast. Almost from the days of its first invention in 1839, women have taken an interest in photography; and while, numerically, male photographers have outnumbered female ones, they have done so only to a moderate degree. At the turn of the century, it has been estimated, a third of professional photographers were women, specialising, many of them, in the tricky art of taking studio pictures of children.[9] Today, almost every tolerably prosperous home has a camera. It is estimated that 45 billion still photographs are taken each year, a rate inviting comparison with other more biological rhythms in our lives. (In their economically most advanced condition, human beings may release the shutter of a camera more often than they have sexual intercourse. They may also derive more pleasure from the first release than from the second.) There are huge imbalances, though, in the representation of the two sexes in certain areas of photography; and, most obviously, in the passion for cameras as objects of fascination in their own right – for instance, cameras that are old.[10]

Once launched into this region of obsolete hardware, there are, first, questions of strategy. Do you join the thousands of collectors of old Leicas, to whom the prospect of mint condition is as central as it is to the stamp collector, and in whose world thousands of dollars, pounds or yen turn on the rarity of a serial number? Or do you look for a memorable object with which you can also take photographs? If

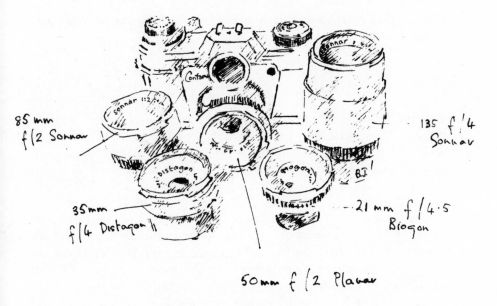

85 mm
f/2 Sonnar

135 f/4
Sonnar

35mm
f/4 Distagon

21 mm f/4·5
Biogon

50mm f/2 Planar

The Contarex Cyclops 1958

you opt for the second path, you could choose the Zeiss Contarex Cyclops; in its day, nearly thirty years ago, the finest single lens reflex system in the world. The quality of its weighty glass lenses, you read, has seldom been equalled and never surpassed. The old Zeiss catalogues speak of the 2,450 engineering drawings and 25,000 measurements that went into the camera body's design; the 1,100 individual parts and the 4,000 tooling operations, each accurate to within 0.001mm. Every time you use your Contarex, you celebrate the halcyon days of post-war German engineering, when, still, quality was sovereign and questions of cost could be left to look after themselves. (Such cameras have personalities. A specialist dealer recently remarked that when he sold an old Leica, he did not give it a second thought; but when he sold a Contarex, its loss stayed with him for some days. He likened the experience to going for a walk and leaving his dog indoors.)

There are discoveries in store – an 18mm lens in an out-of-the-way shop, or an original Contarex case. There are adventures too, like the move to a larger format; not just to a finer quality of image, but, curiously, a more static one. To the outsider, these must seem like exercises in nostalgia; but it is through his intimacy with these objects, inanimate though they plainly are, that the enthusiast shares magical properties and powers.

... OR EMERALDS

The implications of this interplay between the technical and the magical are most easily grasped in the context of another field of obsessive fascination: gemmology. As a branch of geology, gemmology might be thought imaginatively inert. The knowledge, say, that, like aquamarine, emerald is a form of beryl and that the chemical composition of both is aluminium beryllium silicate does nothing to make the spirit leap. Likewise, the information that the green of the emerald arises from the presence of chromium or occasionally vanadium in the beryl, which in its pure state is colourless; whereas the blue of the aquamarine comes from the presence of iron. Or that the absorption spectra of the two stones differ. But to look for the first time though a jeweller's loupe into the heart of a fine emerald can.

In everyday practice, the expert gemmologist brings together two sorts of knowledge. On the technical side, there is the knowledge that all emeralds have flaws or inclusions, their 'jardin'; and that the precise nature of these inclusions helps identify a stone as coming originally from Colombia, say, as opposed to Tanzania; and, within Columbia, as coming from the Muzo mine rather than the Chivor. There is the knowledge, too, that emeralds can be confused with other naturally occurring stones: the green garnets, grossular and demantoid; also diopside, dioptase, hiddenite, peridot and tourmaline. It is part of the gemmologist's everyday wisdom that inferior emeralds are often oiled to improve their colour temporarily; and that fakes abound, ranging in ingenuity from two layers of beryl cemented together with green-tinted Araldite, to emerald-like crystals grown artificially in a laboratory. In making the necessary discriminations, experts have at their command detailed information about the hardness of the stones in question, their refractive indices, their absorption spectra, their appearance under ultraviolet light, and so on. But they also know that such guidelines are fallible and that rude surprises abound. Recently, it has been discovered that the two largest diamonds in the world, the Cullinan 1 and Cullinan 2, though cleaved by Joseph Asscher in 1908 from a single rough stone, fluoresce differently under ultraviolet light.[11]

Chivor Mine, Columbia

Behind the expert's powers of discrimination, there lies a sense not just of the emerald's commercial significance but its history. As one authority says, 'emeralds are the magical link between the eye and the deepest recesses of the earth'.[12] The finest were mined by the Incas at Muzo and Chivor, pillaged by the Spaniards in the sixteenth century, and sold to maharajahs, whence they have filtered back into western markets, often by discreditable means, to be recut, reset and resold. For an expert to look into an 'old mine' emerald, then, is not just to exercise a finely balanced, technical skill; nor simply to entertain calculations about money. It is to experience access to a world of fabulous monsters and exquisitely concentrated desire.

This access unites what are at times disquieting dissonances of meaning: the sense of a history in which beautiful things are steeped in duplicity and greed; and the irony that the search for these re-markable stones often culminates in the adornment of individuals ill-equipped to appreciate them. Most primitively remarkable of all, there is the thought that objects containing such intense concentra-tions of meaning are released by pick and shovel from the earth's bowels; only to be returned, in the finest instances, to subterranean vaults for safe keeping. It is these reverberations of history and myth which give the apparently purely technical concerns of the gemmol-ogist their singular edge.

INSTITUTIONAL LIFE

If, as we have claimed, the effect of the wound is to create an en-during sense of dislocation, it must follow that men (and especially 'male' men) will be dependent on their work as a source of existential security and affirmation. If the adult man's exercise of agency has its origins in the male child's rejection of his mother's intimate comfort, an act of agency remains for him both a feat of arms and an act of symbolic repossession. Granted the intimacy of their original con-text, one would expect such feats to carry with them freights of seemingly arbitrary anxiety – ones that must somehow be contained. Institutions are ideally suited to do this, both because they create a sense of security, and, more particularly, because they give indivi-duals within them the freedom to act not as themselves but as the in-cumbents of a role. His career and its institutions will serve the 'male' male as his exoskeleton, then; and it is within this exoskeleton that his sense of agency will be exercised.[13]

The men like Thomas Sprat who established the Royal Society in the middle of the seventeenth century, did so long before scientific research took on a corporate character, and were conscious as they did so of fashioning for themselves a haven. While 'the consideration of *Men*, and *humane affairs*, may affect us, with a thousand various disquiets', wrote Sprat in 1667 in *The History of the Royal Society of London*, 'it was *Nature* alone' which 'permits us, to raise contrary im-aginations upon it, without any danger of a *Civil War*'.

Significantly too, they, like their counterparts in France and Ger-many, were at pains to exclude women. Although not banned by statute, women were not elected to full membership of the Royal Society in London until 1945. Towards the end of the seventeenth century, Schiebinger shows, one in seven of German astronomers were women, working as artisans within the craft guilds.[14] Such women, like their more aristocratic counterparts, were omitted from the professional institutions of science then taking shape. It seems, more generally, that there is a tendency for men to exclude women from their activities as a new conceptual challenge looms. It is as if, during the seventeenth, eighteenth and nineteenth centuries, men could gear their imaginations to the impersonal challenges of science and technology only by some collective repression of the 'feminine' in themselves and their surroundings; a manoeuvre of which gifted women are the natural butt. If women are now admitted to science as equals, this is presumably because the impersonality of the discipline is now established beyond question.

Not only do institutions like those of modern science provide a structure and haven, they also enable their members to know where they stand. Scientists can calibrate one another's excellence (in terms, for instance, of their fellowship of the Royal Society) in ways without parallel in the arts. That such honours depend on processes of judgement in which conformity, nepotism and intellectual snobbery play significant parts is widely acknowledged. But such admissions do little to blunt the sense that, in becoming a Fellow of the Royal Society, men (and the occasional woman) have had the stamp of impersonal authority placed on what they do.

The relation of the 'male' male to his institutions also has two less obvious properties. The first concerns the sense of 'the real action' – the potential for breakthroughs in science, the exercise of power within a bureaucracy – and where this lies.

The knowledge that their institutions contain real action is one most men find vitalising. At the same time, such happenings are elusive. From the vantage point of the individual, they usually occur at a distance. At any one moment in a given branch of science, it seems, there are only a few sites where the 'music' is right. You sense their excitement, even as a visitor; while, for the insider, the experience is closer to levitation. It is in them, intuitively, almost osmotically, that there passes from mind to mind a sense of where the treasure is: an awareness not just of the right question and the moment to ask it, but of the hidden rhythms of successful inquiry; its cadences and sense of style.[15] The corollary, though, is that for the vast majority, *the experience of doing science is one of exclusion*; of failing to get access to, or actively being excluded from, the juicier gratifications their discipline promises. Such access, our theory suggests, will in any case be perceived as psychologically dangerous. Even in hard science and mathematics, the prospect of discovery implies a collapse of boundaries; and, attendant on that collapse, distant echoes of engulfing intimacy. It would seem to follow, then, that most scientists collude in their exclusion from the real action, comforting themselves as they do so with the imagery of worthy endeavour. They picture themselves as practising what has come to be called 'normal science' (the routine exploitation of an idea for which someone else has already taken credit), and preach the cardinal virtue of 'scientific respectability'.[16]

The second significant feature of institutional life complements the first. In encouraging us to act not as accountable individuals but as incumbents of roles, institutions sanction forms of behaviour – deceit, for example, and vindictiveness – that are otherwise unacceptable. As Alexander Mitscherlich has said, '*When a temptation offered by a role is succumbed to, a step is taken into the pathological*'; and as he goes on to say, 'The fragility of a role's purpose is much greater than we admit. *It is in institutionalized roles that preverbal brutality finds its organ of speech*' (our italics).[17] Mitscherlich had in mind the anti-Semitism of German officials, but what he says applies equally to all forms of institutional life. A scientist committed to absolute veracity in his research may feel himself free to cheat and finagle in competing with professional rivals for funds; and, in his administrative capacity, to look adversaries in the eye and lie without scruple. Successful administrators, like successful scientists, often act as robber barons – 'raiders', Alistair Mant calls them – and do so in direct contravention of the declared values and procedures of the institutions through which they rise.[18]

A consequence is a sharp discontinuity between values governing life at the interface of an institution with its public and those governing life at that same institution's heart; between what is said in documents and speeches and what is said behind the hand. The freedoms the insider enjoys are hidden from the outsider; and they are frequently ones that, if he knew about them, the outsider would regard as outrageous. There exists, then, *a formal equivalence (or isomorphism) between the structure of the male psyche and that of the institutions in which the 'male' male feels at home.* On the outer surface of both, the appearance and often the substance of reason; inside each, the styles and sentiments of catch-as-catch-can. The institution serves, in other words, as a giant reverberator for the suppressed (and often turbulent) psychic lives of those who inhabit it and make it work. Sometimes the emotions this reverberator expresses are specific to individuals and their quirks, but the likelihood is that they are also collective: the frustrations inseparable from projects – the exercise of power, the discovery of the truth – which, in the experience of all but a few of those caught up in them, offer their gratifications to someone else.[19]

MIGRATIONS OF SEX AND GENDER

The perceived 'maleness' of working venues like those of science and administration can none the less change; and such changes are bound in practice both to influence, and to be influenced by, the number of feminine women and androgynous men who move into or out of the venues in question. In turn, shifts in recruitment may alter the habits of thought such venues typically foster. A serious incursion of gifted women into the various experimental sciences could well make science's dominant tone less buccaneering, and soften the pathological edge its institutional life so often displays. In the same way, women and androgynous men could move in appreciable numbers across other boundaries; that, for example, now separating architecture from civil engineering and quantity surveying. Likewise with a boundary internal to the world of music. In the past, women have often excelled in musical performance, but women composers of the first rank have been as rare as distinguished women civil engineers.[20] In fact, a significant migration of women across this invisible boundary is now under way, and the link between maleness and composition could dissolve.

All such gender migrations are natural experiments, nevertheless, and their outcomes are hard to predict. Once initial prejudices are overcome, women may find that there is nothing intrinsically 'male' about the work of the civil engineer or quantity surveyor, say; nothing that leaves women at a disadvantage or that they find antipathetic. The work of women architects and engineers may quite quickly become indistinguishable in character and quality from that of their male rivals. Equally, women may make a contribution that is distinctive. The buildings put up by women architects and engineers may prove detectably 'feminine' in the sense, say, that they take into account the needs of the people who are going to live inside them. Alternatively, the distinctive contribution made by women may prove to be one more of process than of product. Women architects

and engineers may develop more collaborative decision-making processes, allowing clients and users to articulate their own perceived
needs. Or, yet again, the migration may peter out. Women may conclude that there are features of the construction industry that, finally,
they find alien. It may be, for example, that there are extremes of in-
strumentality inseparable from the business of putting up buildings
that women find hostile to their own natures; and that they can
accommodate only by forms of professional commitment they are
increasingly unwilling to make.

Disciplines evolve, in any case, of their own accord. The demands
made by the construction industry or musical composition, painting
or astronomy, may change radically in the course of the next twenty-
five years; even within the next five. Evidence of such transformation is particularly clear in technology; in the collapse, for example,
of the German camera industry in the 1960s. Companies like Zeiss
and Leitz had become superb exponents of the technology of glass
and metal, but could not adapt to the part played in the design of the
modern camera by electronics. This, on the other hand, the Japanese
accommodated with what seemed, to the outsider, like effortless
fluency. In the Western world, not only is industry intensely masculine, but technological advance is seen as stemming from the exercise
of conventionally masculine virtues: competitiveness, abrasion,
courage – in a phrase, controlled force. The indications are that these
virtues do not play a similar part in the factories making Nikons and
Canons.[21]

Such arguments apply equally, of course, to migrations where the
issue is not biological sex or gender identity but object choice, and
where the populations in question are male homosexuals as opposed
to male heterosexuals. If homosexual men have so far had relatively
little influence on the course of science and technology, elsewhere
their impact can be remarkable, as the response to the AIDS epidemic shows. This has led to concentrations of homosexual male
doctors, nurses, counsellors and aides in and around AIDS hospitals
and hospices. These are men committed not only to help those with
AIDS control their symptoms, but also to challenge orthodox medical assumptions about the management of infectious disease and
death. Every effort is made to deny that AIDS is a disease from
which patients can properly be said to suffer; and to insist that it by
no means necessarily kills.[22] In certain AIDS wards, too, staff do
their best to create the atmosphere of a social occasion: the presence
of alcohol and soft drugs, friends and lovers, and the privacy in

which to have sexual relations. This effort represents a significant challenge to medical conventions and folkways, and is a far cry from the rigours of the cancer ward or the squalor of the VD clinic.[23]

Without wishing to belittle the scale of such gender migrations, or the benefits that may flow from them, we are convinced that differences of sex, gender identity, object choice and presentation of self will remain features of working life. Many existing biases are expressions of prejudice and sectional political interest, but some are a legacy of the wound.[24] For the foreseeable future, for example, we would expect instrumental forms of technology like bridge-building and rocket engineering to be dominated by 'male' men. If the evidence were to show that the distribution of 'male', genderless and effeminate men were precisely the same among civil engineers as it is among interior decorators, we would see the story we have told about the wound and its implications as undermined. We would also see it as undermined if, when examined in detail, the work done by 'male' and effeminate engineers (or 'male' and effeminate interior decorators) turned out to be indistinguishable. We would see it as undermined, too, if we found that engineers were outstandingly 'male', but that they only became so in the course of their training – if, before their trainings began, future civil engineers were indistinguishable in terms of their gender identity, object choice and presentation of self from future interior decorators. Faced with such evidence, we would have to concede that, in part at least, we had nailed our colours to the wrong mast – that, in as much as there was a point, it had passed us by.

MALE AND FEMALE BRAINS

Our view of the male wound and its consequences, as we have already stressed, is in no sense reducible to biology. We see the wound, once in being, as a feature of the male's internal life which is self-sustaining and self-sufficient. It does not depend on there being sizeable differences of anatomy or function between male and female brains, or between the brains of men who are 'male' and those who are more androgynous. The wound, we predict, will give rise to differences of the sort so far discussed, even if the dissimilarities between the male and female brain were limited to those in the hypothalamus. Our claim, in any event, is not that 'male' men are more (or less) gifted than women or androgynous men. Rather, that the 'male' man is impelled towards certain imaginatively charged extremities of thought and action in ways which most women and androgynous men are not. What is at issue is not ability as such, but accomplishment of the kind that only a driven need can bring about.

It does seem to us, nevertheless, that our argument would gain an added dimension of interest if differences between brains prove to be sex- or gender-linked. The reason is simple. The more separate but related sources of variety an adaptive system contains, the more subtly differentiated its effects become. A system that encompasses sex- and gender-linked differences at several discrete but interacting levels (those of brain structure and function, psychological development, stereotypical perception, and social institution) may be able to generate a subtlety of response which a system with a single generative source of variety cannot.

The idea of inbuilt biases of response should shock no one. Nor should it be seen as startling that such advantages and disadvantages are linked to identifiable social groups. Twins tend on average to have slightly lower IQs than other children.[25] Similarly, there are tendencies for first born and only sons to excel academically;[26] and for girls to learn to read sooner than boys, but, eventually, to be less good than boys at reasoning spatially.[27] Just as no sane person would use such evidence as grounds for discriminating against twins or younger sons, so they would not use it as grounds for discriminating either against boys or against girls.

No one is clear to what extent such differences are at root ones of motive as opposed to sheer ability. No one is clear, either, about the extent to which they are inherited or acquired. The evidence of patients with strokes does hint, though, that they have an identifiable basis in brain structure and function. Where damage to the relevant parts in the left hemisphere usually destroys language capacity in men, for example, it typically does less radical and more readily reversible damage in women.[28] In terms of what an adequately sceptical research worker would regard as established, the study of sex differences in brain organisation is for the moment a zone of wisps and vapours. Nevertheless, evidence is accumulating, and the security of the foundation it provides may well improve. Much of this evidence concerns the relation between the two cerebral hemispheres, and this has implications not only for men and women, but for the left- and right-handed of either sex. It is in terms of handedness that these implications are most easily approached.

LEFT AND RIGHT

In the last twenty years, simple-minded notions about the local-
isation of functions in the brain have had to be abandoned. The idea
that the left cerebral hemisphere is the seat of reason, while the right
is the home of the imagination is a myth. Nevertheless, some forms
of thought do appear to have a special relation to one hemisphere,
some to the other. Not only the right side of the body but certain
crucial elements of language skill are usually under the control of the
left cerebral hemisphere, while other skills – for example, the spatial
and musical ones – appear to be dependent on the right. In his
seventy-fifth year, and at the height of his powers, the composer
Maurice Ravel was struck on the head in a traffic accident, the
damage being to his left hemisphere. Although not paralysed, he lost
his ability to communicate verbally either in writing or by word of
mouth. On the other hand, it seems that his musical memory and
judgement were largely unimpaired. He immediately recognised
tunes, and detected the slightest mistake in the performance of his
own work. It was not his powers of musical thought he had lost, but
his capacity to transfer that thought to the page.[29]
    In the left-handed, one might expect such deployments to be
straightforward reversals of those in the right-handed, but in many
left-handed people it is still the left hemisphere which is dominant for
language. Only in a minority is the right hemisphere dominant, or is
dominance confused. The present view is that some 70 per cent of
left-handers have the left hemisphere dominant for language, 15 per
cent have the right hemisphere dominant, and 15 per cent have language represented in both hemispheres equally. As a result, the left-
handed can suffer language disability from damage to either hemisphere, but recover from it better than do right-handers. In terms of
their brain organisation, left-handers not only differ from right-handers, they also differ among themselves, there being not one form of
left-handedness but several. As one might expect, left-handedness is
associated with a number of different and at times apparently contradictory patterns of disability and skill. In comparison with the
standards set by the right-handed, some groups of left-handers are
verbally handicapped, while others are particularly verbally adept.[30]
Sometimes left-handedness has been found linked to weakness in
spatial reasoning, sometimes to special strength. Having worked a
good deal with painters, craftsmen, designers and architects, it is cer-

tainly our impression that extremes of visual sensibility are often associated both with left-handedness and with dyslexia.[31]

The consensus, now, is that left-handedness runs in families; that the disposition towards it is probably genetically transmitted; and that it is tied in complex ways to brain structure, brain function, specific cognitive skills and disabilities, and even to qualities of personality.[32] The left-hander may be heavily over-represented as a result in classes of backward readers; but is also over-represented on the tennis court, as the wealth of left-handed champions demonstrates. The right-handed opponent on the receiving end of John McEnroe's service and of his temper may face someone whose special gifts and special frailties arise from a pattern of 'wiring' different from his own.

Just as questions of brain organisation may help explain differences between the left- and right-handed, so they may help explain differences between men and women.[33] Marked sex differences are apparent, for example, among the mathematically gifted. Camilla Benbow describes research based on very big samples of able 12- and 13-year-old boys and girls, and on the follow-up of such samples to the college level and beyond.[34] Her data show large advantages in favour of the boys. These have been consistent over a period in which the attitude towards women and women's education has undergone radical change, and become more pronounced the more advanced the levels of mathematical reasoning in question.[35] Benbow discusses a number of environmental explanations of this evidence but finds them unsatisfactory, and turns instead towards biology. She is struck by the relation of exceptional mathematical ability in boys to left-handedness, allergies and myopia; and concludes that this form of giftedness could be linked to bilateral representation of the relevant thought processes in the brain. In turn, she suggests, this pattern of brain organisation may derive from excessive levels of testosterone encountered in the womb.

It is clear though, even if Benbow is on the right lines, that the interactions are going to be complex. The research on spatial ability shows this. Usually but by no means always treated as the ability to manipulate two- or three-dimensional shapes in the mind's eye, spatial ability is characteristically more pronounced among adult males than adult females.[36] But this deficit on the part of women only becomes apparent, it seems, after the onset of puberty; and is most marked in those who reach puberty early.[37] There is also evidence that spatial ability varies in the adult female with the menstrual cycle. The evidence, however, holds a further surprise; for among adults, spatial ability in both sexes is associated with androgyny, both 'male' women and 'female' men tending to have better spatial ability than their peers. It is for this reason, perhaps, that skills like those of the interior decorator often seem so pronounced among masculine women and effeminate men.

The present position is that psychologists can detect sex differences using paper and pencil tests, that physiologists can detect sex differences of a physical nature, and that both can be shown to correlate at modest levels of predictive efficiency with sex differences observable in the world at large. There remain, none the less, serious discrepancies of scale. Where, on the evidence of students' scores on psychological tests, one might expect sex differences of, say, two or three to one among samples of gifted mathematicians or civil engineers, we find them of the order of 100 or 1,000 to 1. Such discrepancies indicate that the correct explanations are going to lie not in the realm of raw ability, innate or otherwise, but in the interplay between that raw ability and motive. At stake are not the various forms of verbal, numerical and spatial intelligence *per se*, but the passionate inclination to use these for particular purposes, and the highly specific powers of intuitive discrimination and judgement that result.

A study of chess players illustrates this. At its highest levels, chess is to an overwhelming extent an activity dominated by men. Chess players become masters, it seems, not because they have wholly exceptional powers of spatial reasoning, but because they put what powers they do possess to exceptionally good purpose. Masters and relatively weaker players have been compared under two conditions. In one, each player was shown a chess position for a few seconds and then invited to reconstruct it from memory. The masters clearly outstripped the weaker players. But when the experiment was repeated with the pieces deployed at random, the masters' superiority disappeared. Masters excel not in spatial ability, pure and simple, but in the ability to identify and organise familiar constellations of chess pieces, and in doing so to draw on their understanding of the tactical significance each such constellation possesses.[38]

CHAPTER 6

PASSIONATE ABSTRACTION

THE EMBODIMENT OF the male imagination as we have so far portrayed it is Isaac Newton: in the words of Wordsworth's inscription on the memorial to him in Trinity College, 'The marble index of a mind for ever voyaging through strange seas of Thought alone.' Viewed from the outside, as it were, it is for the unparalleled accomplishments of his youth that Newton is remembered: the law of gravitation, the three laws of motion, the theory of light as composed of corpuscles, and the development of the calculus. All this he achieved, in principle at least, by his mid-twenties. Viewed more from the inside, it was, in Maynard Keynes' judgement, Newton's intuition which was 'pre-eminently extraordinary', allied to preternatural powers of concentration. Newton was, he says, 'the last of the magicians, the last of the Babylonians and Sumerians'. His deepest instincts were 'occult, esoteric, semantic – with profound shrinking from the world, a paralysing fear of exposing his thoughts, his beliefs, his discoveries in all nakedness to the inspection and criticism of the world'. He was 'wholly aloof from women'; and published nothing except when pressed by others to do so. 'Until the second phase of his life, he was a rapt, consecrated solitary, pursuing his studies by intense introspection with a mental endurance perhaps never equalled.'[1]

Newton conforms, too, to the pattern of maternal deprivation and loss. Newton's father, an illiterate yeoman, died before his son was born; and Newton consequently enjoyed his mother's undivided attention. But, just after his third birthday, she remarried. Moving house, she left her son to be reared by his maternal grandmother – a departure he resented and perceived as a betrayal.[2] From the age of nineteen, when Newton went to Cambridge until he left for London thirty-five years later, he was a recluse. At the age of fifty, he seems to have become 'transiently psychotic'. Whatever the precipitating

cause, Newton suffered depression, sleeplessness and a sense of per-
secution. He broke with Pepys, accused the philosopher Locke of
attempting to embroil him with women, and never again concentrated as he once could. It was from this depression that he was to
emerge – in Keynes' phrase 'slightly gaga' – to become 'the Sage and
Monarch of the Age of Reason'.

DIAGNOSTIC FEATURES

To the extent that the forms of imaginative energy fuelling scientific
inquiries like Newton's have the wound at their root, we would expect them – in however attenuated a form – to carry their history
with them. They should reveal, that is to say, certain diagnostic
features. In this chapter, we illustrate five:

- A preoccupation with *control* – usually symbolic, but sometimes
  literal;

- The use of apparently abstract and technical ideas as a means of
  executing *primitively psychological* manoeuvres;

- A commitment to formal models, hobby-horses and *fixed ideas*
  pursued, sometimes, with a fervour that can seem scarcely sane;

- A preoccupation with *violence* – again, usually symbolic, but
  sometimes literal; and

- '*Spillage*', whereby delicately poised abstraction is surrounded,
  apparently as a matter of course, by personal feuds, political
  finagling, bullying and abuse.

All five features are by no means always detectable in the work of
any one man. Emphases vary from individual to individual and discipline to discipline.[3] Taking each feature in turn, our examples
centre on science but begin with psychology and extend into philosophy, mathematics and technology. In several, there are unmistakable indications of the male mind's binary cast: its tendency to
approach the world by means of theories in which fissures are nego-
tiated and dialectical oppositions resolved. In the fourth and fifth, the
structural isomorphism of male mind and male institution is mani-
fested in the form of ugly imagery and brutal rows. Although one
might expect such eruptions to be associated with professional frustration and failure, they prove to invade some of science and technology's most conspicuous triumphs too.

CONTROL

No one even distantly interested in the course psychology has taken over the last fifty years can be blind to the influence exerted on it by Burrhus Frederic Skinner. It was Skinner who developed methods of shaping the behaviour of an organism – *any* organism, human or non-human – by manipulating its schedules of reward. It was he, too, who designed a utopian community; devised a missile steered by the pecking beaks of pigeons strapped inside it; and bought up his baby daughter in a box.

J. B. Watson first popularised the idea of behaviourism, but it was Skinner who lent it intellectual conviction. It comes as a surprise to learn that Skinner first launched himself on the world, not as an scientist or engineer but as a writer. In his autobiography, Skinner speaks of submitting poems to literary magazines while a freshman at Hamilton College, and of a 'sudden bout of dramaturgy': a blend, he says, of Ibsen and Shaw.[4] He took courses in stagecraft and creative writing, and, encouraged on his way by the poet Robert Frost, decided when he left Hamilton to take a year off and write a novel. Frost had looked at three of Skinner's short stories, and his praise must have been intoxicating: 'I ought to say you have the touch of art. The work is clean run. You are worth twice anyone else I have seen in prose this year.' Skinner built himself a study in the attic of his parents' house in Scranton, but 'the truth was, I had no reason to write anything. I had nothing to say...'[5]

'Floundering in a stormy sea', he sought refuge in making model ships, painting in pastels, playing Mozart sonatas on the piano, designing scenery for the local theatre, and helping with marionettes. Rescue came in the form of popular articles written by Bertrand Russell. Later, in Russell's *Philosophy*, Skinner read with delight as German idealism was dismissed out of hand, and Watson's behaviourism advocated in its place; the philosophy that 'holds that everything that can be known about man is discoverable by the method of external observation'. Although he did not entirely agree with it, Russell says, he regarded the behaviourist's method as desirable, and one which should be developed to the fullest possible extent. 'The refreshing thing', from Skinner's point of view, was how quickly Russell 'got around to facts'.[6]

Skinner applied to Harvard, went there as a graduate student in psychology in 1928, and his career as an experimental psychologist and visionary began. Intellectually, this career was to express an obsessive preoccupation with the idea of control – a control, Skinner believed, that must be exerted exclusively by relating stimulus to response. To enter into the discussion of what went on in the mind was tantamount to a breach of the rules on which rationality was built. His attitude revealed other distinctive features besides. Taken together, these formed a pattern soon to become familiar in experimental psychology departments on both sides of the Atlantic: a passion for facts; hostility to introspection; literal-mindedness; a contempt for theory; a quasi-religious commitment to the idea of progress; and a fascination with experimental gadgets which, in his case, usually proved not quite to work (an exception being the Skinner Box, a device for teaching skills to rats, which has since had an honourable career as an item of laboratory hardware).

Skinner's literalness is startling, one of the odder features of his autobiography being his description of his own sexual endeavours. He writes as if speaking, quite open-handedly, about the sexual performance of a pigeon. In this respect, it is a cast of mind reminiscent of Alfred Kinsey's. He is also quirky; and it is the baby box or 'air crib' which captures this quality best. Faced as a young parent with the prospect of his infant daughter and her soiled nappies, Skinner devised a solution that, in many people's eyes, makes him a monster. In order to remain warm, the infant has to be swaddled, he reasoned; but given her incontinence, she is bound to be in a state of chronic discomfort. She will as a result suffer, and her parents with her. Why not, therefore, put her into an air-conditioned box with paper towelling on the floor which can be renewed whenever it is soiled? She can then lie in comfort and be taken out in the ordinary way to play.

Baby Skinner smiles happily out at us through the shatter-proof glass of her box in the illustration Skinner supplies. The shock it inspires is little altered by Skinner's subsequent claim about other parents who have used the air crib. When surveyed, all but 3 of the 73 parents who had used it in bringing up 130 babies described the device as 'wonderful'. When first home from the hospital, the temperature that suited his daughter best, Skinner discovered, was 86 degrees Farenheit. As she grew older, it was possible to lower the temperature gradually so that by the age of eleven months she was most comfortable at 78 degrees, with a relative humidity of 50 per cent. 'The discovery which pleased us most', he writes, 'was that crying and fussing could always be stopped by slightly lowering the

Skinner's 'air crib'

temperature.... During the last six months she has not cried at all
except for a moment or two when injured or sharply distressed – for
example, when inoculated.' Instead, she exercised her lungs healthily
in 'shouts and gurgles'. The need to appear rational here becomes
detached, most of us feel, both from humanity and good sense.[7]

It is evident from his autobiography that his background exerted a
powerful influence on the shape Skinner's imagination took: his
mother and father, certainly, but also the environment of plenty in
which, in the early years of this century, his home town of Sasque-
hanna was set. His mother was the dominant member of the family.
'She had *consented* to marry my father, and there was an element of
consent in her behavior with respect to him throughout his life.'[8] She

was derisive, too, of her husband's achievements: two girls he had saved in a flood, and an unpublished short story he had written that hinged on the invention of a gun which shot bullets round corners. An old family friend once said that 'Grace made quite a man of Will Skinner'. It was an achievement, her son remarks, 'of which my mother was not entirely unaware'.

Skinner's father had escaped from work in the mechanical engineering department of the Erie Railroad by gaining a qualification as a lawyer; but neither his legal practice nor his ambitions as a Republican Party politician bore fruit. A long-suffering man who yearned for a warm relationship with his son but did not know how to achieve it, his response to disaster was 'closer to despair than anger'. There was fear that he might commit suicide; but to kill himself would have been to confess his failure. 'Other men', his son concludes, 'had not believed so strongly in progress.'[9]

In the midst of these tribulations, Skinner's mother acted as her husband's confidante; but she was also, it seems, subtly disloyal. 'When I was a child my mother had occasionally rubbed my head, and she still did so from time to time. . . . It was quite possibly a kind of affection which she no longer gave my father; indeed, she may never have given it, because it would have led in a direction she found distasteful. Once when we were alone and she was rubbing my head, she said that she thought my father was jealous, and she giggled, but it was not a giggling matter.'[10] She was, her son surmises, frigid, and gave her husband little sexual satisfaction. She did what was right, but did it 'in a spirit of martyrdom'. 'Will Skinner', the same family friend observed, 'would be a better man if he went to see the chippies now and then'; but his son was sure he never did.[11]

These unresolved domestic tensions are off-set, in Skinner's autobiography, by the rapturous descriptions of the physical world with which they were surrounded:

I grew up in a bountiful world, in which many wonderful things were to be had for the asking. Our backyard offered black cherries, red cherries (shared with the robins), purple plums, green plums, Concord grapes, currants, raspberries, rhubarb, horseradish, and mustard. None of them needed any care; they were simply there in season. . . . Susquehanna was a dirty, unkempt town, but the great sweep of the river valley was magnificent. . . . In spring we knew where to find the delicate trillium, arbutus, fringed gentian, and jack-in-the-pulpit; and we did not even have to look to find honeysuckle, columbine, and dogwood.[12]

It was a world shared with animals too. He caught chipmunks and
tried unsuccessfully to train them; killed snakes, including the occasional rattlesnake; trapped fireflies under drinking glasses and
watched them glow; caught bees in the petals of hollyhock blossoms,
and made 'ladders and teeter-totters' for captured turtles to perform
on.

It seems clear that the young Skinner identified with his father, and
carried over into his own adult life certain of his father's qualities: his
deep commitment to the idea of progress, his odd opacity about
other people, and his curious openness – his father had no secrets
from his wife, and, later, would confide in his son too. Most indelibly of all, however, Skinner must have carried away from life at
close quarters with his father the memory of despair in a principled
man; a painful recollection he was subsequently to hold at bay with
visions of a utopia in which misery is abolished by the application of
science. Skinner wrote *Walden Two* in the years immediately after the
Second World War, and in the wake of the failure of his ORCON
project, the pigeon-guided missile.[13] In it, he sought to demonstrate
that men and women could live together in peace if their society
were structured along the correct behaviouristic lines. It is a vision
now entirely devoid either of superficial excitement or of more principled allure. Skinner's powers of invention seem to forsake him,
leaving him to create an arrangement as politically implausible as it is
bloodlessly polite.

As in Descartes' thought, the intellectual stance of the behaviourist
is organised around the philosophical distinction between mind and
body. The behaviourist's solution to this ancient puzzle is to concentrate, for all practical purposes, on the body – on what the living
organism can be seen to do – and to ignore the mind entirely. Such a
manoeuvre can be dressed up as a question of method; a means of
getting effective scientific inquiry under way. Our claim, though, is
that it is a manoeuvre in which needs intimately associated with the
wound are also gratified.[14]

It is when the male imagination returns from its secure basis in
science or technology to subject-matter manifestly human that the
linkage between this binary tendency and visions of control becomes
clear. Ludwig Wittgenstein was an engineer before he was a philosopher; and more immediately of our own time, Edmund Leach was
an engineer before he was an anthropologist. Like Skinner – and like

Freud – both these superabundantly original men gave the impression of being ill at ease with the finer shades of human intimacy, even of being insensitive to them. All four squared up to human phenomena in terms which were finally binary or dialectical.

Wittgenstein's two remarkable philosophical utterances – *Tractatus Logico-Philosophicus* and *Philosophical Investigations* – in effect contradict one another, the *Tractatus* expressing in extreme form the view that all that can be known can be known clearly, while the *Investigations*, elusive, aphoristic, trace out certain of the routes whereby ordinary language becomes invested with intelligible meaning. It is as if, in Wittgenstein's imagination, the mind's mysteries could be contained by means of two thought-systems, each of which contradicts the other, in style and content, but each of which is dependent upon the other as the context from which its significance derives.[15]

In Leach, this binary quality of mind was even more pronounced. Stephen Hugh-Jones begins his recent obituary memoir of Leach by describing him as a man of paradoxes:[16]

> There were always two sides to his character and to what he said and did, coexisting in uneasy but creative tension. They made him unpredictable and highly original, difficult to understand but exhilarating and stimulating to know.... To tell the story of a man such as this is to enter a hall of mirrors – only to find that he has been there before us to warn us of the distortions to come.

Predictably, Leach was attracted to Lévi-Strauss's version of structuralism, in which myth and ritual are treated dialectically, as the resolution at the symbolic level of the otherwise irreconcilable conflicts a culture contains. As Hugh-Jones says, it was not that Leach outgrew his engineering background in turning to the analysis of primitive people like the Kachin; engineering providing him with the foundation on which his theoretical work as an anthropologist was subsequently built. Leach's first major book, *Political Systems of Highland Burma*, provided an analysis of what, to the conventional ethnographer, would in all probability have seemed a shapeless array of separate tribes. Leach argued that each of these tribes represented, on the contrary, a different facet of a wider social system in a state of unstable equilibrium. Within this, individuals could compete for power and influence, validating their positions by appeal to myth and use of ritual, each inherently ambiguous.

As he aged, Leach brought his analytic flair increasingly to bear on the concerns closest to him: his family background, on the edge of the wealthy Anglo-Argentinian community; and, although a non-believer, on the Bible. His turn of mind was oppositional, it seemed, whatever its focus. In the late 1960s, before he became its Provost, he was invited by King's College to contribute to a college entrance examination, designed to identify candidates of originality, irrespective of their previous academic record. What he produced was untidy and extraordinary. Each candidate was furnished with material with which to plan a journey halfway round the world, but which in practice forced him to choose between two different sorts of solution: one based on airline timetables, the other based on travellers' tales of human sacrifice.[17]

Without any symptom worse than intermittent explosions of unbridled rage, Leach was subsequently to survive the contradictions of his own reign as the head of a college itself in unstable equilibrium. In the late 1960s, King's was already moving from a position of aristocratic privilege in the direction of democracy. It was also moving from a forthright commitment to the humanities in the direction of hard science; and from the celebration of homosexual and bisexual values and folkways towards the social norm. Leach managed to mediate each of these transformations, and to do so in a style of characteristic equivocation. In his time, the 'Hall was turned back to front, the servery became a self-servery, the high table was made low, and English not Latin became the Provost's language in Chapel. More significantly it was under his Provostship that King's, after years of discussion and contention, finally decided to admit women as undergraduates and fellows'.[18] Although Hugh-Jones does not say so, it is characteristic that Leach's posture, throughout the wrangles on the college council, was one of hostility to its dissident members – those who were young and untenured, and who were urging the changes of which, at heart, he presumably approved.

SOPHISTICATED MANOEUVRES AND PRIMITIVE PSYCHOLOGICAL NEEDS

At the turning point of his life, as we have already seen, Freud gave up sexual intercourse with his wife on grounds that were at root aesthetic. It can scarcely be coincidental that the theory he subsequently espoused with such fervour had the sexual urge as its central tenet;

not can it be coincidental that his inquiries took a specifically autobiographical turn.

Among a great deal else, Freud and Fliess were to devote considerable arithmetical ingenuity to the precise birth dates of the Freud
children: Mathilde, Martin, Oliver, Ernst, Sophie and Anna.[19] Mathilde and Martin, they calculated, were born 783 days apart; an inter-
val they could link arithmetically to those between the births of the
remaining children by means of Fliess's magic numbers 23 and 28,
the male and female biorhythms. Freud and Fliess also analysed the
dates of birth of Freud's sister Marie's children. With a little tinker-
ing, all three were shown, similarly, to have been born on dates reducible to a system of 23- and 28-day cycles. The manoeuvre,
patently, was one whereby the untidy processes of conception and
parturition were made safe by being transformed into the purity of
arithmetic.

Far from being an isolated quirk on Freud's part – or Skinner's –
this urge to tidy up unruly and potentially disgusting human nature
has a distinguished philosophical pedigree. In *The Unconscious Origin
of Berkeley's Philosophy*, John Oulton Wisdom shows that Berkeley's
imagination was dominated by two ideas, each of which resonates on
the other.[20] Berkeley believed in the insubstantiality of the material
world: that the chair on which he sat and the table at which he
worked existed only in the minds of the people perceiving them.
Technically speaking, what Berkeley was propounding was 'theo-
centric phenomenalism' – a solution to a grumbling awkwardness at
the heart of the tradition in philosophy which treats as central our
evidence for believing in the external world. The claim is that, at
root, we rely on the evidence of our senses, our 'sense data'; and that
when no one is there to perceive them, chair and table go on existing
because perceived by God.

In fact, Wisdom argues, Berkeley was in the grip of an urge to rid
the body of philosophy of the idea of matter. It was as if matter were
compromising, dirty, while thought itself was clean. As in the
everyday idiom of our own time, 'bad' thought came to be equated
in Berkeley's imagination with excrement.[21] In later life, he also
came passionately to believe in the virtues of tar water, an emetic that
rids the physical body of faecal matter, and – by extension – serves as
a panacea, setting all our physical ailments to rights. He had used tar
water successfully, he claimed, in treating smallpox, eruptions,
ulceration of the bowel, distemper, consumptive cough, pleurisy,
erysipelas, indigestion, gravel in the urine, dropsy and asthma. In his

book *Siris: A Chain of Philosophical Reflexions and Inquiries Concerning the Virtues of Tar-Water*, published in 1744 when he was nearing sixty, he extolled the emetic's virtues as a medicine, and linked its remarkable powers to the nature of the divine being. The book went into six editions in its first year, was translated into French, German and Dutch, and launched a craze for tar water's medicinal use. As with Skinner and his air crib, Berkeley seems to have perceived himself as surrounded by a rising tide of excrement, which it is the function of disciplined thought magically to cleanse.

While his philosophy can be seen as mistaken, and his passion for tar water as evidence of a brilliant man wandering in his wits, to dismiss Berkeley would be unfair. The phenomenalist tradition is a powerful one, fertile to this day, in the social sciences especially. His zeal for tar water was no more far-fetched than were the obsessing preoccupations of other great minds of his own or other times; and although in his case surprisingly literal-minded, Berkeley's hostility to matter expresses a tendency common to all thought inspired by visions of pure reason.

IDEES FIXES

A curious feature of scientists – one that both Skinner and Freud vividly exemplify – is their tendency to become obsessed with certain fixed ideas or thought-formulae. An instance is the idea of 'g', the general factor of intelligence. If you construct an intelligence test in the conventional way using various sub-tests, and give it to samples of individuals, you find a tendency for those who do well on one sub-test to do well on all sub-tests; and for those who do poorly on one, to do poorly on all. You can show, too, that such skill tends to run in families; and there is also evidence – confused, admittedly – which suggests that it is to an appreciable extent inherited.[22] If you subject your correlations to one form of statistical analysis, you can elicit from them a general factor. This is usually labelled 'general intelligence' or 'g' and is assumed to be a quality that all sub-tests measure to greater or lesser extent. If you subject your results to another closely related form of analysis, on the other hand, you distribute this statistical overlap between various factors which are more specific, and these you may label, if you wish, 'verbal ability', 'numerical ability', 'spatial ability', and so on. In itself, the choice is of little importance, and largely a matter of personal taste. British psychologists have usually favoured the first policy, Americans the second.[23]

In the minds of some psychologists though, 'g' ceased to be a purely descriptive feature of complex test results, and took on a moral and mystical significance. For Cyril Burt, a working lifetime's devotion to the structure of intelligence culminated in an increasingly dogmatic preoccupation with 'g' as the reality underlying his vision of a natural aristocracy. In his own mind and those of others, it came to stand as a bulwark. It was, he declared, 'central and all-pervading' and also 'inborn'. 'Neither knowledge nor practice, neither interest nor industry, will avail to increase it.' An American enthusiast even likened it to the Rock of Gibraltar.[24] Until they learnt caution, it also seemed to some to justify a less demanding educational provision for children who were black.[25] The general factor came to stand for the hereditary view of human nature as against environmentalism, for biology against social science, for elitism against egalitarianism – and, in political terms, for the right against the left. In certain embattled imaginations, it also stood for reason against unreason; and in those more embattled still, for the social decencies against weird haircuts, sexual permissiveness and domestic chaos: hence Burt's inspiration in founding Mensa, the society for those with high IQs, its meetings modelled on those of the Arthurian legend.[26]

To challenge an expert on the evidence in a field as technical as mental measurement may seem a straightforward issue, but it is not. In practice it is almost always received as ideologically motivated and menacing, as though it were a military threat among nation-states. The expert may go through the moves of meeting the challenge on its own factual terms, but in reality will give ground to someone he does not implicitly trust only in circumstances which are wholly exceptional.[27] Not only do visions like Burt's seize the imagination; they become principles in the service of which it seems appropriate to overlook difficulties in one's own data and more actively to cheat.[28] When, in his old age, Burt invented two collaborators, 'Miss Howard' and 'Miss Conway', and fudged his data about identical twins, he was cutting corners; but doing so, almost certainly, in the service of what he saw as a higher truth. The tradition is a long-standing one. It seems that Galileo claimed to have made observations which he had not; and, when in altercation with his German rival Leibniz, Newton tidied up certain measurements in his *Principia*, in order to give a better fit between theory and data.[29]

The role that *idées fixes* play in the processes of discovery is by no means entirely mischievous, however, as the astronomer Kepler's discoveries show. In *The Sleepwalkers*, Arthur Koestler tells us that Johannes Kepler, Keppler, Khepler, Kheppler or Keplerus was conceived on 16 May, AD 1571, at 4.37 a.m., and was born on 27 December at 2.30 p.m., after a pregnancy lasting 224 days, 9 hours and 53 minutes. The five different ways of spelling his name were all Kepler's own, Koestler says, as were the figures relating to conception, pregnancy and birth, recorded in a horoscope which Kepler cast for himself. The contrast between his carelessness about his name and his extreme precision about dates reflects, from the outset, a mind to whom 'all ultimate reality, the essence of religion, of truth and beauty, was contained in the language of numbers'.[30]

Kepler was born in Weil, a town in south-west Germany, his forebears and relatives, in Koestler's phrase, 'degenerates and psychopaths', his upbringing 'ghastly'.[31] His father was a wanderer who deserted his family to fight as a mercenary and narrowly escaped being hanged; his mother was an innkeeper's daughter, brought up by an aunt who was burned as a witch. She herself was accused in old age of consorting with the devil and narrowly escaped the stake. Johannes was their first-born, a sickly child, suffering continuous ill-health, with thin limbs and a large, pasty face. He was four when his mother followed his father to the wars; five when they returned and began restlessly to drift. He attended school only irregularly, and from nine to eleven had no schooling at all. Of his own health, Kepler says that he almost died of smallpox, that his hands were badly crippled and that he suffered continually with skin ailments and the scabs of putrid wounds on his feet. On the middle finger of his right hand he had a worm, on the left a huge sore. In early adulthood, he suffered from headaches and a disturbance of the limbs, and also from mange. When as a young man he was offered 'union with a virgin', he achieved this with the greatest possible difficulty, 'experiencing the most acute pains of the bladder.'[32]

Only two childhood memories counterbalance the overwhelming impression of squalor and hypochondria. At the age of six, the young Kepler was taken by his mother to look at a comet; and at the age of nine, he was called outdoors by his parents to witness an eclipse of the moon.

Kepler had hoped to become a clergyman. It was only by chance that he taught mathematics, a job in a distant town opportunely falling vacant. A year after taking up his new duties, he was drawing a figure on the blackboard for his pupils one day, when struck by an idea with such force that he believed he held the key to the secrets of creation in his hand. This sudden insight was to remain his driving force and inspiration for the rest of his working life. 'The delight that I took in my discovery', he exclaims, 'I shall never be able to describe in words.'[33]

His insight was simple, and he published it in his book *Mysterium Cosmographicum*, when he was twenty-five. Why were there just six planets? And why were there just five perfect solids – five three-dimensional figures, that is to say, with sides which are identical and which fit neatly inside or outside a sphere: the pyramid, the cube, the octahedron (contained by eight equilateral triangles), the dodeca-hedron (contained by twelve pentagons), and the icosahedron (con-tained by twenty equilateral triangles)? The truth dawned. The orbits of the six planets must be arranged so as to allow the five perfect solids to fit between them, thus forming the planetary system's in-visible skeleton. The octahedron fits between Mercury and Venus, the icosahedron between Venus and Earth, the dodecahedron be-tween Earth and Mars, the pyramid between Mars and Jupiter, the cube between Jupiter and Saturn. QED. Geometry and astronomy are joined, and the puzzles of the universe solved.

It is perfectly normal for a scientist to be seized with an idea that seems to him unchallengable, a bolt from the blue so dramatic as to arrive as a revelation; and normal too, for a life's work in science to be built around such a dazzling insight. It is also commonplace for such insights to be false, as, of course, was Kepler's. What was re-markable about Kepler's revelation was not that it was unshakable and false, but that, in spite of its falsity, it led him to discover the three laws for which he is rightly famed, and to destroy, once and for all, the pre-Copernican view of the planetary system centred on the Earth. He reached the right answers, or answers which were nearly right, and did so because in the grip of a vision which was com-pletely mistaken.

Even among the most fiercely driven, of course, there is still an important distinction to be drawn: between those who assimilate all evidence to their abiding vision, and those who, like Kepler, eventu-ally allow the evidence to break through. 'Why should I mince my words?' he asks. 'The truth of Nature, which I had rejected and chased away, returned by stealth through the backdoor, disguising itself to be accepted.' He had rejected his original equation for the orbit of Mars and turned to a new one, not realising that both described the same path, an ellipse. But the truth did in the end

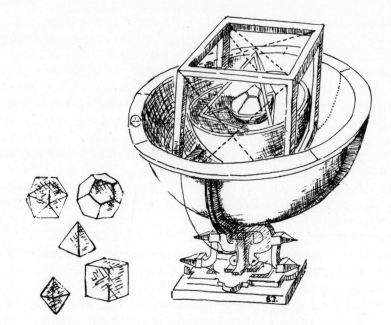

Kepler's perfect solids

dawn. 'I thought and searched, until I went nearly mad,' he says. 'Ah, what a foolish bird I have been.'[34]

In ways not immediately obvious to the non-scientist, Kepler's exclamations imply an arena in which the temptations and acts of courage associated with more traditional views of morality are re-enacted. Forthright frauds in science are very much the exception.[35] The high-handed redrawing of the boundary between appearance and reality, on the other hand, is an everyday feature of laboratory life. If his data fall out awkwardly, the scientist will be tempted to massage them; and there are dozens of ways of doing this which fall short of wilful misrepresentation. The reasons leading him to do so are at least as various as the opportunities the grey area provides: his department's need for a research contract, the blow to his pride inseparable from losing an argument, his addiction to the illusion of intellectual control. The temptations, too, are beguiling. He knows that a proportion of the awkwardnesses in any scientist's data will turn out to be trivial, and that many will resolve themselves of their own accord. He also knows, though, that it is in confrontation with genuinely anomalous evidence that the prospect of a better explanation lies. To look such anomalies in the eye requires a form of courage that few of science's critics will have experienced at first-hand.[36]

VIOLENCE, SYMBOLIC AND LITERAL

Psychologists disagree about the extent to which science is fuelled by hostility.[37] It remains true, nevertheless, that the psychic space which the wound creates is one in which aggressive impulses can easily and fluently be deployed. In exercising his agency in a belligerent way, a 'male' man both celebrates his freedom and punishes the world at large for requiring that he be free (and insecure) in the first place. Science, philosophy and technology become ideal venues, in other words, for the psychic manoeuvres of revenge; and violence, as a consequence, is often a distinguishing feature of science's language and preoccupations.

Together with his mentor Roger Guillemin, Robert Schally won the Nobel Prize in 1977 for the discovery of TRF (thyrotropin re-leasing factor), a major feat in the world of endocrinology. Schally's career had been that of an outsider.[38] He was born in Poland, but grew up in Scotland. He moved to London to work as a laboratory assistant; then to Canada, where he became a Canadian citizen; and finally to America where he became an American citizen. He did not take his first degree until he was twenty-nine. About his status as a refugee, and about the competitiveness of his struggle, Schally is quite explicit. 'Guillemin and I, we are immigrants, obscure little doctors, we fought our way to the top; that's what I like about Guil-lemin; at least we fought, and now we have more awards than all of them.'[39]

The search for TRF was a violent endeavour in the literal sense that it could be won only in minute amounts, a milligram at a time, from several tons of hypothalami delivered from the slaughterhouse. It was also Napoleonic, in that Guillemin and Schally sought to wrest TRF from the hands of the physiologists, who were already using the substance in its unanalysed form, and carry it off to biochemistry – a feat that could only succeed with massive allocations of research money, and the grinding labour of chemical refinement and analysis. As Schally says: 'Nobody before had to process millions of hypotha-lami. . . . The key factor is not the money, it's the will . . . the brutal force of putting in 60 hours a week for a year.' And again, 'It's like fighting Hitler. You have to cut him down.'[40]

As it happens, hostile impulses also fuelled the imagination of the man who established the prize Schally and Guillemin won: Alfred Nobel himself. Nobel was born in Stockholm in 1833. When he was eight, he moved with his family to St Petersburg so that his father could set up a torpedo works there. At the age of seventeen, he went to live for a short while in America, but then returned to Russia and thence to Sweden. Thereafter he was to move time and again. As Anthony Sampson says of him, he 'seemed to belong to no country or place'.[41]

Before he was thirty, Nobel had succeeded in making nitroglycerine explode, and soon he and his brother Emil established a small explosives factory. One day there was an accidental explosion in which five men were killed, Emil among them. Alfred was to remain haunted by this disaster, and his father never recovered from it, but the fascination with explosives remained. Within five years, Nobel had discovered a means of mixing nitroglycerine, a lethally unstable substance, with a form of clay, thus making it safer to handle. This new concoction came to be known as dynamite, an invention from which a vast fortune flowed. Later, he discovered a form of cordite; and, at the age of sixty, bought the Swedish armaments firm of Bofors. However his interest in explosions, he liked to explain, was essentially impersonal: 'it is rather fiendish things we are working on, but they are so interesting as purely theoretical problems, and so completely technical, as well as so clear of all financial and commercial considerations, that they are doubly fascinating.'[42]

As a businessman, Nobel proved bitterly litigious, travelling the world to defend his patents and creating for himself a monopoly comparable to John D. Rockefeller's Standard Oil. Despite his energies as an inventor and industrialist, his temperament was melancholic. He suffered from migraine, viewed women with suspicion (the 'fair, but usually repulsive sex'), and preferred dogs. Personally, he was disconcerting, moving jerkily with a mincing step, his conversation disjointed and often macabre: 'without rudder or compass', he once said of himself, 'a wreck on the sea of life'. Despite his lifelong obsession with explosives, Nobel was an advocate of pacifism, and saw himself as a political reformer, even a Bolshevist. He also wrote poetry in the style of Shelley. In later life, Sampson claims, one of Nobel's favourite schemes was his 'suicide institute': an establishment on the Riviera, with beautiful views and a first-class orchestra, where prospective suicides could end their lives in dignity and style (in its own way, an innovation as technical as his experiments with nitroglycerine).

PURITY AND 'SPILLAGE'

One could be forgiven for assuming that if scientists harness their intimate emotions to their work, the further one moves across the academic spectrum from the arts towards pure science, the calmer would be the outward behaviour of the individuals concerned. In fact, some of the most bitter – and bitterly *personal* – rows the academy has witnessed have been instigated by the purest of the pure: theoretical physicists and mathematicians.

In a famous row which disfigured the life of the Princeton Institute for Advanced Study in the 1970s, renowned mathematicians like Andre Weil, brother of the French mystic Simone Weil, were pitted against the Institute's director Carl Kaysen, an economist. The point at issue was Kaysen's determination to build up the Institute's strength in the social sciences; and, with this end in view, to invite to the Institute as a member of its permanent staff a sociologist from California, Robert Bellah. As with the roughly concurrent quarrels in psychology over race and IQ, this exceptionally bitter dispute had all the outward signs of a political brawl: orthodox scholars rebutting the efforts of a brilliant and worldly but abrasive new director, intent on getting his own way – the battleground, the legitimacy of modern, 'soft' sociology.[43]

From the outset, though, the Institute had had a history of personal animosity and political strife. Set up in the early 1930s, it was committed to the cause of academic purity: 'the usefulness of useless knowledge'. In the words of its third director, Robert Oppenheimer, it was 'an intellectual hotel, dedicated to the preservation of the good things men live by'; and it became home for some of the world's greatest theoretical physicists, mathematicians and logicians, among them Einstein, Von Neumann and Gödel. Some, like Gödel, lived in a world where logic merged into mystery, his gift being to detect illogicalities in arguments which, until that moment, everyone else had assumed to be sound. As a young man, he had demonstrated that, contrary to the belief expressed by Russell and Whitehead in *Principia Mathematica*, mathematics cannot be derived from a handful of axioms whose truth is self-evident. This insight subverted a mechanistic view of mathematics; and, by implication, of all other aspects of the mind's functioning. By the

mid-1970s, shortly before his retirement, Gödel's presence at the Institute was treated by visitors as god-like; a man with access to forms
of knowledge denied to lesser mortals. To have talked to him – if
only about Leibniz – was to have engaged in conversation of super-
natural significance. (In personality, Gödel was hypochondriacal,
unworldly, depressed. Implausibly, in his early thirties, he had married a night-club dancer. Although childless, the marriage lasted
until his death forty years later. As he grew older, he became increasingly convinced that his food was being poisoned; and when his
wife underwent surgery and had to stay for a while in a nursing
home, he ceased to eat altogether, and starved himself to death.)[44]

While the Institute had had success in recruiting brilliant theoreticians like Gödel, the recruitment of representatives of untidier disciplines like economics, politics and the humanities was troubled. Its
first and second directors, Abraham Flexner and Frank Aydelotte,
found mathematicians and theoretical physicists unwilling to accept
such lowly beings as colleagues. The third director, Oppenheimer,
father of the atom bomb and director of the atomic research laboratory at Los Alamos, was an altogether more formidable figure;
but he, too, experienced extremes of difficulty over appointments,
being opposed on principle by Von Neumann and other mathematicians, who accused him to trying to pack the Institute with flam-
boyant but unproductive generalists.

It was Kaysen who succeeded Oppenheimer; a man in his mid-
forties, at the height of his powers, one of the recruits from Harvard
who had lent the Kennedy administration its lustre of intellectual
quality. While other members of the administration were preoccupied with the Cuban missile crisis, Kaysen had been for a while
'vice president in charge of the rest of the world'. Returning from
Washington to Harvard, Kaysen became a professor of political
economy. His work was applied; and, at the Institute, the titles of his
books were to be held against him: *United States v United Shoe
Machine Corporation, an Economic Analysis of an Anti-Trust Case; The
American Business Creed; Anti-Trust Policy; The Demand for Electricity
in the United States.* On the other hand, his fellow economist John
Galbraith is said to have characterised Kaysen as 'the most perfectly
informed man I have ever known'.[45]

Despite his political acumen, Kaysen in turn fell foul of the Institute's permanent academic staff, and departed. It is arguable that
Flexner, as founder and first director, was bound to run into trouble;
that Oppenheimer was past his best; and that Kaysen was wretchedly

ill-advised in his choice of Bellah as a social scientist with whom to confront restive colleagues, his work offensive not only to the Institute's mathematicians but also to its historians. It is true, too, that the Institute's trustees had twice appointed directors, Oppenheimer and Kaysen – whose distinction in the application of knowledge was sharply at odds with the Institute's declared aims. It is true, yet again, that the permanent staff of the Institute were, from a director's point of view, an impossible group with whom to deal. Many had been given life tenure on the strength of remarkable accomplishments, but were now in the trough of inanition that awaits fine minds once their best work is done.

These reservations granted, the implication must still be that no one could have run the Institute in its formative years; no one, that is to say, unwilling to bow to the intense hostility of distinguished mathematicians and theoretical physicists towards scholars whose work was less pure than their own. The fact that, within its own grounds, John von Neumann had developed the first electronic digital computer is one about which the Institute is to this day revealingly uneasy. Arguably, this uneasiness is attributable to the computer's first use: the calculation of the thermonuclear consequences of the first H-bomb explosion, at the time, the largest calculation ever undertaken. The indications are, though, that its real source is symbolic. Von Neumann and his team had sullied the Institute's purity with 'a nuts-and-bolts, angle-iron-and-sheet-metal *machine*'. Now in the Smithsonian Institution, it has 'a stack at the top, a flue, an exhaust pipe up which the heat of all the glowing filaments and vacuum tubes inside could escape'.[46] The site of this remarkable achievement remains uncelebrated, and is used as a stationery store.

The wound not only fuels the male imagination, such battles suggest, but also constrains it. For although, superficially, the forms of scientific and philosophical thought are various, their underlying preoccupations are few. The 'male' man is evidently drawn to the dramas of purity and cleansing, of force, and of the penetration of mysteries. Uniting such concerns, invariably, there is a preoccupation with the idea of order: of structures and of boundaries which define and limit. More specifically, and especially when the subject-matter is human, the processes of the male imagination appear, time and again, to come to rest on dualities and schisms, and on the task of resolving these by the power of reason.

CHAPTER 7

MALE VICES

W E MOVE NOW from the patterns of behaviour men display in public to the more shadowy domain of private life. There remains the same sense, though, of actions controlled and driven. If our argument about the wound is correct, the adult heterosexual male *must* view the intimately personal – and, more specifically, the intimately sexual – ambivalently. On the one hand, it is a chance magically to recover a primitively symbiotic comfort. On the other, it represents a return to a state of defencelessness. Either the male holds himself back from intimate experience, treating the people he desires as objects; or he abandons himself to it, thereby exposing himself to anxiety, even psychic annihilation. In the first mode, he is less than wholly human; a copulatory gadget. In the second, like a cortex without its skull, he is exposed to intolerable extremities of psychic pleasure and psychic pain. In the first case, he retains his sense of agency, and sees himself in instrumental terms, seeking intense but containable discharges of pleasure. In the second, he will experience a collapse of agency, and the need, thereafter, to effect repairs; to gather himself back together as a being who has boundaries to maintain and a life of threats and challenges to endure.[1]

The male, separated from his source of primitive comfort, an agent, his imagination fuelled, will also be susceptible in ways that the female is not to elaborations and displacements of sexual appetite. He is more likely than the female to displace his desire for a person onto part of that person or onto an object; and he is more likely to act out such desires in literal terms, rather than simply fantasising about them. In as much as a man finds his chosen form of sexual endeavour cutting him off progressively from primitive comfort, he is likely, too, to infuse his behaviour with misogynous resentment or hatred. He may resort inappropriately to violence or become promiscuous. He may also become a pervert.

The wound leads us to expect, in other words, a functional equivalence between certain acts of arbitrary violence, sexual promiscuity
and perversion. All three are expressions of the same proclivity; the
tendency of men, when in the grip of powerful feelings, to think of
people as emotionally charged figments. Here, therefore, we are
going to look at the linkages between maleness and forms of sexual
behaviour which are in various ways aberrant. In doing so, we lay
the foundation (in the form of a diagram) for the bridge that will
carry us, in the next chapter, into the terrain of art.

SEXUAL CRIME

In terms of criminal behaviour, our predictions are confirmed by the
evidence. The rate of men convicted of sexual offences in English
courts is between 30 and 40 times higher than that of women.[2] The
male is overwhelmingly more likely than the female to display sexual
aberrations of any kind, and especially those that constitute a legal
offence: to rape women, molest children on buses, make obscene
telephone calls, display his member to passers-by, set fire to buildings in order to have orgasms, have intercourse with corpses, and so
on. Reviewing the literature, Bancroft shows that in nearly all the
rape and sexual assault cases that come to court, the victim is a
woman and the perpetrator is a man; only 0.2 per cent of the sexual
assaults on women in the United Kingdom are homosexual ones in
which the assailants were other women.[3] For anatomical reasons, it is
not possible for a woman to have sexual intercourse with an unwilling man. But granted that some women are physically stronger
than many men, and that groups of such women could easily overpower and abduct a man, one might expect an appreciable number of
sexual assaults by women on men. Whether acting singly or in
groups, however, sexual assaults on men by women are rare. Bancroft cites an American murder trial in which a homosexual man was
accused of killing a woman who, he claimed, had raped him. This
might well have been an instance, though, of coercive intercourse
between a heterosexual woman and a man who was actually bisexual
– an act in which the man had at the time colluded. Such cases, in any
event, belong to the American law's bizarre fringe.

Bancroft also notes that in cases of incest it is usually men who are
the guilty parties. In the twelve-month period examined, the bulk of
those convicted in British courts were fathers (and step-fathers) who

had had sexual relations with their daughters (72 per cent), or brothers who had had sexual relations with their sisters (24 per cent). Of the remainder, 3 per cent were cases of sexual relations between mothers and adult sons; 1 per cent of sexual relations between grand-father and granddaughter. In all, 124 males were convicted of incest; only 5 women. In not one case was a mother convicted of sexual re-lations with a son who was still a child or adolescent. While the atti-tude of some mothers to their sons may well be highly eroticised, the impression is strong that it is typically males, not females, who act to breach the taboos with which incest is surrounded.

The home is the context not just for incest, but also for a sub-stantial proportion of lethal violence. Recently Black and Kaplan have pointed to the high proportion of murders committed by men on their current or erstwhile wives or lovers.[4] Home Office statistics indicate that of the 234 female victims of homicide in England and Wales in 1989, 48 per cent were killed by a spouse or lover. A further 17 per cent of these homicides occurred within the family, and another 16 per cent were committed by people whom the victim knew.[5] In other words – and the statistics allow that this may be an underestimate – in four out of every five cases in which a female is murdered, the event occurs, not as a bolt from the blue, but within a web of personal relationships.

INTIMATE VIOLENCE

Statistics make clear the personal roots of such violence, but cannot reveal the dynamics of the spillage from one area of passionate con-cern to another. For this purpose, case histories or the detailed recon-struction of criminals' lives are indispensable. Only in the grain and texture of such accounts does one grasp quite how the pertinent tran-spositions occur.

In *The Executioner's Song*, Norman Mailer offers a re-creation of the life of the murderer Gary Gilmore, and in it details the steps whereby his brand of violence was unleashed.[6] Gilmore is often labelled a psy-chopath, and his two murders are dismissed as gratuitous. But to view Gilmore solely in this light is to overlook the relation of passion to violence, and the circumstances in which emotional spillage occurs. Where the two killers of Capote's *In Cold Blood*,[7] Dick Hickock and Perry Smith, seem sub-human, Gilmore emerges from Mailer's book as fully human but as, in some crucial respect, flawed.

The contradictory facets of his character are those of more normal males, but the dampers which smooth the performance of the normal male into a tolerable impression of consistency were in Gilmore's make-up weak or lacking. He was also fiercely intelligent.[8]

When Gilmore left prison in 1976, he was a small-time crook in his early thirties, who had just finished a twelve and a half year sentence for armed robbery. The son of a con-man who travelled under various names and who had close connections with show business, Gilmore had spent a substantial proportion of his life locked up. With the support of relatives, the newly released Gilmore found a job of sorts, but two passions quickly seized him. One was for a white pick-up truck. Freshly painted but with 100,000 miles on the clock, it was selling for $1,700, which Gilmore did not have and could only steal: he had 'fallen in love with a paint job'. The other passion was for his 'little elf', Nicole Baker, a young woman, living on society's margins, hopelessly promiscuous, but in her own elusive way principled. She loved him in return, but they quarrelled viciously, and she hid from him, frightened of the violence she discovered he could do.

One oppressively hot day in mid-summer, Gilmore at last got his hands on the white truck, and was given forty-eight hours in which to find the first payment of $400. At the wheel, with Nicole's deranged younger sister April for company, Gilmore went looking for Nicole and for $400. Apparently at random, Gilmore entered a petrol station, menaced the attendant with a gun, made him lie on the floor of the lavatory face down with his hands beneath him, and shot him twice in the head from close range. Dollar bills in his pocket and coin changer in his hand, he then walked to his truck and drove away.

The next day, Gilmore had his weekly session with his parole officer. For the first time, he seemed to confide: that he wanted to give up drinking because it might help win Nicole back, and that he felt he had difficulties as a lover. At last, his parole officer sensed, they were making progress. That evening, Gilmore left his truck at a local garage, complaining that it would not start properly, entered the City Center Motel, shot the manager and walked away with the pistol in one hand and the motel's cash drawer in the other. When the police caught up with him, he had almost reached Nicole's mother's home where, as it happened, Nicole was spending the night with her two children. When asked, much later, he sounded unequivocal: 'I killed them', he said, 'because I did not want to kill Nicole.'[9]

Part of the difficulty between Gilmore and Nicole Baker was sex-

" I got to have that truck " . . . .

ual. Physically their relationship was not a success. More significantly, Nicole was promiscuous, Gilmore was not. Mailer's narrative makes it clear that the causes were not an excess of sexual energy
on her part and a lack of it on his (Gilmore masturbated incessantly
while incarcerated). What she sought from other men, however
fleetingly, was reassurance, physical intimacy. What Gilmore sought
from Nicole, on the other hand, was eroticised possession; a need
which, when thwarted, threw bolts of violence in all directions.

Throughout Gilmore's imprisonment and trial, and the bizarre
sequence of events culminating in his execution by firing squad,
Nicole remained loyal. A flood of love letters passed between them,
more articulate on his side, more obviously heartfelt on hers. In the
course of this correspondence, the question of her unfaithfulness was
explicitly broached. At one point, she wrote to Gilmore saying: 'It's
such an ugly thing to do. I spend so much time either getting drunk
or getting fucked.' In response, his violence leaps from the page:

> Baby the jailer just brought me your letter. You're always writing
> and telling me about getting fucked, getting fucked, getting
> fucked, getting fucked. Everybody fucks Nicole. Everybody.
> Everybody picks her up hitchhiking or sees her 3 or 4 times a week

just for the vibes the beautiful vibes feel the beauty just friends just company don't even have to know her just sit and listen to her talk about how much she loves Gary then fuck her. Goddam mother-fuckin son of a goddam bitch.... If you feel so much mother-fuckin sympathy for someone that you'll fuck him why oh Jesus Jesus Jesus fucking Christ Goddam Goddam fucking damn. Baby Jesus Christ help me understand...[10]

Four days later, he is calmer, but it is not a mood that inspires trust. Later still, he becomes rhapsodic, but this inspires little trust either. As Mailer observes, Gilmore will implore 'Little elf, how can you do this to me?' But then, at the top of the next page, as if he had just 'swallowed a lightning bolt of rage...FUCK, SHIT, and PISS would be written in letters two inches high'.[11] An air of calculation hangs about these letters to Nicole, just as there did about so much of what Gilmore said and wrote. Passion is there; but, at the same time, a wary intelligence is being exercised, and a remorseless succession of manipulations is being wrought.

One of these manipulations took the form of a suicide pact with Nicole. She attempted to keep her side of the bargain, overdosing herself with Seconal and putting herself to bed to die with a picture of Gilmore under her pillow. He did not keep his. Where Nicole had faced death in a mood of exhausted surrender, to Gilmore the relationship with death and the 'other side' remained one of will: 'Like about everything else in life', he told Nicole, '*you* gotta remain in control'.[12]

PROMISCUITY

Men are nowhere more objectifying than in their promiscuity. Forty years ago, Kinsey noted that even the most promiscuous women rarely had as many sexual partners as some men. He saw, too, that promiscuity among males was particularly marked among homo-sexuals. Of his homosexual males, 8 per cent reported having more than 100 partners, a figure that few of his heterosexual males and none of his female homosexuals approached.[13] As Roger Brown has pointed out, the comparison between male and female homosexuals is in this respect especially illuminating, because heterosexuals of both sexes may modify their own inclinations in the light of the dis-crepant needs of the people they desire.[14]

Published some twenty-five years later, Bell and Weinberg's study

of male and female homosexuals, also from the Institute of Sex Research, suggested a massive increase in promiscuity among the men,
these changes being part, perhaps, of a wider shift towards sexual
permissiveness influencing homosexual and heterosexual alike.[15] Bell
and Weinberg claim that of 574 white homosexual males interviewed
from the Bay Area of San Francisco, 15 per cent reported having had
between 500 and 999 partners; and 28 per cent reported 1,000 or
more. Only 1 per cent reported having had 4 partners or fewer; three
quarters reported 100 partners at least. The figures for women are of
a different order. Only 2 per cent of 227 white female homosexuals
reported having had at least 100 partners. While easily the most common response among the males was '1000 or more', easily the most
common among the females was 'between 5 and 9'.[16]

Clearly, there are important distinctions to be drawn. The first is
between promiscuity and satyriasis – between needing to have sexual
relations with very large numbers of strangers, and having a sexual
appetite which is huge. Of Bell and Weinberg's white male homosexuals, only 4 per cent reported a frequency of sexual contact of at
least one a day. On the other hand, 4 out of 5 reported that at least
half their partners were strangers; and 7 out of 10 said that more than
half their partners were men with whom they had sex just once.
Only 1 per cent reported never having had a partner who was a
stranger; and, similarly, only 1 per cent reported never having had a
partner with whom they had sex just once. The figures for white
female homosexuals were 62 per cent and 38 per cent respectively. In
psychology, one does not often find differences so marked; and their
significance is clear. Among the men (but not the women) Bell and
Weinberg studied, it was not sexual energy *per se* that was at issue,
but an urgently eroticised idea: the thought of sex allied to that of the
unfamiliar.

Also pertinent is the distinction between promiscuity and anonymity – the need not to know who your sexual partner is. Bell and
Weinberg collected ethnographic material as well as statistics. Both
promiscuity and anonymity, this material suggests, were circumstances which the mores of the Bay Area in the 1970s made it easy to
contrive. One ethnographer reports: 'Upon entering the men's room
of the X Theater, I saw five middle-aged men standing in the door-
way of the stall to the toilet. One man had his pants dropped, while
another man was performing fellatio on him, and another was performing anal intercourse from behind. Two men were leaning
against the wall and masturbating. I was told I would have to stand

in line.'[17] They also speak, as does Bancroft, of holes bored in the walls dividing lavatory cubicles, which allow the penis of a man on one side of the wall to be fellated by a man on the other side, entirely anonymously. 'Glory holes', Bell and Weinberg call these, and they comment that they have seen them carved in marble, plastic, metal and opaque glass. In some cases, it was work which must have taken weeks to complete.

It is arguable that such segregation of the sexual from the personal is one of the needs the wound establishes in all males, homosexual and heterosexual alike. One can also insist that, although squalid, such practices may have a prophylactic function, releasing tension otherwise disruptive. In doing so, they may allow the individual to express his imaginative energies in other directions, the novelist Georges Simenon being a celebrated case in point.

In all, Simenon wrote between 400 and 500 books of fiction, the majority psychological thrillers, in which human nature's darker recesses are explored. Simenon produced each of his works in a sustained period of creative effort lasting between a week and a fortnight; 'states of grace' he called them, times of nervous tension sufficient to make him vomit, and during which he habitually lost appreciable weight.[18] By all accounts, a deeply unquiet man and a fantasist, Simenon was also a womaniser; and in matters of sex, he claimed, his needs were imperious.[19] Late in his life, in the course of a discussion with the Italian film-maker Federico Fellini, he said he had had sexual relations with '10,000 women', a figure he later adjusted to 'tens of thousands'. Simenon's prodigious feats of application as a writer could well have been part of a broader deployment of psychological boundaries and defences, then, in which sexual desire was split from the rest of his experience, and was expressible only in arbitrary terms. Transparently, his estimates of his own prowess are in Mailer's term 'factoids'; fables designed to manipulate the emotions of an unseen audience.[20] Far from being at variance with Simenon's career as a weaver of compellingly life-like fictions, in other words, his stories about his own sexual energies are integral to that career. Even if his factoids are accepted as only distantly approximating to fact, Simenon still stands as an example – a gloomy one, admittedly – of the bifurcation often seen in the creative and scholarly arts, between fastidiousness of expression within the medium allied to an urgent crudity of response outside it.

While there is nothing discreditable in the idea that sexual promiscuity and anonymity may serve an equilibrating function, the impression lingers that something is amiss; that there is something wrong with the man who urgently needs, say, to be fellated by an unseen stranger on the far side of one of Bell and Weinberg's 'glory holes'. The imaginative energies fuelling such a venture seem actively – one might almost say, creatively – stunted or distorted. To take this interpretative step, however, is to move towards the heart of one of psychology's most strife-torn zones. In it, certain facts are available; and for the most part these are uncontentious. What is at issue is their significance.

THE PERVERSE

The list of sexual perversions (or 'paraphilias') is a long and distressing one. At least at the level of public behaviour, it is dominated, yet again, by men. Among pedophiles, offenders are always or almost always men; likewise the exhibitionists and peeping toms – the incidence of offences by women being so low that, in reviewing the field, Bancroft fails to take them explicitly into account. In the case of exhibitionists, Rosen takes an unequivocal view: 'the perversion of genital exhibitionism', he claims, 'does not occur in women'.[21] As with sexual assault, there is no physiological reason why women should not molest children, exhibit their genitalia to unsuspecting members of the public or peer in at bedroom windows. The statistical evidence makes it plain, nevertheless, that while there may well be venues in which such interests are pursued by women in a more socially accepted way, their expression in criminal form is entirely or almost entirely a male preserve. A detail cited by Bancroft from another sexual hinterland helps make the nature of the difference plain. Both men and women cross-dress. In mild and qualified form, cross-dressing is one of the staple ingredients of the *frisson* high fashion creates; and in forms more whole-hogging can express both complexities of gender identity and a homosexual object choice. In addition, though, cross-dressing can arise from a fetishistic preoccupation with the clothes worn by the opposite sex. On the present evidence, Bancroft concludes, this fetishistic aspect of cross-dressing is exclusive to men.[22]

No one knows why some people become perverts, others not. No one knows, either, why perverse interests take quite the form they do: why one man becomes fascinated by fur coats, say, while another needs to be whipped. Nor is there any agreement about where the relevant lines are to be drawn. In a recent and widely publicised case, the English police were said to be investigating the deaths of boys thought to have been killed during the filming of pornographic videos: ones aimed for private circulation among pedophiles, in which boys were sexually violated and then murdered while the cameras roll. Whatever the facts of the matter prove to be, the vast majority of people would agree that such an undertaking is grossly depraved, and most would say wicked. Some would deny, nevertheless, that, in itself, pedophilia is a perversion. Like homosexuality, they would insist, it is merely an 'orientation'. Following this line of reasoning, the American psychiatric profession has in the quite recent past agreed to remove homosexuality from its *Diagnostic and Statistical Manual of Psychiatry (DSMIII)*, the list of conditions which it regards as illnesses; but it drew the line at pedophilia.

While such changes of mind are of genuine sociological interest, they leave the issue of theoretical principle unresolved. In Britain, the opinion of psychiatrists and psychoanalysts remains divided. Some, like Comfort, urge us to ask of a sexual practice not 'Is it normal?', but 'Is it a resource or a handicap?' and 'Is it socially tolerable?'[23] Others remain convinced that the needs of both homosexuals and pedophiles are of their essence perverse, and are so irrespective of whether or not they are socially tolerable or are a handicap or a resource.

Predictably, the psychoanalytic notion of perversion is exacting. Rycroft defines it admirably crisply as 'any form of adult sexual behaviour in which heterosexual intercourse is not the preferred goal.'[24] In psychology and psychiatry, however, neat definitions never seem quite to work. Thus Rycroft's would categorise as perverse much of what happens inside happy marriages, because sexual pleasure or intimacy (rather than intercourse) is its goal; and it might also admit as normal some cases of incest. In practice, the sexual perversions form a loose-knit cluster of fantasies and behaviours, sharing some or all of six characteristics. The perversions are:

- Biologically maladaptive, in the sense that they are unrelated to reproduction;
- Activated by anxiety, disgust or hatred;
- Shocking or forbidden;
- Specialised to the point of seeming, from the outsider's point of view, bizarre;
- Necessary, if orgasm is to occur; and

- Subject, in terms of sexual excitement, to the law of diminishing returns.

The conviction with which one can identify an act or fantasy as perverse varies, needless to say, from the grossly aberrant (the coprophile who can only have orgasms with the faeces of a desired woman in his mouth) to the more marginal (the man who can only have orgasms with a woman he dislikes). A number of different but closely related claims are made about the nature of the psychological distortions or disturbances underlying such aberrations. Stoller has argued both that perversion is the erotic form of hatred,[25] and that behaviour is perverse it it carries us away from intimacy rather than towards it.[26] Khan argues that perversion is inseparable from alienation, and that perverse sexuality is the sexuality that results from intention rather than desire.[27] Grunberger suggests that perversion arises from damage to our feelings of intrinsic worth and connectedness, and from the hostility this damage provokes.[28]

These four claims, and the arguments that support them, overlap rather as the circles in a Venn diagram do; and, cumulatively, the picture they paint is congruent with our own. However, one element – a fifth Venn circle – is missing, and it seems to us the centrally placed one. Without it, the phenomena of perversion fail to make sense. Our own claim is that, under the influence of the wound, male desire tends of its own accord towards the impersonal; and that under the influence of hostility, fear or alienation, this tendency becomes specialised, self-perpetuating and addictive. Like all men, and especially 'male' men, the pervert moves in a world where the categories of person and thing are to some extent confused; but in him that confusion of people-as-things and things-as-people serves a particular erotic purpose. If his perversion focuses on objects (like fur coats), he treats them as though they were people or parts of people. If his perversion focuses on people (like the video-making pedophile's victim), they are people whom he treats as though they were objects. Once they are the focus of a pervert's desire, other people's thinghood frees him, as if by the wave of a wand, from any compunction he might otherwise experience towards them. In some cases, the perverse system of need becomes exclusive; in others, as with Eric in Chapter 2, two erotic systems – the ordinarily transactional and the blithely guilt-free – exist side by side.

Whether focused on a thing-as-person or a person-as-thing, the perverse desire expresses intense ambivalence, erotic fascination being mixed with (and temporarily acting to disguise) hate or fear. If it is women in rubber garments who become essential to the pervert, it is her body's surface that concentrates the sense of her thinghood. If he is a masochist and must be chastised in order to have an orgasm, it is his own body and its sensations that acquire the properties of otherness and thinghood. In each instance, the focus of the perverse desire – whether on thing-as-person or person-as-thing – becomes, in effect, a *fetish*: an object imbued with potently magical and irreducibly personal meaning. And such manoeuvres, we are claiming, are 'male', not just because they occur largely or exclusively among men, but because they acquire the shape and force they do because of the wound's lasting influence.

THAT RARE CREATURE: THE FEMALE FETISHIST

Men are not alone, of course, in having perverse sexual fantasies; women have them too. It is overt sexual perversions which are rare among women; and we would predict that when they do occur, they will be associated with disturbances of gender identity – a point neatly illustrated in a case study by Juliet Hopkins of a girl fetishist.[29]

Hopkins' patient, 'Sylvia', was first brought for therapy at the age of six. She was deeply disturbed. The psychiatrist who had seen her was uncertain whether to diagnose her as 'psychotic' or 'borderline'; and the psychologist found her untestable. She had been born prematurely and had been in intensive care for sixteen days. Her mother recalled Sylvia's early months as a nightmare: feeding three-hourly, taking an hour and a half to feed, and when not feeding, screaming. Sylvia did not speak fluently nor was she toilet trained until she was five. At six, she was still wetting her bed. Now she was at a school for maladjusted children and was unmanageable. Her usual manner was angry and menacing. On the other hand, her face would light up from time to time with a smile which Hopkins describes as radiant.

The psychiatrist, Sylvia's social worker and Hopkins herself were all convinced, on first meeting Sylvia, that she was a little boy. Hopkins says that Sylvia succeeded in appearing unmistakably male, although in fact her hair length and clothes were equally suited to either sex and her features were not masculine. It must have been her slightly swaggering gait, aggressive manner and assertive body postures, Hopkins concludes, that conveyed so strong an impression of masculinity.

It transpired, in the course of two years in therapy, that Sylvia's grandparents had wanted Sylvia's mother to be a boy; and that she in turn had wanted Sylvia to be a boy. Sylvia's father, a violent man, had been killed in a car crash when Sylvia was just short of her fourth birthday, and from that point Sylvia had insisted that she was a boy. In her dealings with her, Hopkins says, it was clear that Sylvia at least half-believed that she had a penis, and could urinate like a boy. 'Willies' (penises) were a source of intense excitement to her; an excitement which, Hopkins felt, masked equally intense anxiety.

It also became clear that Sylvia experienced intense erotic excitement about shoes and feet. This had first been evident, her mother claimed, as early as seven months, when she appeared fascinated by her father's shoes. She would draw herself up to them, salivate on them and then suck her thumb. Only shiny leather excited her in this way; suede would not do. In the clinic's waiting room, she embraced and slobbered over other patients' boots and shoes in a manner that bystanders found shocking. She was fascinated, too, by bare feet, becoming wildly excited at the prospect of paddling, of smelling feet, or of seeing pairs of bare feet together. These strange events had their precursors. There are indications that Sylvia's father had encouraged Sylvia to play with his feet, and had been unduly sexually intimate with her. (She spoke of her father's 'nice friendly willy'. But she also said once that 'willies are sick' and 'I'm sicking out white like a willy'.) When she was two, she had screamed at the prospect of taking a bath, and would take one only if sitting in her father's lap, which she used regularly to do.

In the course of her therapy, Sylvia's fetishistic excitement with shoes and feet subsided, to be replaced by fantasies of bodily damage. At the same time, Sylvia ceased to be a 'boy'. Both social worker and therapist noticed this independently. A beautiful boy had changed into a plain – and sometimes 'loathsome' – little girl. The terror and radiance had gone, and with them the masculinity too. Hopkins likens this transformation in her patient to exorcism.

OTHERNESS

The novelist and poet Thomas Hardy observed that 'the highest flights of the pen are mostly the excursions and revelations of souls unreconciled to life.'[30] The same could well prove to be true of the sexually aberrant. Gilmore's homicidal violence; the promiscuity of certain heterosexuals and homosexuals; Sylvia's fetish: we have presented them here, side by side, because we see all three as extreme expressions of states of mind which, in principle at least, coexist within each person, and each passionate act. All erotic expression, we are saying – male or female, normal or perverse – is imaginatively *complex*; and, in the male, this imaginative activity is particularly subject to distortion. The sexual behaviour of the supposedly red-blooded male, summarily copulating with every attractive and available female, is often depicted as being as spontaneous and unreflective as that of a stallion or dog. But in truth, we are suggesting, such episodes are shaped (and, both before and after the event, represented) in such a way as to resolve the ambivalences with which sexual desire (and especially sexual desire in the male) is riven.

The expression of desire in an intimate human context – most particularly, in the birth canal of an identifiable woman with a life and needs of her own – is a social performance in which conflicting systems of sexual and extra-sexual meaning must somehow be resolved. If the resulting action often appears arbitrary, it is so because the mind is organised in such a way as to permit abrupt discharges of activity across boundaries separating one preverbal or nonverbal meaning-system from another. Where the need for the arbitrary becomes engrained, this happens not because, rhythmically, imperiously, our biology overrides our psychology and sociology, but because these are expressions of the erotic imagination which have taken an unusually stunted and stereotypical form.[31]

Sexual acts occur within a system of imaginative representation which, in principle at least, is incessantly mobile. It is also a system within which sexual and non-sexual elements coexist, sex expressing a multiplicity of psychological states, many of them non-sexual. In Gilmore there was violence and a cold-hearted propensity for calculation – yet the letters he wrote to Nicole embody a passion that is both erotic and also rudimentarily poetic. For Simenon – imperative, repetitive – sex served, one senses, to deny emptiness and celebrate power (and especially the power of the professional fantasist). While in Sylvia's remarkable transformation, things – shoes, feet, willies – were the pivots on which the movements of her gender identity turned.

Each of these lives – Sylvia's no less than Gilmore's and Simenon's – raises the same question: that of the part played in the erotic by thoughts not of the comfortingly familiar, but of the strange or alien.

Common sense suggests that such ideas became enmeshed with
desire in those three lives precisely because the individuals in
question were psychologically disturbed. There is, however, a more
radical possibility: that thoughts of the erotic and thoughts of the
alien are inseparable – the lives of the psychologically disturbed
merely demonstrating this link most clearly. 'Le désir de l'homme
est le désir de l'Autre,' Lacan claims, 'l'Autre' or 'the Other' being
equated within his system of thought with what is repressed.[32] Far
from being harmonious with the intimately familiar, in other words,
desire lies at a tangent to it. Kingsley Amis catches this implication
neatly in *A Point of Logic*:[33]

> Love is a finding-out:
> Our walk to the bedroom
> (Hand in hand, eye to eye)
> Up a stair of marble
> Or decently scrubbed boards,
> As much as what we do
> In our abandonment,
> Teaches us who we are
> And what we are, and what
> Life itself is.
>
> Therefore put out the light,
> Lurch to the bare attic
> Over buckets of waste
> And labouring bodies;
> Leave the door wide open
> And fall on each other,
> Clothes barely wrenched aside;
> Stay only a minute,
> Depart separately,
> And use no names.

It would seem to follow that, within an intimately familiar relationship, voluptuous physical experience occurs only if the participants
can recreate within it a sense of the alien. Yet again, we confront the
nest of antitheses inherent in the wound, and the unstabilities to
which these give rise:

> similar : different
> familiar : strange, alien
> acknowledged : denied, repressed
> civilised : feral, barbarous, engulfing

There is the otherness that is a property of other people, especially strangers. There is also the otherness belonging to those facets of the personality that are normally hidden, but to which desire gives us access. Both partners bring to bed, that is to say, both the consciously acknowledged and the hidden components of their own desire. The adult male may lodge himself for all practical purposes of everyday life among the adjectives on the left-hand side of the antitheses just listed, and express desire exclusively by means of sorties among those on the right. Typically, though, solutions will be more complex: erotically significant but only partially acknowledged similarities will be explored within a context of perceived differences, and vice versa. Usually, it is not the alien in itself which is convulsively exciting, but *the alien in the context of the intimately familiar, and the prospect of the intimately familiar amid the alien.*

THE SIX-FOLD TRAFFIC OF DESIRE

Erotically, it seems, the qualities two people find significant in one another have three sources. For a heterosexual man, these will be:

- His wife or mistress as she acknowledges herself to be;
- The 'otherness' within himself which erotic excitement makes available to him; and
- The 'otherness' within her which, he discovers, erotic excitement makes available to her.

These properties of intimacy can be spelt out in terms of a simple diagram. It concerns any two people in any form of sexual relationship, but bears especially on those that are committing and sustained. Its four elements are states of being: two individuals as they ordinarily acknowledge themselves to be, and the two people, normally unacknowledged or only partially acknowledged, who those same individuals become when their consciousnesses are invaded by desire. For the sake of simplicity, the diagram is approached from the heterosexual male's point of view:

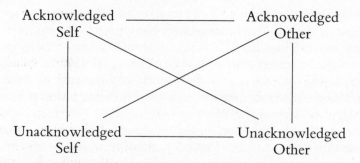

Each of the diagram's four elements is simultaneously a vantage point and an observable psychological entity; a system of self which perceives and construes and, at the same time, is perceived and construed.[34] Implicit in the interlocking of these four elements are six separate but mutually reverberative traffics. The first is the one dominating instruction manuals of sex and marriage: that between the manifest selves of the two partners. This is usually seen as posing issues of novelty, habit, mutual compatibility, and so on. In our own terms, it is more nearly a shadow-show, in which the controlling influences are rarely visible, and in which the exercise of common sense usually serves to disguise what those influences are.

It is the five remaining traffics which carry the intimacy's real freight. Two of these are internal: one to the man, the other to the woman. In each, a reconciliation is sought between those aspects of the self which are acknowledged and those 'other' aspects which are revealed only when the individual in question is seized by desire. Beyond these, there are three more traffics. Two consist in the negotiation of meanings between individual and partner, where one is lodged in everyday consciousness and the other is erotically seized. The last traffic of the six consists of the sense the partners make of one another when both are seized or transported.[35]

Although both parties' perceptions will tend to crystallise around certain stereotypical preoccupations and themes, the scope for dissonance and contradiction these traffics provide is limitless. An intimacy, normally congruent, may reveal gross incompatibilities when either or both parties to it are sexually enflamed. A man previously decorous may become brutally forceful, a crazy solipsist; and afterwards, in reaction, a woman may be overwhelmed by thoughts otherwise alien to her, of barely stifled dislike. An activity that makes sense when both parties to it are in the grip of desire may well seem grotesque the moment that grip is relaxed.

From the man's point of view, however, there is a more important perception. It is in intercourse with his wife or mistress that – unwittingly, subliminally – he learns one lesson above all others. He will discover *on what terms she allows him access to a state of symbiotic intimacy, and on what terms she allows him, once that access is achieved, to retrace his steps.* The crucial issue is that of 'symbiosis anxiety'; and the possible outcomes are several.[36] There may be no access; merely the urgent contiguity of bodies. There may be access, but to an interior landscape which is threatening. Or there may be access to a landscape which is reassuring; one from which he may, or may not, be able to retrace his steps with comparative ease. Because our culture is largely silent in such matters, consequent upheaval will be grasped in terms of the arbitrary and literal. Princes and princesses will become frogs over night, and energies previously turned on will be turned off. Boredom, irritability and a sense of mechanical repetition are the six-fold traffic's presenting symptoms when it is in disarray. If the imagined play of similarity and difference is not possible within a stable intimacy, the male may translate the need for it into literal terms, and seek to gratify it by repeating the same experience with different partners: that is to say, in driven promiscuity. Intimate violence and perversion may result too.

Not all surprises need be malign, though; and some will be life-enhancing. Where the ambiguities of similarity-in-difference and difference-in-similarity implicit in the six-fold traffic generate the variety of which they are in principle capable, both parties will experience intercourse, not as repetitious, but as each time anew.[37] This traffic can also generate life-enhancing surprises of another kind: all those works of art which originate in sexual desire but reach beyond it. These are our focus as we carry our argument into the world of the creative arts.

THE OTHER SIDE OF THE COIN

CHAPTER 8

BEYOND DESIRE

THE MALE IMAGINATION has two facets, we have argued. In terms of abiding preoccupations, one reflects the need to treat the impersonal as though it were personal, things as though they were people. It is this need that expresses itself most clearly in science and technology. The dominance men enjoy in disciplines like mathematics and physics stems from the wound, we claim, in the form of a driven need to create and explore formal structures. Such a need might also account for the superiority men have in the past enjoyed in certain aspects of the arts; musical composition, for instance.[1] The other facet, obvious in the field of sexual perversion, reflects the need to treat the personal as though it were impersonal, people as though they were things. Interpretatively speaking, in other words, the previous chapter opened a second avenue, the obverse of one expressed in science and technology. It pointed to the tendency of men, again stemming from the wound, to invest people, parts of people and objects with intense erotic significance. The implication is that men may be distinguished in the arts by their need to produce works which have their point of origin in sexual desire.

Pursuing this idea, we shall tread warily. Psychology and psychoanalysis are notorious for their crassly reductive explanations of the aesthetic impulse. The task we set ourselves is to explain the male artist's tendency to produce works of art that spring from his passion for his 'muse', but transcend that passion. They do so, we shall argue, because two propensities interact. One is the impulse that, in other contexts, can lead to an obsessing preoccupation with pure form; the other is the one that, in different contexts, can lead to fetishism. Where, however uneasily, these two propensities strike a balance, there results work of special quality; texts and images that contain an erotic charge but at the same time embody the formal relationships on which art (and love) depend.

139

The present chapter is devoted to points of principle. It offers, in effect, a thumbnail sketch of a psychology of aesthetics. In it, we identify what we see as the crucial distinction between a creative art and a science, and describe three features which we see as essential to the artistic endeavour itself. Then, in our final chapter, we look more closely at the lives of a photographer, a poet, and a painter, each committed to the transformation of the women with whom they were intimate into art; and at the patterns of cost and benefit within which their feats of transformation were achieved.

ART AND SCIENCE

The projects of scientist and artist are in many ways alike. Both demand the reconciliation of intuitive judgement with technical control; both demand experiment; both can be fuelled by fantasies of mastery.[2] Intriguing questions also arise at the points where the sciences and arts overlap: in the relation of the formal to the mysterious in mathematics and in non–figurative painting like Mondrian's, for instance; and in the issues posed by photography - part technology, part art, part alchemy.[3] But although they interconnect, the arts and sciences are different terrains. It is often said that the scientist grasps the truth literally, while the artist does so in terms of illusion and metaphor. There is another difference, however; less obvious but more fundamental. The clue to its importance lies in the fact that while old science is dead science, great works of art remain vividly alive. Kepler's laws and Newton's are little more than curiosities to the modern astronomer or physicist. Shakespeare's texts and Titian's canvases, on the other hand, are still vibrant. This difference arises, we believe, because *the sciences and arts are the products of sharply dissimilar attitudes towards ambiguity*.[4]

Whatever the context, scientific or artistic, we achieve meaning by sifting continually between perceived similarities and differences. It is only by recognising these properties in an array, whether of people or rhododendrons or elementary particles, that we are in a position to attach significance to any one of that array's elements. We categorise and differentiate, and do so, typically, in terms of minute detail and nuance. In science, the aim is to reduce the ambiguities implicit in such judgements to a minimum: to offer a statement which is *unequivocal*. In the arts, in contrast, ambiguity – far from being analysed out and removed – is set to work. Ambiguities are *assembled into systems, within which they are allowed to reverberate.*

In the previous chapter, we depicted sexual intimacy as offering the male a gratification that he perceives unstably: as profound but also as potentially menacing; as necessary to him, but at the same time as fleeting or elusive. In many men, there is as a result an urge not only to form ideal sexual intimacies and revel in them, but to render them permanent. Accordingly, they 'petrify' the women in their lives by turning them into patterns on photographic paper, sentences on the page, painted marks on a stretched canvas. While few may achieve it, the ambition to remove the object of desire from time and space in this way – to transfix or eternalise it – is widespread; and it is the gratification of this urge that, in turn, furnishes our culture with many of its most compelling icons and texts.[5]

THREE PRINCIPLES

It was Freud's reluctant conclusion that 'before the problem of the creative artist analysis must, alas, lay down its arms'.[6] In our view, it need do nothing of the kind. What we envisage are neither straightforwardly affirmative claims about the liberation of human potential, nor the explanation of the non-perverse in terms of perversion. Rather, an account of the steps whereby, in art no less than in science, a profound psychological dislocation becomes a source of strength. But if ideas like that of the wound are to be used in making sense of the more intimately personal of the arts, three points of principle must first be set in place. These principles are ones we see as applying to men and women alike, but as having a special poignancy for men. The first concerns the human context in which the translation of erotic sentiment into art occurs, especially:

- The dependence of all creative thought in the arts on relationships of like-with-unlike – relationships, that is to say, which are *asymmetrical*.

The second focuses on our ability to use images and texts as containers and transmitters of vivid intuition. In particular:

- The importance of the distinction between what we know, in a civilised way, and what *pierces or transfixes* us.

And the third deals, as the theory of the wound indicates that it must, with:

- The deep formal significance, within a work of art, of *ambiguity which is focused and contained*.

This third principle deals, that is to say, with the part played in works of art by perceptions of difference-in-similarity and similarity-in-difference, and the unstable reversals to which these give rise; and with these perceptions and reversals as the components from which containing systems – individual paintings or poems – are fashioned, each with its own formal integrity.

ARTIST-AND-MODEL

The transformation of the artist's desire into a work of art occurs within a nexus of personal relationships, the chief of which, typically, is that of Artist-and-Model. The asymmetry of this relationship is sometimes seen as ideologically unsatisfactory. Certainly, when one thinks of asymmetrical relations in a historical context, it is usually Master-and-Servant that comes first to mind; and it is also true that the notions of asymmetry and complementarity have been used to suppress women's rights, women being seen as designed by God to provide the nurture that the man of will and deed requires. It is important to grasp, nevertheless, that almost every relationship of emotional or cultural significance turns out in practice to be asymmetrical, both in broad outline and in detail: not just Artist-and-Model, but Parent-and-Child, Teacher-and-Pupil, Doctor-and-Patient, Psychoanalyst-and-Analysand, Biographer-and-Subject, Playwright-and-Director, Director-and-Actor, Composer-and-Conductor, Enterepreneur-and-Financier, Lawyer-and-Client, Politician-and-Administrator, and so on. Most harbour uncomfortable tensions; some productive, others erosive. Rarely are these resolved or resolvable.

It is not just that asymmetrical relationships are the norm we all grow used to. It is that, within the constraints of almost any task worth performing, symmetry is so awkward that, in practice, it prevents good work being done. A shade rashly, perhaps, we would want to claim that relationships are unrewarding and unworkable *unless* they rest on complex and shifting patterns of asymmetry; and that, from the relation of Parent-and-Child onwards, asymmetries are the stuff from which human endeavour is made. In putting this book together, to snatch an example close at hand, one of us (LH) has acted as writer, the other (BJ) as editor. One (LH) types, the other (BJ) makes notes on the typescript in long-hand. In terms of the product that goes first to friends, then to publisher, we operate as a committee-of-two. What does not satisfy either of us is altered until it does. In verbal matters, one of us (BJ) is orderly, the other (LH) intuitive. One (BJ) – as the relevant research suggests – is right-handed, with left cerebral hemisphere plainly dominant; the other (LH) left-handed, with a pattern of cerebral dominance more confused. The net effect, when we operate in unison, is consistently better than either can produce alone.[7]

The relation of Artist-and-Model is at the heart of the processes of 'petrification' we are committed to explain, and two of the three examples we discuss in our final chapter centre on it. It is unusually imaginatively potent, we would want to claim, not just because it is asymmetrical, but because it permits the full range of personal investment, from hostility and cynical exploitation to erotic fascination and love.

There is a famous photograph by Brassai of Henri Matisse and one of his models in Matisse's studio. In the centre of the image stands a nude woman, posed slightly awkwardly, as if already part of a painting; her hands clasped above her head, her legs crossed below the knee. To the left stands a painting of Matisse's, still in its easel and only half-finished; and, in the background of this unfinished painting there is a sketch of a nude, her pose roughly echoing that of the woman. To the right of the photograph sits Matisse, an old man with a beard in a white coat, seventy at the time it was taken. Under the white coat, he wears a neat collar and tie. His trousers have a crease, and his shoes shine. His air is almost that of an ageing professor of medicine conducting a demonstration for this students. He is serious, though, to the point of melancholy. In his hand, there is a drawing pad; and while he may be drawing, he seems for the moment immobile. He looks, in fact, a little like Freud (who died in that same year, 1939).

Female : male. Young : old. Naked : respectably clothed. Passive : actively deliberative. Physical : cerebral. Desirable : beyond desire perhaps, but not beyond its recollection. Everything in this image is asymmetrical, even its pattern of gazes. The model looks down at the floor to her side; the artist gazes fixedly at her naked form, focusing somewhere in the region of her midriff, possibly as high as her breasts, perhaps as low as her genitals. While she looks away, he looks at her. At the same time he seems to look through her or beyond her, to the painted image which her physical presence in-

Matisse and his model

spires in him: the translation of bodily sensations into an array of colour, light and paint texture. The artist stares at his model's body in just the way that the Musician stares at Venus's in Titian's great painting in the Prado, *Venus and the Organ Player*.[8] Figuratively, it is as if the arts – music, painting, poetry – will spring from the female body if it is subjected to a sufficiently intense male gaze.

Once more, notions of 'otherness' assert themselves, and the need for a second diagram. This has the same form as the one in the last chapter. Again, there are four elements, and a six-fold traffic; and again the structure supporting the fabric of our argument shows through:

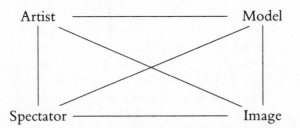

It is within the triangular pattern of relations linking Artist, Model and Image that the crystallisation or petrification of desire is achieved. The process does not just snatch desire out of time and place, though; it renders desire public. For that reason, the Spectator has a significant place in the diagram too. In fact, it is on the relation of Spectator to Model, individuals who in real life will rarely meet, that the whole enterprise of the representational art of the person depends.

However closely you view the relation of Matisse and his model, you find not a single point of symmetry. The model is employed by Matisse and is in that sense in his power; but she is necessary to him in a way that he cannot be to her. Without her, almost within arm's reach, the translation which obsesses him cannot begin. She makes possible the imaginative movement which turns perceptions of a body, not into a life-like representation of that body, but into new projects within the painter's formal language of colour, texture and light. Matisse was explicit about this. He described himself as being 'absolutely dependent' on his models. They kept him, he said, 'in an emotional state, like a kind of flirtation which ends in a rape'. The rape in question, though, is not an attack, literal or symbolic, on the woman in front of him, but on his own involvement with her. It is this attack that provides his work with its 'orchestration' and 'architecture'. While a seventeenth-century painter like Rembrandt or a nineteenth-century painter like Degas would automatically have conducted their scrutinies of the body's pleasurable or more disquieting properties in terms of a recognisably life-like representation of his model's body, a modernist like Matisse appears to attack the body. But in truth what he attacks are the impulses within himself which his model's body inspires. It is in the course of this attack that his response to her is translated not just into symbolic but into abstract terms.[9]

Further asymmetries arise if we consider Brassai no longer as a hidden spectator but as an artist in his own right – if both Matisse and his model become Brassai's models, and the image ceases to be a painting and becomes a black-and-white pattern on photosensitive paper. The terms of Brassai's relation to his models are different from Matisse's. Far from parading his own creativeness, Brassai lured his subjects into registering their permanence through him, and wished them to do so in full consciousness, as parties to an artistic event. But although more passive, he was no less emotionally engaged. As he once said of himself, 'in the absence of a subject with which you are passionately involved, and without the excitement that drives you to grasp it and exhaust it, you may take some beautiful pictures, but not a photographic *oeuvre*.'[10] In this case, what his image objectifies is an untidy meeting of minds (fully dressed old man, naked young woman and invisible photographer), creating out of it a moment's stillness, imaginatively fertile but unresolved. And where, on common-sense grounds, one might expect such an image to have a fugitive significance, offering none of the subtler gratifications of a painting, it continues to cast its spell over us – the photograph's spectators – half a century after it was taken.

PLEASURABLE SURRENDER

Underlying the argument we have deployed about the wound and its influence, then, there is a series of transpositions; ones that unite the individual's erotic endeavours into a project. The preoccupations formative in the context of the wound itself – those with differences-in-similarity and similarities-in-difference, and with people-as-things and things-as-people – reassert themselves in the adult with each expression of sexual desire. Transposed again, they structure the artist's relation to his model; and, if the artist's skill and sensibility are sufficiently refined, they also structure the spectator's response to the image or text he creates.[11]

There is still a problem, however. The language of desire, which psychology has inherited from biology, is too assertive to do justice either to the sensibility with which many artists' work is imbued, or to our own response to it as spectators. It is a language more adapted to the creation of pin-ups and pornography than of art. We need to accommodate thoughts not just of amorous mastery but of rapturous surrender too. The rudiments of a more appropriate language are already to hand, but they need to be set in place with a little care.

Baron Sacher-Masoch was a minor nineteenth-century novelist

who explored the erotic reverberations of physical cruelty. The perversion Krafft-Ebing named after him concerns sexual arousal caused by our own experience of pain; also, the excitements of being humiliated or of being in someone else's power – being urinated upon, for instance, or being tied up. It can include, too, the elaborated fantasies and daydreams of humiliation with which, for many people, male and female, sexual excitement is routinely accompanied.[12] To treat all masochism exclusively as a perversion, though, is to miss a vital lesson psychoanalysis has to teach: namely, that masochism exists as a propensity in each of us, and as such is normal and non-perverse. Further, there are halfway houses on the continuum that separates masochism's perverse from its normal manifestations. There is the fascination with bodily violence, for example, imagined from the point of view of the victim; the excitement some men experience at the thought of the woman they love in bed with another man; and the morbid preoccupation with her loss or her death. Various of these intermediate manifestations of masochism have, as we shall see, played their part in the creation of works of the highest aesthetic quality.

Leo Bersani has broached this relation of masochism to art. In *The Freudian Body*, he advances what is, in effect, 'an aesthetics of masochism'; a view of the response to art that takes masochism as its central tenet. The insight at the heart of Bersani's argument, never quite clearly stated, is that the aesthetic response, our ability to relinquish our defences and allow a work of art to take control of us, only makes sense if seen as a surrender.[13] Arguments like Bersani's focus on the spectator; but they can equally be used to make sense of the artist's response to his model. At the centre of the lives of ordinary people, these arguments suggest, there exists a mechanism which enables us to fall under the spell of a work of art in just the way that we fall under the spell of a person. In the presence of the person by whom we are besotted, as in the presence of works of art or of any other feature of our world that moves us deeply, our defences collapse. Rather than organising our responses in the usual tolerably competent way, we allow ourselves to be flooded with intense and uncontrollable feeling. Structures carefully set in place are washed away. Reason goes by the board. Specialised, and carried to extreme, this mechanism yields the aberrant: the cabinet minister spanked and the call girl spanking. But, in itself, the impulse to succumb is normal; and without it, our lives would scarcely be worth living.

But surrender is dangerous, for the artist no less than for the scientist. So the artist recreates the experience of surrender in symbolic form; a feat that serves (as we shall see in the next chapter) both as a celebration of magical access and as a defence against thoughts of real access and its concomitant terrors and ambivalences. It is only the audience for whom this experience of surrender is safe; its terrors and ambivalences held at arm's length.

STUDIUM AND PUNCTUM

Towards the end of his life, the French semiologist Roland Barthes wrote two books in which his central preoccupations – with love and art – come increasingly sharply into focus. The word-play, so disfiguring a feature of recent French avantgarde thought, drops away to reveal Barthes' vulnerability and passion. Although he was himself homosexual, his insights are one heterosexuals of either sex find it easy to share. Again, as with Bersani's arguments, Barthes' are easily transposed from the vantage point of the spectator to that of the artist; and, in being transposed, they make crucial features of the artist's surrender plain.

In *A Lover's Discourse*, Barthes announces the impossibility of describing the lover's experience in normal narrative by organising his argument alphabetically. The list begins (where else?) with *s'abîmer*: the lover's craving to be engulfed; and ends with *vouloir-saisir*, his 'will to possess'.[14] The lover is fascinated, but he is also trapped, and what threatens him in his trap is not abandonment but destruction.[15] Words fail him. Worst of all, he cannot anchor the loved person in terms of any knowledge or principle outside the relationship of love itself. 'I am caught in this contradiction: on the one hand, I believe I know the other better than anyone and triumphantly assert my knowledge to the other ("*I* know you – I'm the only one who really knows you!"); and on the other hand, I am often struck by the obvious fact that the other is impenetrable, intractable, not to be found...'[16]

At the end of *A Lover's Discourse*, one is left adrift, flummoxed. In matters of love, the utterance of anything other than banalities seems impossible. Three years later, though, in 1980, the year of his death, Barthes finished his last and most accessible book, *Camera Lucida*.[17] Though no photographer himself, he speaks there about certain memorable photographic images and the places these occupy in his own intimate life and affections. In doing so, he makes a distinction of great importance: perhaps the most useful of any drawn in this century for the understanding of art – and, by implication, of intimacy too. It harks back to the thought of surrealists like Max Ernst, and, via them, to Freud's vision of the repressed unconscious and Schopenhauer's distinction between will and representation.[18]

Far from being the vehicle of our true experience, common sense is, the surrealists believed, a barrier placed in the way of it. It is for this reason that they saw art as inherently subversive. Its role is to catch us momentarily off our guard; to jar our defences briefly loose on their moorings. Barthes draws on this tradition and separates from within it two distinct perceptual regimes. In our pleasurable appreciation of photographs, he points out, our tendency is assimilative. The ideal medium for this process of assimilation, although Barthes does not mention it, is the better class of Sunday newspaper. Skimming here, dipping enjoyably there, we garner a vast array of images and items, each with its own charge of interest and excitement. Gathered up, they are found their place in the great quilt of things we care about, which protects our status as civilised beings and separates us from the Goths. To this assimilative activity, 99.99 per cent of the pleasurable and appreciative looking we do, Barthes gives a label. In French, there is no word that quite serves his purpose, nor is there in English, but Latin comes to his rescue: *studium*. Barthes uses *studium* to mean not so much study as commitment; one which is exercised with enthusiasm but without special acuity. It is by means of *studium* that we 'participate in the figures, the faces, the gestures, the settings, the actions' a memorable photograph might contain.[19]

The second element of the distinction Barthes propounds transfers agency from the viewer to the image. One can sense the ghosts of Freud and Schopenhauer guiding his hand as he makes this move. 'This time it is not I who seek it out (as I invest the field of the *studium* with my sovereign consciousness), it is this element which rises from the scene, shoots out of it like an arrow, and pierces me.'[20] The Latin word that designates such a piercing, inflicted by a pointed instrument, is *punctum*. It also means 'sting, speck, cut, little hole – and also a cast of the dice'. It suits Barthes' purpose all the better, he says, because 'it also refers to the notion of punctuation', the photographs he has in mind being 'punctuated, sometimes even speckled with these sensitive points'. 'A photograph's *punctum* is that accident which pricks me (but also bruises me, is poignant to me).'

In the first half of *Camera Lucida*, as in *A Lover's Discourse*, the bruises and poignancies Barthes has in mind are those of fascinated desire. He is particularly seized by a Robert Mapplethorpe nude self-portrait. Barthes saw in it an image that 'launched desire beyond what it permits us to see... toward the absolute excellence of a being, body and soul together', and did so with 'just the right degree of openness, the right density of abandonment'.[21] It is only later that he talks of the death of his mother and his grief. One photograph – of his mother as a child, the 'Winter Garden Photograph' – captures her for him precisely, and fills him with an inexhaustible astonishment. It is not so much that the Winter Garden Photograph enables him to recapture lost feelings about his mother; it is that, looking into the image, Barthes finds his mother for the first time as she actually was. 'During her illness, I nursed her', he writes, 'held the bowl of tea she liked because it was easier to drink from than from a cup; she had become my little girl, uniting for me with that essential child she was in her first photograph.'[22]

Not surprisingly, Barthes withholds the Winter Garden Photograph from us. He knows that it cannot puncture us as it does him. But other photographs he displays enable us to follow the intersecting lines of his argument and gaze. When Barthes extols Mapplethorpe's self-portrait, we see what he means. While at the same time drawing back from the homosexual nature of the image's appeal, a heterosexual man or woman, looking over Barthes' shoulder, can see why he is seized. In the same way, we can share his sense that the image of Nadar's mother (or is it wife?) offers something 'supererogatory', above and beyond what the camera can normally be expected to provide. His distinction between *studium* and *punctum* allows us to grasp, more generally, that there are two modes in the management of our psychic lives. In the first, our more poignant feelings are automatically regulated, alienated; in the second, control is forsaken and our access becomes direct. His distinction also allows us to see what it is that, in surrender, the male artist loses and gains. The implication must be that the bifurcatory regime which normally regulates his imaginative life – that of things-as-people and people-as-things – collapses and that, however briefly, he is free to perceive the world as it is. *He is free, that is to say, to see people as people and things as things.*

REVERBERATIONS

How is it, though, that a photographer, painter or poet can structure a work in such a way that it in turn will puncture; and do so not idiosyncratically, piercing the defences of individuals here and there, but predictably and consistently over a wide range of those to whom the truth about human experience remains of concern?

In the last twenty years, the nature of this undertaking has been explored by French theoreticians of language, notably Jacques Derrida.[23] This theorising has a particular bearing on literary texts, but, by implication, it encompasses the non-verbal too. It bears, in fact, on any utterance that is not exclusively literal and technical. The claim is that the elements of any such sign system have no significance in themselves; they become significant in their conjunction with one another, and in the differences we detect between them. In Meit's carving of *Judith and Holofernes*, the object in Judith's right hand has, of course, an identity: we recognise it as the handle of a sword. However, it draws its imaginative meaning from its conjunctions – its proximity to her naked abdomen and vaginal cleft and to Holofernes' severed head. These proximities, in turn, alert the eye to nuances (the casual way in which she holds the sword handle); and to notions of a more general kind (the thought that, in her nakedness, she has dismantled Holofernes, segregating his power and sexual energies from his head).

Similar processes are at work when we read a poem:

> Only a man harrowing clods
> In a slow silent walk
> With an old horse that stumbles and nods
> Half asleep as they stalk.

> Only thin smoke without flame
> From the heaps of couch-grass;
> Yet this will go onward the same
> Though Dynasties pass.

> Yonder a maid and her wight
> Come whispering by:
> War's annals will cloud into night
> Ere their story die.[24]

'A man harrowing clods', 'an old horse that stumbles and nods', 'heaps of couch-grass': Thomas Hardy uses these images in writing

In Time of 'The Breaking of Nations' as nodes with which to create an imagined space; and it is within this space – part semantic, part formal, part fantasised – that, as readers, complex patterns of cross-referencing and differentiation become available to us. Hardy has chosen with care; and he uses his images to propound certain themes. In his third verse, for example, the ideas of love and war are broached. But reading poetry is not a process of detecting correct meanings; rather, of casting ourselves into a space within which meanings have a tendency ceaselessly to migrate.

Such migrations of meaning occur of their own accord, and do so for a variety of reasons. Some are to be found in the culture on which Hardy drew; in this instance, the Book of Jeremiah, and God's judgement against Babylon:

> Thou art my battle axe and weapons of war: for with thee will I break in pieces the nations, and with thee will I destroy kingdoms; And with thee will I break in pieces the horse and his rider; and with thee will I break in pieces the chariot and his rider; With thee also will I break in pieces man and woman; and with thee will I break in pieces old and young; and with thee will I break in pieces the young man and the maid . . . Behold, I am against thee, O destroying mountain, saith the Lord, which destroyest all the earth: and I will stretch out mine hand upon thee, and roll thee down from the rocks, and will make thee a burnt mountain.[25]

Other reverberations are autobiographical. Initially private to the author, these become available to his readers through his other autobiographical writings. In his *Life*, ostensibly written by his second wife Florence but in fact written by himself, Hardy says: 'I believe it would be said by people who knew me well that I have a faculty (possibly not uncommon) for burying an emotion in my heart or brain for forty years, and exhuming it at the end of that time as fresh as when interred.'[26] He gives *In Time of 'The Breaking of Nations'* as his instance. He wrote it, he says, during the First World War, but it recalls a feeling that moved him many years earlier, during the war between the French and the Prussians. It harks back, that is to say, to a time when he was in love with his wife-to-be, Emma Gifford. For Hardy, the poem's imagery signifies a particular day – 18 August 1870, the day of the battle of Gravelotte – when he and Emma read Tennyson together in the rectory garden at St Juliot, talked about the war, and looked down on the horse and ploughman working in the valley below. In pencil, on the end papers of a book he was reading at

B.J.

the time, Hardy noted 'Sc. rusty harrow – behind that rooks – behind him, 2 men hoeing mangle, with bowed backs, behind that a heap of couch smoking, behind these horse & cart doing nothing in field – then the ground rising to plantn.' Some time that same day, Emma sketched her lover as he sat on a fence with makeshift flag in his hand; and the next day Hardy sketched her as, sleeves pushed back and ringlets falling forward, she groped in the water for a picnic tumbler which had fallen between the rocks of a waterfall. Both these scenes, the harrowing horses and the lost tumbler, were to remain eloquent to Hardy of the love for one another which he and Emma were to destroy, yet which was to resurface, paradoxically, after her death.[27]

In Time of 'The Breaking of Nations' is a poem about war, and our response to it will be conditioned by the immediacy of our own experience of loss. It is also a poem about love, and our response will be conditioned, too, by the precise state of our personal life, and the extent to which thoughts of love and loss stir disquietingly within us. More specifically, it is a poem that moves and unsettles us in as much as the experiences of war and love have not merely mingled inside us but coalesced; if we fear that love can turn in our imaginations (as it did for Thomas and Emma Hardy) into a 'burnt mountain', a killing field. Finally, in its last verse, it becomes a poem about the life that survives the desolations of war; a theme that was to obsess Hardy in the years after Emma died, as we shall see in the next chapter.

As this line of reasoning indicates, meanings within a poem like Hardy's migrate for another reason. Any image or text that moves us deeply is bound to implicate our powers of suppression and repression. There must exist a traffic, in other words, between a work that stirs us imaginatively and thought that is to some degree unconscious; a traffic open not just to the processes of civilised transformation, but to eruption and land-slip. Any imaginatively conceived text, it follows, must contain hidden networks of meaning: some partially accessible to the author, some partially accessible to the reader – and only a proportion accessible to both alike. A poem like Hardy's, as a consequence, may have an enduring impact for reasons that neither author nor reader properly understands. Author, text and reader can hover in relation to one another like three versions of the same dream – as did artist, image and spectator in the case of 'The Slave Ship', the horrific work that Turner painted and his mentor and ardent admirer John Ruskin owned.[28]

What we confront in a poem like Hardy's is a structure of emotionally charged, partially graspable ambiguities of meaning, set within the formal bounds of a scheme of rhythm and rhyme, and informed by our sense of the poet's voice. Instead of resolving the emotional tensions this structure generates, as a psychologist might seek to, the poet leaves them to reverberate disquietingly in the mind. A product of intelligence achieves the status of 'work of art' in as much as it articulates (but does not resolve) deep-seated and inherently unstable ambiguities. A determinate structure, it is none the less one within which meanings are, as in the imagination, inherently mobile. Without its reverberations and echoes, a poem like Hardy's is reduced to the status of an entertainment; no longer able to puncture, it becomes a box of tricks.[29]

A PHOTOGRAPHER, A POET, AND A PAINTER

WHILE THE WOUND encourages men to objectify the women they find desirable, it also ensures that such manoeuvres are inseparable from risk. Granted the necessary technical skill, the resulting works can sometimes achieve a two-fold reconciliation: of the ideal with the carnal, and of the fleeting with the permanent. In them, as if by magic, the wound seems healed. But in practice, we are going to show, the successful reconciliation of the erotic with the formal is as precarious an achievement as it is rare.

Where the scientist segregates the world of *Arbeit* from that of *Liebe*, the artist fuses the two. Advertently or inadvertently, he may as a consequence destroy the intimacy he sets out to celebrate. We return, in other words, to the metaphor of swings and roundabouts and to equations of cost and benefit. With luck, the male artist (and the artist in each male) will be drawn to women who find it gratifying to be objectified, and who create of their own accord the kinds of intimacy resilient to the consequent wear and tear. But wear and tear there is bound to be. While the wound may be healed in the artist's finished product, the intrusion of the objectifying on the personal will be evident, at each step along the route. The price paid may well be intimate relationships drained of vitality or in other ways despoiled. Such art easily coexists, too, with misogyny. Hence William Gass's warning: 'So to the wretched writer I should like to say that there's one body only whose request for your caresses is not vulgar, is not unchaste, untoward, or impolite: the body of your work itself.'[1]

In this last part of our story, we return to Thomas Hardy, but begin with a photographer, Edward Weston, and conclude with a painter, Pierre Bonnard. We consider all three in the context of the women they loved and the work this love produced. For the photographer, it was as if falling in love carried him across a hidden aes-

thetic threshold. The character of his work changed subtly but categorically, and, for a brief period, he could do no wrong. Soon,
though, his work altered again, and its air of effortless lucidity evaporated. In the case of the poet, a clarity of utterance previously
denied him was achieved only late in life, retrospectively, once the
challenge of the actual was removed. It is only in the painter that the
work seems to have evolved satisfactorily from one phase to the
next. In him, it is as if, step by step, progressive adaptations to the
contradiction between the erotic and the formal were sought and
found, his achievement a summation of the challenges faced and only
partially surmounted by the other two.

Each of these men used women not only as inspiration but as raw
material, and all three trod stony paths at least partially as a consequence. In the work of the photographer there is a contradiction
between erotic subject-matter and a self-imposed asceticism of philosophy and technique; in that of the poet, a contradiction between
rival systems of obsessive preoccupation, one amorous, the other
morbid. Although the tensions in the work of the painter are less
dramatic, they too are unmistakably evident in the images themselves.

THE VERIDICAL IMAGE

The perils inherent in the translation of personal life into art arise in
all media, but are clearest in the case of photography. Since its
earliest days, the camera has been pointed at the nude model; usually
but by no means exclusively by men at women. Most of the images
produced are in varying degrees banal. Only a tiny minority are of
aesthetic significance. Rather than offering an imitation of the nude
as it has evolved in painting and sculpture, many of these repond to
an opportunity quite new. For, pre-eminently, the technology of the
camera offers the visual artist a property all other media lack: *verid-
icality*. Where a painting can be life-like, the photograph presents
itself to us as a form of representation categorically more literal. A
'take' rather than a 'representation', as the critic Rosalind Krauss
says, it is as if the photographic negative were a 'deposit of the real
itself'.[2] (The word 'veridical', incidentally, is fruitfully ambiguous. It
means truthful. It also refers to those insights that reach us in dreams
or reveries and are subsequently discovered to be true. It is on just
this movement between the real and the imagined that the power of

the photograph depends.)

A high-minded tradition of nude photography exploits this special property. Although the woman photographed is often a professional model, it is not uncommon for her to be the photographer's wife or mistress. In some, parts of the model's body are considered in isolation. In others she is both without clothes and recognisably herself, the effect being that of a nude portrait. A pioneer of the genre was Alfred Steiglitz, his model the painter Georgia O'Keeffe. The most obvious of the hazards they faced were legal. Until surprisingly recently it was a crime to send an image through the United States mails showing a single pubic hair. More specifically psychological are the dangers of making the private public; ones the photographic image poses with particular clarity. In principle at least, the man who photographs the body of the woman he desires makes that body available to alien males far and wide. The resulting ambivalences may short-circuit his desire, and do so in ways beyond his control. The costs for his model are real too. 'I have simply bared to the world a woman's life,' Steiglitz declared.[3] But in baring O'Keeffe, he helped turn her into an item of lubricious speculation and gossip; vulnerable, to the suggestion – originating, we believe, with Truman Capote – that she was the kind of woman who carried a dildo in her handbag.[4]

CHARIS AND EDWARD

Even more remarkable than Steiglitz's images of O'Keeffe are Edward Weston's photographs of his model and later wife, Charis Wilson. Both Weston and Wilson wrote about their relationship, and what they say illuminates the processes whereby idealised images of a desirable (and, in this case, conspicuously literate) woman are produced.

When they first met in 1934 at a concert, Weston was in his late forties. With sons by a marriage long since lapsed, he was at the height of his powers, and renowned, particularly, for his ability to turn women into nudes of a compellingly formal beauty – 'a small, gentle person with violent insides'.[5] Later, when their paths recrossed, Charis became his model and mistress. There are doubts about Weston's ability to invest himself wholeheartedly in their relationship, but there is no doubting the quality of the images it produced.[6] In terms of visual quality, there is perhaps no advance over the best of his earlier work; but, almost for the first time, these are nude *portraits*. Where, in the most remarkable of his previous nudes – those, for instance, of the dancer Bertha Wardell – the bodies are headless, the model's face being cropped or hidden, Charis's is usually fully in view. As she puts it, there were to be 'no more "bits" and "pieces", only whole people in real places'.[7]

Weston's self-imposed discipline as a photographer was stringent. He worked with unwieldly cameras – many of the nudes of Charis being taken with a camera producing 8 × 10 inch negatives – and he sought meticulous rendering of detail, with the greatest possible depth of field. In effect, he brought the technical requirements of the still-life photographer to bear on the live model. Weston's expectation of himself, what is more, was that he must take all the aesthetic and technical judgements implicit in each photograph before the shutter was released. His images – of rocks, trees, vegetables, shells, delapidated buildings, dead birds, clouds, nudes – were then transferred from negative to positive with the minimum human intervention. Arguably, this discipline served Weston as a defence against the ambivalences his subject-matter inspired in him, and was the equivalent of the alarmed psychologist's resort to 'methodology'. His precision, allied to the beautifully graduated tones of his black-and-white prints, nevertheless transformed the naked female body into visions which have about them an air of inevitability, and are often characterised as 'platonic'. Their poise and meticulousness, the overwhelming atmosphere of technical control they convey, now make them seem the work of one of the medium's old masters. In its own day, this was none the less a radical form of image-making, subversive as well as revelatory, and influential in the political circles of the far left.[8]

The couple married in 1939, and separated in 1946. Quite soon thereafter, Weston, already in the grip of Parkinson's disease which was to kill him ten years later, took his last photograph. Plainly, his incipient illness may have produced changes in his relationship with Charis; and these, in turn, could have influenced the character of the photographs he took. Such a relationship, though, seems to have its own trajectory. As revealed in the nudes he took of Charis, the evolution is by no means an entirely comforting one. First, there is the transition from 'bits and pieces' to 'whole people in real places'; the implication being that, when sexually infatuated, the male tends to imagine the female body in terms of its component parts, and that it is only when he is in love that he perceives the woman in question both erotically and as a whole person. But even within the regime of 'whole people in real places', Weston's nudes reveal readily discernible stages. There is the purity and candour of the first phase; the famous images of Charis in the sand dunes. Then a phase of carnal energy – those taken in New Mexico in 1937, characterised by a formal concentration on Charis's genitals. And, finally, a phase of quirky dislocation and humour: the image of Charis floating in a pool, in which she looks as though she might be dead; and, even more disconcerting, the one taken in 1942 of her posed in the nude but wearing a gas mask. The position of the carnal in this unfolding pattern is neither that of starting point nor of resolution, but of an intermediary step. Far from being an upwelling of instinctual energy, there is the suggestion that the resort to the carnal in image-making is one psychic manoeuvre among several, each occurring in the face of an intractable ambivalence, and each in itself unstable, ambiguous. Perhaps it is significant, too, that Edward and Charis should have married not during the first or second phase, but at the beginning of the third: in the year of the 'dead body in the pool'.

THE NUDE AND MISOGYNY

A relationship as exceptional as Edward and Charis's raises the possibilities of self-deception and false consciousness. It is not far-fetched to suggest that, far from being at ease with the female body, Weston was uncomfortable with it; even that he was at heart a woman-hater, his imagination seething with partially repressed fantasies of disgust, against which his immaculate imagery was a species of defence. It is as if, in his fascination with the body as a thing-in-itself, Weston was pursuing to its bitter end a project in which the natural focus of male desire – the female body – is exhausted of its capacity to excite. 'Why this tide of women?' he once asked himself. It may be that women volunteered themselves as his models with such alacrity not because he could turn them into art, nor even because he could give them back their own bodies in idealised form, but because they sensed the nature of his conflict and were unconsciously stirred by it.

Evidence of misogyny in Weston is indirect, and the interpretation is certainly one which Charis Wilson herself rebuts.[9] The point is none the less important because, in the history of the nude, it is the misogynous (or, at least, the cripplingly ambivalent) who have played a formative part. As Manet once remarked to Berthe Morisot, Edgar Degas was 'incapable of loving a woman, even of telling her so'.[10] Degas was drawn to women, it seems, but was fearful of them. Even so, he was arguably the first male artist since the Renaissance to produce images of the female body which do not presuppose the existence of a predominantly male audience, and in which the woman appears neither as an object of erotic allure nor as a meta-phor, but as a focus of contemplation in her own right.[11]

If Weston's misogyny remains in doubt, that of his Czech con-temporary, Frantisek Drtikol, is beyond question. A flamboyantly eccentric bisexual, Drtikol's attitude to women was one of attraction confounded by distrust. In recommending himself to a young woman with whom he was in love, he wrote: 'You must bear in mind that. . . . I have finally decided that I despise all women who are content to be inferior beings, and that I denounce, in word and deed, women who are nothing but beautifully female.' His imagination was now dominated, he says, by 'a type of black woman, sun-scorched, with the psychic and physical force of a man – a snake with breasts as hard as steel, without stomach, and with *un sexe spécial*'.[12] In eventually renouncing photography for painting and theosophy, his misogyny is undisguised: 'In the male, there's one half which is god, another which is animal. Woman is only animal. . . . More and more, I like women in general, and above all I love them spiritually and at a distance. As soon as a woman comes closer to me, and I pic-ture myself holding her and making love to her, everything in me rebels, and I sense an immense disgust.'[13]

The vigour of Drtikol's dismay is completely at odds, however, with the nature of his best nudes, in many of which the models are recognisable as individuals, their facial expressions the key to the precise form of the consciousness each image conveys. His images capture an erotic sensibility at the same time urgent and poised; and, like Degas', do so without a trace of belittlement or dislike. Far from being an isolated freak, this relation of intense ambivalence towards women's bodies and the ability to create profoundly memorable images of them is characteristic, we believe, of the steps whereby the tensions associated with the wound are accommodated. Not only can the contradictions inherent in the wound express themselves in the artist's image or text; occasionally, and remarkably – as with Weston and Drtikol – they can be resolved within it. The conse-quence is not solely, as one might expect, erotic nudes that are fright-ening (Meit's *Judith*) or unflattering (Rembrandt's *Diana*, aptly described by Adrian Stokes as 'the sagging repository of jewels and dirt, of fabulous babies and magical faeces'),[14] but one that members of either sex can view with a sense of constantly replenishing exhilaration.

THE WESSEX DEPRESSIVE

Such tensions are expressed with particular clarity in the life and work of Thomas Hardy. He and Emma, a full-bosomed creature of great vitality, with bright blue eyes and a mass of blonde hair, had married for love. But as husband and wife they proved incompatible – he gloomy, introspective, evasive; she outgoing but spoilt – and they were bitterly unhappy together. He neglected her, and she took refuge in evangelical religion. In her unhappiness, her extraversion hardened into oddity; and the inhabitants of Dorchester grew used to her presence among them, astride her bicycle though massively overweight, delivering more 'beautiful little booklets' advocating the strictest adherence to the tenets of the Protestant faith. In their eyes, she was half-mad.

Eventually, Hardy became famous. He was offered a knighthood, which he declined, but accepted honorary degrees and the Order of Merit, and was perhaps the richest writer of his day. He was often away; and when at home would shut himself in his study to grapple with the proofs for the Wessex Edition of his own works. Habitually, he and Emma met only at dinner, and did so in silence. Much of the time, they were in a state of war. Later, she was in great pain from gall-stones. In those days, morphia or chloroform were often prescribed; and although surgery had become possible by 1912, both Emma and Hardy viewed it with horror. The point was reached when, each Sunday, Trevis the gardener had to push Emma to church in a newly acquired bath-chair. When Emma's death came, Hardy made a public show of surprise, insisting that it had come unexpectedly. In a letter to a friend, Mrs Florence Henniker, he says; 'Emma's death was absolutely unexpected by me, the doctor, and everybody. . . . I have reproached myself for not having guessed there might be some internal mischief at work.' It is hard to avoid Robert Gittings' conclusion, nevertheless, that 'Hardy shut his own eyes to his wife's state, and tried to shut the eyes of others after her death'.[15]

But, in the years after Emma died, Hardy wrote love poetry to her of great eloquence, the emotions he 'exhumed' being those of their courtship. He did this although, at the time of Emma's death, he was in love with another much younger woman, Florence Dugdale, and although Emma's death enabled him, quite soon thereafter, to marry Florence.

The poems Hardy published in the period immediately before Emma's death are conspicuously cynical; and they deal, a number of them, with some of the more brutal ironies of marriage. In *At a Watering-Place*, one bystanding male comments to another on a 'smart proud pair', about to be wed:

> ... How little he thinks
> That dozens of days and nights on end
> I have stroked her neck, unhooked the links
> Of her sleeve to get at her upper arm ...

In a second, *At the Draper's*, a dying husband overhears his wife ordering the fashionable dress she will wear at his funeral. A third, *In the Nuptial Chamber*, eavesdrops on a husband and wife's first coupling as a band plays outside:

> 'O that mastering tune!' And up in the bed
> Like a lace-robed phantom springs the bride ...

The tune, the husband believes, is the townsfolk's compliment to their marriage. But his bride – 'my innocent' – has another view:

> 'O but you don't know! 'Tis the passionate air
> To which my old Love waltzed with me,
> And I swore as we spun that none should share
> My home, my kisses, till death, save he!
> And he dominates me and thrills me though,
> And it's he I embrace while embracing you!'

The love poems which Emma's death released in Hardy, are quite different in tone, and, in the judgement of many, the best he ever wrote. They numbered fifty or more over the next two years; works of intense emotion, and all the more compelling for being obliquely expressed. Naively, one might imagine that Hardy would use these poems, in his own phrase, as an 'expiation'. He must by now have realised that he had been able to ignore Emma's suffering because, for the past five years, he had been devoting 'all his best care, tenderness, and consideration' to Florence. At first sight, they do seem an unguarded confession of guilt; but, as Gittings points out, they are more complex than this and more devious. In *The Going*, one of the earliest in the sequence, Hardy asks:

Why, then, latterly did we not speak,
Did we not think of those days long dead,
And ere your vanishing strive to seek
That time's renewal?

And he concludes:

I seem but a dead man held on end
To sink down soon.... O you could not know
    That such swift fleeing
    No soul foreseeing –
Not even I – would undo me so!

'I seem but a dead man held on end/To sink down soon' seems grimly heart-felt. But it is hard to read 'no soul foreseeing' and 'not even I', as anything other than circuitous; part of an obfuscation, both to the world at large and to himself.

The fact of Emma's death was to become the Hardy household's dominant preoccupation, his desk calendar remaining set at Monday, 7 March, the day of their first meeting. Emma's notebooks, although for twenty years largely given over to harsh comments about her husband's shortcomings, were now of obsessive concern to Hardy, their contents becoming part of the poems now flooding from him. Insights and turns of phrase are Emma's, and the voice too; a strange feat of retrospective possession. Often, Hardy writes of himself as seen through Emma's eyes, and on occasion, as in *Lost Love*, allows the resentful bafflement and despair of her last years to shine through:

I sing my songs once more,
    And presently hear
    His footstep near
    As if it would stay;
    But he goes his way,
And shuts a distant door...

More usually, he puts himself in Emma's shoes, but provides his own version of her perception of him. In *A Man was Drawing Near to Me*, he becomes Emma, as she sits in the St Juliot rectory, waiting. He was then an architect's clerk, and had travelled all day, with a view to surveying the church's neglected fabric. Her journal records his arrival: 'At that very moment the front-door bell rang, and the

architect was ushered in. . . . I was immediately arrested by his familiar appearance, as if I had seen him in a dream.'[16] In Hardy's hands,
this becomes:

> . . . There was a rumble at the door,
> A draught disturbed the drapery,
> And but a minute passed before,
>   With gaze that bore
>   My destiny,
> The man revealed himself to me.

In psychological terms, perhaps most intriguing of all is *Under the
Waterfall*, in which Hardy uses his interrogatory, question-and-
answer mode to invade the fine grain of his dead wife's imagination:

> 'Whenever I plunge my arm, like this,
> In a basin of water, I never miss
> The sweet sharp sense of a fugitive day
> Fetched back from its thickening shroud of gray . . . '

> ' . . . And why does plunging your arm in a bowl
> Full of spring water, bring throbs to your soul?'

> 'Well, under the fall, in a crease of the stone,
> Though where precisely none ever has known,
> Jammed darkly, nothing to show how prized,
> And by now with its smoothness opalized,
>   Is a drinking glass . . .

> . . . By night, by day, when it shines or lours,
> There lies intact that chalice of ours,
> And its presence adds to the rhyme of love
> Persistently sung by the fall above.
> No lip has touched it since his and mine
> In turns therefrom sipped lovers' wine.'

In these Emma poems, Hardy engages in what was to become a
more general commitment of his extraordinary last years: the rewriting of his own history in terms of loss. For not only was he
driven to idealise Emma and at times to impersonate her; he felt
compelled to disguise himself and his origins. The evidence suggests
that, from very humble beginnings, Hardy's father had built up a
successful business, first as a bricklayer and subsequently as a master-
mason; and far from being improvident, as his son liked to suggest,
he earned a reputation (as would his son) for being tight-fisted.

About the fact that his mother was one of seven children brought up on parish charity, Hardy was totally silent; similarly that close relatives, like his uncle John Hardy, were labourers, that several were disreputable or drunk, that his mother, and both his grandmothers, had been pregnant well before their marriages, and that the women in his family, with few exceptions, were domestic servants.[17] In common with John Durbeyfield in *Tess of the D'Urbervilles*, Hardy was seized with the idea that his family had once been important, but had come down in the world. 'The decline and fall of the Hardys', he called it; 'so we go down, down, down'.[18]

What is also evident is that, well into his sixties and seventies, Hardy was to remain vulnerable to the 'throbbings of noontide', yet would neglect his desire's object once achieved. That he had been in love with Florence Dugdale seems beyond question; and that she had been his mistress seems likely. He had installed her as his secretary; and Florence being on friendly terms with Emma, he, Emma and Florence had at times lived together under the same roof as an uneasy *ménage à trois*. Quite soon after Emma died, Florence, forty years his junior, came to live with him, much to the scandal of Dorchester society, and just over a year later, in 1914, they married. But, once wed, he neglected Florence too, seemingly oblivious of the anguish that his preoccupation with Emma and all her remembered doings caused her.

There was in Hardy, both as a man and as a writer, something bitterly pessimistic. His autobiography has been described as 'affording an astonishing anthology, or necrology, of mortuary occasions'.[19] Lovingly, he recalls the details of famous murders and the exploits of hangmen; and, in conversation, dwelt relentlessly on the execution of women. His pessimism is not so much suffered, you sense, as indulged; and when you read him, this indulgence is a quality you are continually invited to share. There is the sense, too, that Hardy's pursuit of 'mortuary occasions' was obliquely self-referring. When he speaks of burying an emotion for forty years and then exhuming it, it is as if his own head were a tomb; yet one from which, paradoxically, emotion emerges 'as fresh as when interred'.

Not only was Hardy preoccupied by death and the grotesque; he seemed reconciled in advance to the knowledge that the 'throbbings of noontide' are ones he could celebrate only in retrospect and at one remove. His idealisation of Emma once dead; the clarity of utterance he thereby achieved; his neglect of Florence; the myth of the Hardys as a grand family in decline; the insistence of his preoccupation with

Hardy with Florence Dugdale

the ghoulish and morbid: none of this makes sense unless cast within the framework of tensions the wound creates, and a subsequent commitment to resolve these in symbolic terms. As Millgate observes, 'it is perfectly clear that... what gave Hardy pain was precisely what provided the fuel for his art.' Accordingly, 'There is a sense in which regret for Emma... flourished in a condition of deep melancholy which was to some degree willed, deliberately cultivated – a kind of enclosed mental garden in which Hardy's creativity could uniquely flourish but which he was none the less capable of entering or leaving almost at will.'[20]

PIERRE AND MARTHE

The facts of Hardy's life and work are inseparable, of course, from his depressive temperament. In this respect, he stands in contrast to a buoyant figure like Weston. He also stands apart from Weston in terms of his chosen medium of expression; for if photography is the most literal of media, and in that sense the most recalcitrant, the written word is among the least. Hardy's references to Emma in poems like *The Going* and *In Time of 'The Breaking of Nations'* demand no give-and-take between the idealised and the actual; or none, at least, beyond the requirements which the writer's own commitment to the literal truth imposes.

The third figure we have chosen, the painter Pierre Bonnard, stands midway between Weston and Hardy, both in terms of temperament and of the recalcitrance of the medium in which he chose to operate. He was born in 1867; his parents prosperous, living in suburban Paris but with their roots in the French countryside. At the *lycée*, Pierre excelled in literature, and afterwards began to study law, but, instead, decided to paint. At this stage in his life, he was sociable, mixing easily in the Paris society of painters and poets, and quickly built a reputation for himself as an illustrator. His style was decorative, nostalgic. As one critic says, the feet of Bonnard's people seem always to rest a little uneasily on the ground. The mood, in another critic's phrase, is one of tenuous rapture.

Subsequently, Bonnard was to stand apart from the art world's revolutionary upheavals – cubism, surrealism, abstraction – and follow a more private path. As he said of himself towards the end of his life, he floated between intimism and decoration, a sensibility repellant to a warrior like Picasso, who is said to have characterised one of Bonnard's works as 'piddling'. 'That's not painting,' he announced. 'Painting isn't a question of sensibility; it's a matter of seizing the power, taking over from nature, not expecting her to supply you with information and good advice.'[21] Although often seen as innocently Epicurean, Bonnard's character was more complex than this would suggest. As it unfolded, his work was to reveal paradox overlaying paradox; a development closely tied to the part played in his life by his model, Marthe.

The two met, it seems, in the street. One source says that he was twenty-five at the time, she sixteen; another that they were both in their mid-twenties.[22] She is said to have been working in a shop selling artificial flowers, and perhaps acting as a part-time model. Her real name was Maria (or Marie) Boursin; but, rather more grandly, she called herself Marthe de Meligny. Moderately talented as a painter in her own right, and genuinely appreciative of Bonnard's gifts, Marthe was to prove difficult; and, like Emma Hardy, arguably a little mad. Much given to ill-health, she followed the sometimes far-fetched advice of doctors and quacks about her diet. There are descriptions of her, resentful and self-absorbed, bringing her own food to the table: slabs of raw meat, which she would eat under the outraged gazes of fellow guests and restaurateurs alike. Increasingly, too, she spent long hours in and around her bathtub and in front of her mirror.

The changes in their life together can be charted by means of the photographs Bonnard took. Like Degas, whom he admired, and like his friend Edouard Vuillard, Bonnard, in the early years of his relationship with Marthe, was a keen photographer. His softly focused, often technically faulty snapshots reveal a world of domestic abundance and felicity: friends' children splashing in a pool, adults gathering to eat, dogs, the family cat and – sometimes clothed but more often nude – Marthe.[23] Her unusual body appears before us in these photographs, posing amidst the greenery almost as if she had wandered into the garden from a poem of Verlaine's. (In fact, the movement was in the other direction. Some of these photographs of Marthe served as the basis for drawings used to illustrate Verlaine's poems.) There are also nude photographs of Bonnard taken by Marthe; and, indoors, in their Paris flat, several of Marthe posed, nude, on a bed in front of their stove. Depending on your basis of calculation, Marthe was at the time either in her mid-twenties or her early thirties. Her distinctively slender, small-breasted body was still in its prime. Thereafter, with a single exception, she appears in Bonnard's surviving photographs only in her clothes.

The bulk of Bonnard's surviving nude photographs of Marthe seem to have been taken in a relatively brief period, at the turn of the century. Five or six years later, he took more, now sadly deteriorated, of a model (not Marthe) posing in his studio. Some ten years on again – he was by now approaching fifty – there are also four remarkable photographs of a third model. She is carefully posed and fully dressed, although in one she is taking off her blouse. Where, in Marthe's case, the face is usually indistinct and it is her body you remember, these are portraits, and the model is beautiful. Looking at them, it is easy to believe that he was at least half in love with her,

Marthe

and she perhaps with him.

It is clear, the while, that the Bonnards' social life progressively deteriorated. Furiously jealous of his friends and acquaintances, Marthe drove them off. More and more, the two of them were alone together, and were seen, increasingly, as eccentrics. Although not hard up, they took to living in bare and ugly rooms: he, scruffy, silent; she, garishly clothed, always complaining, her voice 'savage and harsh'. It is said that he was devoted to her; also that he was frightened of her, or frightened at least of her jealousy and temper. Eventually, when he was in his late fifties, they married, his attitude one of gruff acquiescence. Once wed, they headed south in search of a cure for her many ailments, but also into even greater seclusion. She died in 1942, during the German occupation; Bonnard is said to have been desolate.

What makes this gloomy sequence of events noteworthy is the effect it had on Bonnard's painting. Six or seven years after they began living together, and at just the point where he was taking nude photographs of her, Bonnard began to paint nudes of Marthe which were unmistakably erotic. As Janet Hobhouse says in her essay on this strange couple, these early nudes are 'beautiful and worldly images, full of sensuality, conveying the feel of sheets and skin, the airlessness of near bodies in closed rooms'.[24] Perhaps the most famous, *Indolence*, is now in the Musée d'Orsay. The image's power lies close to its centre: legs sprawled carelessly apart, a sparse line of pubic hair, and, curious detail, the big toe of the left foot gripping the flesh on the inside of the right thigh. Uniting these three elements, there are curling wisps of cream paint which, at first glance, might seem to represent a discarded negligée, but only make sense as steam rising from the bathtub, bottom right. Without being in the least bawdy, and even seeming oddly chaste, these creamy wisps create a sense of desire slowly dissolving back into the haze of rumpled bed linen. Not so much an invitation to excitement, as erotic paintings usually are, *Indolence* is more its recollection – already slipping away and, even at the time perhaps, never brought fully into focus or forthrightly enjoyed.

There is something even more distinctive about this image than its composition, however: the paint itself. Bonnard's brush has inched and scratched its way nervously around the shapes, exploring them but at the same time rendering them worryingly insubstantial. Subject matter and treatment exist, in other words, in a state of contradiction. Just this tension was to characterise all Bonnard's best work. On the one hand, apparently life-enhancing subject matter: nudes, sun-drenched landscape, tables laden with food - all set out, eventually, in colour of unparalleled vibrance; on the other, a paint surface which dissolves, when you look at all closely, into a language of marks as seductive as sandpaper.

As the years pass, the explicitly erotic element in Bonnard's nudes fades. Most of the best are identifiably images of Marthe as she was in her thirties, before her body showed signs of age. Often only portions of her appear, the rest of her cut off by a door, say, or by the canvas's edge. But where *Indolence* was largely monochromatic, built up out of shades of brown, black and cream, Bonnard's colour becomes increasingly experimental and increasingly radiant. In the great works of Marthe in her bath – the one in the Tate Gallery, for instance – she appears as a water-borne puppet, afloat in shimmering veils of coloured light. As Hobhouse says, it is as if the obsessing excitement implicit in Marthe's body has abandoned its original locus and suffused the whole of the rest of his perception. You have the impression, in these late nudes, that he is no longer the 'enticed object of the nude's seduction'. His own responses now 'outweigh, overpower and eventually obliterate what he sees'.[25]

His friends saw Bonnard's maturity as a martyrdom, locked in a destructive intimacy with a woman who was scarcely sane. But he none the less transformed this querulous, hen-pecking companion into chaste apparitions. And, granted the internal logic of this process of transformation, it is predictable perhaps that he should produce one of the most sumptuously coloured and formally radical of these visions, her body now dissolving in rainbow hues, her dog sitting as a heraldic presence on the bathmat before her, in the few years that remained to him after she was dead.[26]

FINALLY

It might be said in criticism that the three men we have dwelt on in this chapter all led personal lives which were in varying degrees sad. While the intimacies they formed produced art, they did not produce domestic felicity and they did not produce children.[27] In our defence, we would argue that the serenely happy man and woman who live together with their children, and who create from their intimacy images which the rest of us find electrifying, are utopian figments. Except intermittently, for an hour or two at a time, they do not – and cannot – exist.

It might also be objected that, in each of these three lives, there is the sense of a woman sacrificed to the compulsions of a man. While admitting that this is so, we would argue that more is at stake in intimacy that contentment. There are other gratifications; and to have fuelled the compulsions which drive a talent may be among them. Charis Wilson was happy to acknowledge this. There is no hint in this shrewd woman's account, looking back over her life with Weston, of oppression in a relationship of power. For her, the rewards were conspicuously disinterested. The nudes Weston took of her, she says, were not 'pictures of *me*', they were 'photographs by *Edward* – his perceptions and his artistry'. She had never felt so vividly alive as when being photographed by him. He made his model feel 'more completely *there* than she probably had ever felt in her life'.[28] Bertha Wardell had been even more blunt. 'What you do', she wrote to Weston, 'awakes in me so strong a response that I must in all joy tell you your photographs are as definite an experience to the spirit as a whiplash to the body.'[29]

These are aspects of intimate life crowded with unresolved puzzles, though. Even poor Emma Hardy, delivering Christian tracts on her bicycle, may have sensed, obliquely, that she was necessary to her husband's creative gifts. We do not know what governs the sense that, at root, a relationship is worthwhile; nor can we safely assume that the judgements of the parties to it are always well-informed. One dark November day, quite soon before Emma died, both the Hardys wrote poems. By this time, they no longer spoke to each other. Yet what both wrote – Emma briefly and pathetically, Hardy the first version of *The Bird-Catcher's Boy* – centres on the imagery of birds.[30] It is as if there were still a traffic in intuitive understanding between them. Imaginatively fertile intimacies, this suggests, may be *folies à deux*, in which mutual understanding can be taken for granted. What must be struggled for and protected is mutual separation, difference. In analytic terms, nevertheless, this is trackless ground. Beyond its outward signs and symptoms, little enough is known about marriage; still less about its relation to the imagination.

The territory we have covered in these last two chapters is more modest. In the arts, we have claimed, the male imagination can turn from its natural home in the world of science and technology to the female body from which it initially took flight. From this contemplation it can fashion containers for those forms of erotic consciousness which move men most: not just desire nor simply excitement but the experience of magical access, the 'raw material of grace'.[31] Men like Weston, Hardy and Bonnard seem to have treated the women they loved as sources of that raw material, carrying it off and releasing from it its hidden store of light. Compared with building a bridge or investigating the interior life of the atom, it seems a private thing to do, intelligible to two people at most; yet, remarkably, the light they release reaches us all.

In his forties, Shakespeare used *The Winter's Tale* to explore the pardoxical reversals on which this artistic legerdemain depends; ones inherent in the ideas of people-as-things and things-as-people. In writing it, he reworked a romance published some years earlier by a contemporary and rival: the dissolute Robert Greene, who had died, it is said, from a surfeit of pickled herrings and Rhenish wine.[32] In Shakespeare's elaboration of the original story, the virtuous queen, Hermione, is imprisoned by her husband Leontes, the King of Sicily, who wrongly suspects her of infidelity. When she gives birth to a daughter in prison, he orders the baby to be left on a desert shore to perish. Hermione's son dies of sorrow at his mother's suffering, and hearing of her son's death, Hermione in turn dies. Her husband is grief-stricken. Years pass, and then, at a crucial moment in the plot, he is taken to see a statue which resembles his dead wife in every detail. His grief is intensified, but he then discovers to his astonishment that the status is alive; Hermione did not die after all. In a *coup* of the dramaturgist's art which Hardy would perfectly have understood, the couple are magically reunited.

Images of the living-as-dead and the dead-as-living invade the thoughts of the younger generation too. Perdita, the baby daughter abandoned to die, is rescued and brought up by a shepherd. Subsequently she falls in love with Florizel, the son of Polixenes, King of Bohemia, whom Leontes had suspected of seducing Hermione. Her love is returned. He tells her:

> ... when you do dance, I wish you
> A wave o' th' sea, that you might ever do
> Nothing but that, move still, still so,
> And own no other function.[33]

The resonances and dissonances of 'move still, still so' flow in and out of Shakespeare's text, and permeate spectators' minds as they listen. The while, the poet slips from hand to hand the themes which, if we are right, the wound makes obsessive in the male mind: the thought of paradise regained; the idea of the object of love both moving and motionless, quick and dead, and therefore safe from changes of heart, time, or the depradations of alien males; the thought of a creature potentially dangerous plucked of her sting; and the wish-fulfilling fantasy that desire can go on galvanising the human imagination for ever. The poet lures us into a privileged space in which what seems real usually proves insubstantial, and only what we know to be illusory is capable of being real.

The steps whereby the male child establishes his sense of his own maleness in two respects empower him, we have suggested. They offer him the formative experience of agency, and they make available to him a source of psychic energy he would otherwise lack. He discovers that, at a cost, he can step away from his mother's body and its gratifications, and create a stance of his own. The cost is the wound. If he chooses to heal this directly, in the context of a sexual intimacy, he may find himself vulnerable to destructive upheavals and reversals of sentiment over which he has no control. It is in the world of art, imaginatively removed from the immediately corporeal, that such contradictions can be turned to good account. It is there that impassioned thought is most satisfactorily contained, its finest artefacts acquiring an enduring life and integrity of their own.

These live in the mind and shape our perception precisely because they capture those formal properties of experience, elusively yet transfixing, which characterise love and loss and desire.

INTRODUCTION

1 See, e.g., Greenson (1968), Chodorow (1978).
2 Our interest in the wound stems from our own research on the career choices of
adolescents and adults, on the relation of public life to private life, and on the
various shapes which expressions of the imagination take. The theorising we do
is psychological in the sense that its working parts are not mechanisms underlying states of subjective experience (like the psychic apparatus of classical Freudian theory), but inferred states of subjective experience themselves (Stern,
1985).
3 Closest to our own train of thought is Keller (1985).
4 The natural historian's appeal to 'the facts', needless to say, is always suspect: see
'Hudson's law of selective attention to data' (Hudson, 1972). This law was for-
mulated in the context of rows about race and IQ, but is equally applicable to
work on gender. Very properly, psychology seeks rigour, but at present has no
recipe for finding it.
5 More generally, our view of psychology is that intellectual excitement is keenest
in those areas were psychologists' arguments compete with those being offered
by their academic neighbours and rivals. One of several consequences is that psychology as a discipline tends to be richly developed around its edges, but in its
heartland empty (Hudson, 1985a).
6 In using biographical material, the psychologist is to a considerable extent at the
mercy of the myth-making propensities of both the subjects themselves and their
biographers. We will certainly be galled if we find we have been parroting such
myths. On the other hand, our real purpose is more formal; that of counter-
posing general theoretical statements with forms of evidence which act as 'slices
of life' – ones that stand for (and in that sense represent) the particularity and
variousness of individual experience.
  The dangers of the narrative mode are in no sense local to the psychologist's
use of biography. In the more scientific branches of psychology, one hardly ever
has access to other people's evidence in its raw state, and takes heroic feats of
selection for granted. The reduction of information about a hundred individuals
to a medium–sized correlation coefficient is just such a feat. To read such a correlation as evidence of a causal connection is in most circumstances an imaginative
leap. To treat it as evidence of the same causal connection operating within each
of the hundred lives in question is to make a serious commitment to fantasy.
7 Intuition enters psychological argument in mysterious ways. Material seen by

175

the psychologist as self-evidently luminous often turns out to be recalcitrant. It is as if in psychology, as in art, material is perceived as inspiring precisely because it is subtly alien or 'other' to the task in hand. A good example of this is Freud's use of the 'Irma' dream in *The Interpretation of Dreams* (Standard Edition, 4–5) (Hudson, 1985b).

CHAPTER 1: THE GENDER INDUSTRY

1 Hall (1978), pp. 92, 138. The nature of the changes brought about by reformers like Marie Stopes can be gauged by the letters written to her by ordinary citizens of both sexes, many of which Hall quotes.

2 Robinson (1969, 1976) has written well about the 'sexual radicals', among them Havelock Ellis.

3 Sulloway (1979) remains the best source for the outsider interested in the facts of Freud's intellectual life and the scientific background from which his theorising sprang. Roazen (1975) is valuable too.

4 Freud (Standard Edition, 9), p. 194.

5 Roazen (1975), p. 162.

6 Jung (1963), p. 150. Jung's recollections of Freud, it should be said, were not necessarily accurate or disinterested.

7 Sulloway (1979), p. 138.

8 The bungled operation on Emma Eckstein's nose became the focus of Freud's famous 'Irma' dream: the one in which, he believed, the secrets of the unconscious were revealed. This dream's significance has been the subject of much debate: see, e.g., Erikson's (1968) comments, Kuper and Stone's (1982) ingenious re-analysis of the dream in structural terms, and the relevant chapter in *Night Life* (1985b).

9 Darwin (1887), p. 262.

10 Biographical material about Kinsey can be found in Robinson (1976) and Weinberg (1976). There are close parallels between Kinsey's upbringing and that of Carl Rogers, the inventor of person-centred psychotherapy (Kirschenbaum and Henderson, 1990). They even shared a passion, as young men, for natural history.

11 Weinberg (1976), p. 55.

12 Rycroft (1979).

13 Erikson (1963), p. 266.

14 Freud later claimed that Fliess, like Adler, saw the struggle between the two sexes as the decisive cause of repression. Hence both their theories had 'in common a sexualization of the process of repression'. This Freud rejected. It was, he said, 'Man's archaic heritage' which formed 'the nucleus of the unconscious mind' (Freud, Standard Edition, 17, pp. 200–3.

15 Mead (1935), p. 190. A decade and a half later, in *Male and Female* (1949), she was to make an interesting concession. In fields like the physical sciences, mathematics and instrumental music, she felt, men might always have a marginal advantage. In such fields, it would be men who made new discoveries, women who followed. Equally, women might always have an advantage in those human sciences demanding the type of understanding that, until it is analysed, is labelled intuition.

16 Mead's ideas were discussed, for instance, in Roger Brown's *Social Psychology* (1965), arguably the best psychology textbook yet written. If our remarks in this section betray a trace of warmth, the explanation is simple: we have lived and

worked for two decades and in three universities among anthropologists and sociologists.

17 This ethnographic evidence was summarised by D'Andrade (1967), but its implications seem largely to have been ignored.

18 Vigorous but inconclusive discussion now centres on the concept of 'difference' (Rhode, 1990). There are:

- Those who accept that the sexes are biologically dissimilar, but insist that, morally and politically, they should be treated as equal;
- Those who accept that the sexes are biologically dissimilar, but see women as inherently superior to men;
- Those who believe in the essential sameness of men and women, differences being seen as trivial or illusory; and
- Those who see differences between men and women as real, but as the product of the historically constituted oppression of one sex by the other.

Remedies vary. The traditional feminist policies are those of political pressure and consciousness-raising. A more radical option (e.g., Hare-Mustin and Maracek, 1990) holds that conventional notions of achievement should be 'deconstructed', with a view to opening activities like science, traditionally dominated by men, to women. Sometimes the contribution of women to these activities is seen as distinctively 'female', sometimes not. The effect, Keller (1985) hopes, will be the end of 'hegemony' in science – the assumption that science can only be done successfully in one way. More radical still is the systematic destabilisation of all forms of sex- and gender-based thought (Butler, 1990).

19 Butler (1990), pp. xi-xiii. It is an interesting irony that the enterprise of 'decentring the subject' should stem from the work of men like Lacan, Foucault and Derrida – the 'all-purpose subversives' of French intellectual life (Skinner, 1985) – who are widely perceived as charismatic, and who have proved conspicuously skilled in exploiting the special status this perception affords.

20 See, e.g., Feyerabend (1975). The prior authority often cited is Thomas Kuhn's *The Structure of Scientific Revolutions* (1962), a text that views the history of science through the spectacles of sociology. Kuhn's view is that facts about the natural world can only be established in the light of systems of assumption or paradigms; hence that there can never be objective grounds for privileging one scientific story about, for instance, the structure of the atom at the expense of all others. His view is an accurate characterisation of much of what happens in everyday science, and is a valuable corrective to the excesses of logical positivism. On the other hand, it presents difficulties no easier to surmount. One of the most important of these is that few practising scientists see what he says as believable. The standard sociological response is that scientists are bounded by their own paradigms, so cannot be expected to have views about those paradigms worth listening to. The same logic is not seen as applying, though, to the body of Kuhn's own thought. Kuhn and those inspired by him believe fervently that his view is correct and that others are mistaken.

In hindsight, it becomes clear that Kuhn's theory draws its significance from its dialectical relationship with logical positivism. Detached from this relationship and treated as the truth, it leads to absurdity: the assumption that sociologists and philosophers of knowledge can grasp the truth unequivocally while natural scientists can never hope to do so.

21 Marcuse (1955), Henry (1966). Both Marcuse and Henry saw sexual permissiveness as serving the interests of the market-place, and Marcuse spoke of 'repressive desublimation': the process whereby a capitalist culture offers its citizens

careers as liberated pleasure-seekers in order to distract them from the possibility of effective political action. He also saw the 'desexualisation' of the rest of body and the confinement of erotic pleasure to the genitals as a precondition for the transformation of the body into an instrument of labour. Hirschman's (1982) essay 'On Disappointment' is pertinent too. Marketing is successful, he points out, in as much as it encourages customers to buy something they want but that disappoints them – thus priming them to buy again. Sexual intercourse with large numbers of attractive partners conforms to this purchasing cycle precisely.

22 Technological metaphors have played a significant part in the modernisation of our sexual attitudes, that of the 'turn-on' being attributed by Brown (1986) to the sex expert John Money.

23 If psychoanalysts are notorious for quarrelling among themselves, so too are taxonomists, the recent reclassification of the genus *Rhododendron* being a particularly torrid affair (Royal Horticultural Society, 1980).

24 Keller (1985), p. 164.

CHAPTER 2: SIMPLE CHOICES, COMPLEX SOLUTIONS

1 Brown (1986). The field of sex and gender is a terminological minefield. Kinsey and others have insisted, for example, that the terms 'heterosexual' and 'homosexual' should only be used to describe acts, not persons. Our own policy is to be easy-going over terms, but to be as careful as we can about what is assumed and implied. In using the terms 'sex' and 'gender' we observe a rough-and-ready body/mind distinction, 'sex' referring to aspects of experience which have a behavioural or reproductive component, 'gender' to issues of self-perception and identity. Biological, psychological and social argument and evidence are assumed, though, to be equally applicable to both. It was John Money, incidentally, who, in 1955, first borrowed the term 'gender' on psychiatry's behalf from philology.

Words like 'desire', 'erotic' and 'passion' still seem to us good currency. On the other hand, 'sexuality' (like 'creativity') has been used so indiscriminately as largely to have been drained of meaning. We do our best to avoid it.

2 Hudson (1982).

3 Tanner (1978), p. 57.

4 Ibid., pp. 56, 70. Schiebinger (1989) charts the steps whereby new knowledge of anatomy was used in the seventeenth and eighteenth centuries to establish a relationship of complementarity between the sexes: the broad-hipped, small skulled female being seen as nurturing and supportive; the narrow-hipped, big-skulled male as the creature of will and deed. Wilson (1989) cites untranslated German research which claims to demonstrate an intriguing relationship between width of pelvis and rates of divorce. Men with broad pelvises and women with narrow ones are much more likely than other men and women, it is claimed, to get divorced. The explanation offered builds on evidence that narrow-hipped men and broad-hipped women tend to have conventional sexual attitudes and beliefs; and that marriages between partners whose attitudes are conventional are more likely to remain unbroken.

5 Bell and Weinberg (1978); Brown (1986).

6 Sociobiology, it has recently become evident, is a discipline emerging from its grossly reductive, 'red neck' phase, and the views being offered by evolutionary biologists, animal behaviourists and ethologists now deserve close attention. Hinde (1987) has advanced the claim that the development of gender differences

depends on a 'dialectical interplay' between biological propensities and social forces. These social forces he sees as mediated by family relationships but as derived from the gender stereotypes of the culture in question – stereotypes which in turn are exaggerations of biological propensities. Although it emerges from a research tradition quite unlike our own, we find this formulation astute, and seriously deficient only in that it allows no place for causal processes which are genuinely psychological. Also helpful are the discussion of 'sensitive periods' in Bateson and Hinde (1987), and the clear articulation of the relation between the genetic and environmental in Bateson (1987).

7 The startling phenomena of transsexuality have been examined in detail by Stoller (1968). The work on the assignation of hermaphroditic children to one sex or the other is reported by Money and Ehrhardt (1972).

8 Brown (1986).

9 Cases of foetal androgenisation are described by Money and Ehrhardt (1972); and both this and analogous defects are discussed by Bancroft (1983). The history of research on Turner's Syndrome (see, e.g., Money 1964, Jensen 1969, Hudson 1970) points a pertinent moral, though. It reminds us how unwise it is to base arguments about the influence of genetics on the study of individuals who are, and are seen to be, physically abnormal.

10 Stoller (1968), p. 173.

11 Ellmann (1985), p. 71; also Baker (1969, 1981). Like the Victorians, Hemingway believed not only that the male is weakened by ejaculation, but that his store of semen is limited: that what he spends now he cannot spend later. Physiologically speaking, this belief is mistaken. But if semen is seen as a metaphor for the vital juices of the psyche, it becomes more intelligible. Our capacity to invest ourselves wholeheartedly in acts of intimacy, whether with people or with texts, may well be limited. Once that limit is reached, all experience may become repetitious.

12 See, e.g., Beardslee and O'Dowd (1962), Hudson (1968). Stereotypes are not necessarily in the least factually accurate. Like prejudices, they are powerfully influential none the less. In statistical terms, they produce some of the most striking regularities a psychologist can expect to come across.

13 Hudson (1967a, 1967b).

14 Marcus (1966), p. 16.

15 Hudson (1975).

16 In earlier discussions of these data, it was felt that the stereotypes of the sciences and arts were caricatures of the the the preoccupations of latency and adolescence respectively (Hudson, 1975, pp. 131–43). This is a view we would now want to qualify. Our present view is that sex-linked stereotypes first take shape much earlier, in infancy, and are a product of the steps whereby parents and child, between them, segregate experience into responsible and pleasurable domains. It is the nature of these steps which the next chapter examines.

The status of such stereotypical perception in the development of theory, it should be said, is delicate. The lazy view is that there is no problem: stereotypes are simply by-products of the mental processes which psychological theories aim to describe and explain. A more cautious view raises the reverse possibility. Namely that psychological theories take the shape they do because psychologists, as they sit in their armchairs, fall under the sway of stereotypical systems of thought. These ensure that our theoretical formulations have 'good Gestalt', the ring of truth. Theorising thus becomes a form of sleep-walking. From it, we can be awoken not by yet deeper reading of seminal texts, but by confrontation with embarrassing and subversive evidence.

17 Hudson (1967a).

18 The concept of androgyny, discussed here in terms of mosaics of 'male' and 'female' qualities, was used in the 1970s for political purposes. Bem (1976) employed it to promote the right of women (like Mrs Thatcher) to be powerful, of men to be nurturing, and of either sex to be nurturing and powerful by turns. Androgyny, it was claimed, was a separate dimension of personality, and a sign of good mental health. As a line of inquiry, this proved inconclusive, bogging down in technical confusion and muddles over semantics.

In practice, androgynous cultures seem as prone to stereotyping, coercion and unwitting self-parody as markedly masculine or feminine ones. As institution like King's College, Cambridge demonstrates this. As a male college with a flamboyantly bisexual tradition, it produced – especially in the years between the wars – a conformity as oppressive in its own way as those of the football club or lingerie boutique.

19 In its simplest form, our scheme operates as a decision tree with four layers, at each of which the individual makes a formative choice (Hudson, 1982, fig. 6). This has two obvious weaknesses. The language of choice and decision-making is too rational, few of the choices in question being ones over which the individual exerts much conscious control. There is also the implication that decisions are made in a fixed sequence, those about gender identity, say, always preceding ones about object choice. A more flexible and more realistic (but less controllable) form of modelling is provided by the two- and three-dimensional network or lattice, within which forces have free play, subject to biases and constraints which are either in-built or which the system learns. It is fragments of such lattices which we deploy in the diagrams in Chapters 7 and 8.

20 See, e.g., Woodcock and Davis (1980). The human sciences are nowhere more fashion-ridden than in their theorising. Dissonance theories were popular in the 1960s, are now out of fashion, but are due, we feel, for a revival – not least because psychodynamic explanations are so often dissonance explanations in thin disguise. In the first edition of *Social Psychology* (1965), Brown described cognitive dissonance theories as 'probably the most influential ideas in social psychology'. In his second edition (1986), such work is not mentioned. Should a third edition be published in 2007, it could once again occupy stage-centre.

CHAPTER 3: THE MALE 'WOUND'

1 Tanner (1978), p. 56. Rose, Kamin and Lewontin (1984), on the other hand, point to evidence that actively feminising influences may be at work too.

2 Stoller (1985a), p. 74.

3 Held (1989), Geschwind and Galaburda (1987).

4 Keller (1985) follows a train of thought adjacent to our own. A mathematical biophysicist, she was seized – in mid-stride, as it were – by the need to understand the 'maleness' of the professional enterprise to which she was committed, and subsequently used psychoanalytic and feminist arguments in doing so.

The terrain where psychoanalysis and feminism meet, it has to be said, is one where a good deal of lambasting goes on. In the 1960s, feminist critics dismissed Freud's views on gender out of hand as sexist. Mitchell (1974) took them to task for failing to read what Freud had written. Chodorow in turn characterised Mitchell as an 'apologist'; one who offers 'a zealous defence of every claim Freud makes', and who implies that these claims 'all have equal empirical and method-

ological status and are always valid' (1978, p. 141). As Sulloway (1979) demonstrates, Freud saw psychoanalytic theory as an instinct theory, and differences
between the sexes as a natural (as opposed to a symbolic) phenomenon. To what
extent psychoanalytically minded feminists share these views is now unclear.

5 Greenacre (1952), p. 31, Grunberger (1989), p. 68.

6 Harlow and Harlow (1965), Bowlby (1979), Rutter (1981). Important issues of
fact remain unresolved, even so. Little is known about the long-term effects of
having several 'mothers' rather than a single mother, or a male 'mother' rather
than a female one. Nor is it clear whether there is a balance to be struck between
'too much' mothering and 'too little'. Arguably, an over-intrusive or enveloping
mother does more psychological damage than a neglectful one (Stoller, 1974).

7 Greenson (1968).

8 Bower (1989) and Stern (1985) argue for complex developmental processes early
in infancy. Specifically, Stern claims on the basis of child observation that the infant's sense of self is established in stages during the first 18 months of life, each
corresponding to a formative phase: 'emergent self' (0-2 months), 'core self' (3-6
months), 'subjective self' (7-15 months) and 'verbal self' (15-18 months). By implication, each of these differentiations of 'self' from 'other' occurs before – or in
parallel with – the establishment of a stable gender identity.

9 Between the ages of 3 and 6 months, Stern stresses, infants are already in a position to use their gaze to exert 'control over the initiation, maintenance, termina-
tion, and avoidance of social contact with the mother; in other words, they help
to regulate engagement. Furthermore, by controlling their own direction of
gaze, they self-regulate the level and amount of social stimulation to which they
are subject. They can avert their gaze, shut their eyes, stare past, become glassy-
eyed' (Stern, 1985, p. 21).

10 Rosenthal (1984).

11 Hinde and Stevenson-Hinde (1987).

12 Tanner (1978), p. 58.

13 Greenacre (1952), p. 110.

14 Most psychoanalysts, Stoller (1979b, p. 109) contends, follow Freud in believing
that 'all psychopathology, not just the sexual deviations, results – by such
mechanisms as castration anxiety and penis envy in the oedipal conflict - from
disturbances in the sense of gender identity, that is of masculinity and feminin-
ity'.

It is these mechanisms of penis envy and castration anxiety that Chodorow in-
vokes in the context of what we have called the wound. Although she confesses
herself uncomfortable with it, she follows the orthodox line: that when the son
discovers that his mother lacks a penis, he is seized by castration anxiety, and
separates himself from his mother as a result (Chodorow, 1978, p. 107). While
we accept that mother/infant relations may be intensely eroticised, we view this
part of the orthodox psychoanalytic story with scepticism. Our own view of the
wound is unrelated either to castration anxiety or to the idea of the female genitalia as the wound that results when, in fantasy, the male genitalia are cut away.
Although our argument belongs to the broad family of psychodynamically inspired ideas, its links with classical Freudian theory are few.

15 See, e.g., Bronfenbrenner's (1970) comparison of the pressures brought to bear
on American and Russian school children.

16 Social psychologists (e.g. Tajfel, 1981) see individuals' self-images as having two
components: a personal identity and social identities which correspond to each of
the groups to which the individual in question belongs. Such theorists assume

that whenever individuals join a group, this automatically becomes an 'in-group', perceived as superior to any alternatives. Such theorising is inadequate to cope with the evidence of academic specialisation, though. Young physical scientists plainly choose a profession which they themselves continue to perceive in unfavourable terms (Hudson, 1967a).

17 Lacan appears to take this view (Bowie, 1987, p. 117). Although attractive, it has an obvious flaw. In as much as both boys and girls are subject to parental authority, it suggests, both will experience themselves as 'male' – leaving as determinants of gender identity the relatively superficial questions of noticed similarities and differences of physique, names, ascribed roles, and so on. Rescue is possible; but the difficulty is typical of the puzzles which theories of identification pose.

18 Broadly, psychoanalytic theory admits four sorts of identification: (1) Primary identification – the primitive state which is presumed to exist in the minds of infants before they can discriminate themselves from other people; (2) Secondary identification – the normal developmental process whereby infants model themselves on parents whom they see as separate from themselves; (3) Introjective identification – the process whereby individuals envisage other people (or aspects of those people) as 'inside' themselves; and (4) Projective identification – the process whereby individuals envisage themselves as 'inside' other people. Primary and secondary identification are uncontentious, at least to the extent that they accord with common sense; but the notions of introjective and projective identification constitute a battle ground.

It is also an assumption of much psychoanalytic theorising that the infant's early introjective and projective identifications occur in terms which are semantically stereotyped and binary: hence the psychoanalytic shorthand whereby the mother is seen as fragmented in her infant's eyes into 'good breast' and 'bad breast'. It is easy to see how such primitive distinctions could evolve into the categories which structure the stereotypical perceptions of adolescents and adults: 'exciting'/'dull', for instance, and 'valuable'/'worthless'. But while methods of observing mothers and their infants are becoming increasingly sensitive, as Stern's work shows, there is little prospect, ever, of such semantic activity being directly confirmed. To infer it retrospectively from the fantasies of adults is plainly unacceptable, because those fantasies (like the psychoanalyst's theories) could well be shaped by systems of stereotypical perception acquired at a later developmental stage.

19 This traffic in turn permits the 'export' from one person to another of complex systems of anxiety and need; hence Erikson's claim that 'whatever deep "psychic stimulus" may be present in the life of a young child, it is identical with his mother's most neurotic conflict' (Erikson, 1963, p. 30). There is also the difficulty, as Goffman (1959) has insisted, that so much of our sense of ourselves is dramaturgical.

20 Brown (1986), p. 551.

21 Greenson (1968).

22 Clark (1960), p. 300.

23 Osten and Vey (1969), p. 30; Hibbard (n.d.), pp. 66, 220.

24 See Clark (1960), plate 260; also Hudson (1982), where Meit's image is discussed in more detail.

25 There are female psychologists and psychoanalysts (e.g. Levenson, 1984, Aries and Olver, 1985) who see the absence of an equivalent feat of separation among women as leaving them at a clear disadvantage. Women characteristically have

difficulty, they suggest, not only in separating from their parents, but in functioning autonomously within their own adult intimacies. Chodorow reaches the opposite conclusion. She sees the 'separateness' of the male rather than the 'connectedness' of the female as 'problematic' (Chodorow, 1990, p. 120). What women lack, if our own argument is correct, is not a penis but an in-built sense of agency (of which the penis is sometimes assumed to be symbolic). It is this sense which a woman must subsequently construct, and which – especially if her sense of her own feminity is insecure – she may envy.

26 In adopting the idea of a psychic space which opens up between the male infant's sense of himself and his mother, we become heirs to Winnicott's (1971) concept of 'potential space'. Winnicott envisaged this as an 'intermediate area of experience', which serves as model and precursor of imaginative activity among adults. From our point of view, there are none the less distinctions to be drawn. Winnicott's potential space is established in the child's mind at a much earlier developmental stage than that created by the wound, and in both sexes alike. We are suggesting, in effect, that under the impact of the male wound potential space takes on a significance which is gender-linked.

Lacan's notion of the *nom-du-père* is pertinent too. 'Freud's essential discovery', Lacan believed, was that 'man bears otherness within himself'; that, in the relation of unconscious to conscious, he comes face to face with his own '*excentricité radicale de soi à lui-même*' (Bowie, 1987, p. 118). Lacan follows Freud in taking the Oedipal triad of mother – father – child as given, and assumes that all authority derives from the father: not the actual father, nor even an imagined one, but the symbolic father, *le nom du père*. 'The *nom-du-père*, the original Other, introduces a gap between desire and its object(s) which the subject is bounded by, and bound to, throughout his life and at all levels of his experience. This primordial estrangement is by its very nature destined to recur, and be converted, ubiquitously . . .'. Again, though, distinctions are necessary. Like Winnicott's potential space, Lacan's *nom-du-père* arises in the first year of life; the wound later. The *nom-du-père* is inseparable from the 'Symbolic Order'; the wound relates only indirectly to boy's symbolic capacity. The *nom-du-père* is part of the stock-in-trade of the theoretician who dances; the wound part of that of ones happy to plod.

27 Storr (1988). As Chodorow (1978, p. 177) says, identification among boys and the acquisition of the male role is in any case unlikely 'to be embedded in relationship with their fathers or men but rather to involve the denial of affective relationship to their mothers'.

28 It is presumably for this reason not only that the earth is perceived as female – 'Mother Earth' – but so too are those pre-eminently 'male' pieces of machinery, the boat and the motorcar.

29 Keller (1985, p. 158) correctly insists that there is 'a world of difference' between the objectivity of the scientist who masters his chosen slice of the natural world and imposes order on it, and that of the scientist – she instances the geneticist Barbara McClintock – who 'listens to the material' and develops a feel for it. There is a distinction of principle, in other words, between thought which is objective in the sense that it is abstract or analytic, and thought which is objective in the sense that it is open-minded or dispassionate.

30 The reversal of infantile identity implicit in the wound whereby the father (previously different) is seen as similar, and the mother (previously similar) is seen as different:
SIMILARITY-IN-DIFFERENCE : DIFFERENCE-IN-SIMILARITY

thus leads to a bifurcation of imaginative preoccupation, in which the two components mirror one another:

THINGS-AS-PEOPLE : PEOPLE-AS-THINGS

The step is vital to our argument, and is the first of the three points where our underlying presuppositions show through. It is from this linkage between a reversal of identity and a splitting of imaginative preoccupation that the rest of what we have to say about the male imagination flows. While it is the preoccupation with things-as-people that will dominate our discussion of science and technology, it is the segregation of the two preoccupations – things-as-people and people-as-things – that regulates the male's sexual expression, and does so most clearly in its perverse forms. It is only in the last part of our story, where we discuss the male's distinctive contribution to the creative arts, that, however precariously, these preoccupations with people-as-things and things-as-people are reconciled.

31 The developmental influence of dis- and counter-identification will vary from cost to cost and benefit to benefit. Apparently complex, these interactions are easiest to grasp when tabulated:

| | | The Developmental Influence of | |
		DIS-IDENTIFICATION	COUNTER-IDENTIFICATION
Costs	INSENSITIVITY	Necessary	Reinforcing
	MISOGYNY	Necessary	Counteracting
Benefits	AGENCY	Necessary	Necessary
	ENERGY SOURCE	Necessary	Irrelevant
	ABSTRACT PASSION	Necessary	Reinforcing

This table suggests that the developmental pattern giving rise to abstract passion will also give rise to personal insensitivity – but not to misogyny. Where abstract passion and misogyny do occur in the same man, we would expect the resulting tension to become an organising principle of the imaginative life of the individual in question (as seems to have been the case for the philosopher Schopenhauer, as the next chapter shows.)

32 Hudson and Jacot (1971). These data are derived from *Who's Who*. The samples being large, very high levels of statistical significance were achieved. See also Hudson (1973), where the British evidence is confirmed by American data drawn from the National Surveys of Higher Education, sponsored by the Carnegie Commission.

33 Kuhn (1962).

34 These are effects of the kind which Freud's psychoanalytic colleague Ferenczi labelled 'bioanalytic'. Winnicott's idea of potential space falls into this category.

Stern (1985, p. 26) argues that, in psychoanalytic theorising, the psychic apparatus is assumed to operate apart from subjective experience – in terms, for instance, of repression, the mechanisms of defence, the structures of ego and id, and so on – and to yield subjective experience as its by-product. His own account of self-and-other is unique, Stern believes, in that its 'main working parts' are the inferred subjective experiences of infants themselves.

Our own impression is that some psychoanalysts are more deeply wedded to the experience-as-by-product view than others: Melanie Klein, say, more than

Winnicott. In this respect, nevertheless, we stand with Stern. Once the disjunctions of dis- and counter-identification are in place, there exists, we believe, an apparatus which seeks to resolve perceived consonances and dissonances between emotionally charged alternatives, and does so, not apart from the subjective experience of the individual, but as a centrally placed component of that experience.

35 Lattices are discussed in *Bodies of Knowledge*, in a developmental context; and in *Night Life*, in the context of meaning systems like dreams and poems which are structured but only partially determinate.

36 In making predictions either about individuals or about samples, it follows that simple-minded expectations of the data (like those implicit in the correlation coefficient or the chi-squared test) have often to be abandoned (Hudson, 1977). It is also important to grasp that the differentiation of the pertinent behaviours or perceptions may in practice be sharper within a social group than between groups. In a study of research students and their wives in Edinburgh University, we found the sharpest differences not between those at the extremes of the academic spectrum, but within the discipline of biology, between the 'natural historians' and the 'physical biologists' – for instance between ecologists and geneticists (Hudson, Johnston and Jacot, 1972).

This study exemplified a further point, itself obvious, but easily overlooked when the time comes to analyse quantitative data. Namely, that a marriage is itself a dynamic system, within which differences can gravitate. Although, in this study, the samples were recruited in terms of the husbands' work, the most pronounced differences proved to be those between the two groups of wives. The 'natural historians' had married graduates with whom they conducted dual career marriages; the 'physical biologists' had married non-graduates, and their marriages followed the more conventional pattern. The wives even differed in terms of the age at which they had reached sexual maturity; those of the 'natural historians' having first menstruated relatively late, those of the 'physical biologists' relatively early.

37 The disciplines in which 'male' formats are most contentious are those of the mid-ground: philosophy, social science and of course psychology. It is not clear, for example, to what extent Freud's partitioning of the mind between conscious, pre-conscious and unconscious is advantageous, nor how much mileage psychologists can legitimately make out of developmental models clearly divisible into phases: for instance, Freud's view of the imagination as sexual research, in which an anxiety (the infant's misgivings about where babies come from) is subject to resolution in discrete stages (Freud, Standard Edition, 11).

In Derrida, there is the interesting suggestion – one he attributes to Nietzsche – that the process of differentiation implicit in argumentative formats like Freud's is linked to the idea of force (Derrida, 1981, p. 9).

CHAPTER 4: THE FAMILY NEXUS

1 Sears, Maccoby and Levin (1957), Kagan and Moss (1962). The psychological and social correlates of harsh discipline for sons have since been explored in greater detail (see Hinde, 1987, p. 48). Hinde also reports research on preschool children, among whom it was the shy boys and the non-shy girls who had tense relationships with their mothers; the non-shy boys and shy girls who had relationships with their mothers which were more equable.

Kagan and Moss found long-term effects, too, on sons' and daughters' abilities to score well on intelligence tests. Summarising the evidence of longitudinal studies, Bloom (1964) estimated that 50 per cent of the variance that adolescents display in terms of their aggression, their dependency and the intellectuality of their interests can be predicted from measurements made as early as the age of five. By standards normal in psychology, this is an impressive achievement.

2 Whiting, Kluckhohn and Anthony (1966).

3 Stoller (1974), p. 170.

4 Stoller (1968). States of excessive intimacy between mothers and their sons, like those between fathers and daughters, may be activated by the mother's failure to repress incestuous wishes. There may prove to be an important distinction, in other words, between symbiotic intimacies which are eroticised on the mother's part and those which are not – between those which threaten the son with incest and those which threaten engulfment.

5 The issues of imitation, stereotypical perception, social identity, personal identity and agency are all implicated here. See Brown (1986), pp. 551-74, for a well-poised discussion.

6 This field has recently been subjected to painstaking review by Mackintosh and Mascie-Taylor (1986). Differences of achievement in British schools – for example, between children of West Indian and Asian background – may yet prove explicable in terms not of racial differences nor selective migration, but of the different family structures of the communities in question: one matriarchal, the other partriarchal; one diffuse, the other tight-knit.

7 Carlsmith (1964). Retrospective analyses of this kind are powerfully persuasive, and gratifying to do. Unfortunately, their design never seems quite to be water-tight. In Carlsmith's study, it is arguable that the fathers' absence influenced their sons' intellectual development not because they were away during the first three years of their sons' lives, but because, as returning veterans, the smooth running of their marriages was subsequently disturbed. The literature on sex differences in non-verbal, spatial and mathematical reasoning is still unsettled: see, e.g., Coltheart, Hull and Slater (1975), Harris (1978), Nyborg (1983) and Benbow (1988); also Chapter 5 below.

8 Hudson (1960).

9 This biographical material comes from Leishman (1964) and Leavy (1965).

10 Leavy (1965), pp. 178-9.

11 Ibid., p. 6.

12 Ibid., pp. 11-25.

13 Ibid., pp. 8, 124.

14 Ibid., p. 168.

15 Ibid., p. 154.

16 Ibid., pp. 155, 182.

17 Snow (1987) sees a crucial step in the evolution of Rilke's work as separating the two volumes of New Poems. These were also written with great rapidity, in 1907 and 1908, when Rilke was in his early thirties.

18 The circumstances of this outpouring are discussed in more detail in Hudson (1972, 1985b).

19 Painter (1983).

20 Baker (1969).

21 Roe (1951, 1953).

22 McClelland (1962). This article itself becomes an exercise in McClelland's re-markable brand of ingenuity. What begins as a literature review leads to a scrutiny of scientists' and non-scientists' tastes in metaphors of nature.

23 Wolpert and Richards (1988), Regis (1989).
24 Stern (1966).
25 The mind/body parallelism, and the attendant distinction between statements that can properly be made about minds and statements that can properly be made about brains, is one that neither Descartes nor subsequent philosophers were satisfactorily to resolve. With the advent of associative networks and 'intelligent' automata, the terrain is one in which everyday usage is becoming increasingly lively.
26 Stern (1966), p. 117.
27 Magee (1983), p. 10.
28 Ibid., p. 11.
29 Ibid., pp. 7, 24-5.
30 Usually punctilious about his sources, Freud denied his own dependence either on Schopenhauer or on Nietzsche. But, as Sulloway (1979) points out, Freud was for five years a member of a pan-German reading society in which the views of Schopenhauer, Nietzsche and Wagner were avidly discussed. Freud, in other words, was fully versed in Schopenhauer's beliefs. Schopenhauer, as Magee points out, was also one of the few philosophers whom Wittgenstein read.
31 Magee (1983), p. 18.
32 Stern (1966), p. 112. His misogyny makes Schopenhauer and his mother of interest to feminists: see, e.g., Battersby (1989).
33 Even the biography of someone famous and only recently dead can present insurmountable problems of documentation, as the scandal surrounding Cyril Burt's actions and motives shows (Hearnshaw, 1979; Joynson, 1989; Hudson, 1989).
34 Storr (1988).
35 Kirschenbaum and Henderson (1990), p. 384.
36 Hudson (1966). The creativity movement blossomed in the 1960s, but had its origins more than a decade earlier, as Guilford's (1950) paper shows. In this respect, the antennae of academic psychologists seem to have been sensitively tuned. In questions of sex and gender, on the other hand, the profession has been more cautious, often letting anthropologists, sociologists and English and French literature specialists set the pace. As ever, needless to say, being first and being right remain separate issues.
37 Rosenberg (1963), p. 1.
38 Ibid., p. 4.
39 Ibid., p. 20.
40 Ibid., p. 21.

CHAPTER 5: MALE STRENGTHS

1 Erikson (1963), p. 264.
2 Data supplied by the Equal Opportunities Commission, 1989.
3 Building Industry Council (1989).
4 The British Psychological Society has five times as many men as women in its Mathematical and Statistical Section. In British universities, the discipline is also fissured between teachers and taught. Four out of five first year students of psychology are female; four out of five of those teaching them are male (Morris, Holloway and Noble, 1990).
5 See, e.g., Allen (1988).
6 Zuckerman (1977), Hudson and Jacot (1986). In the appointment of senior

judges in England and Wales, there remains a massive bias against both women and solicitors. Among the 10 Law Lords, the 27 Lord Justices and 83 High Court Judges, only 3 are women and none is by background a solicitor (Gilvarry, 1991).

7 Steiner (1983), Hodges (1983).

8 See, e.g., Crick and Mitchison (1983). As Steiner's caveat implies, many scientists assumed to be heterosexual could turn out to be homosexual. It could be, too, that certain areas of science will prove to hold a special attraction for homosexual men. If Turing's example is significant, they might display particular virtuosity in those areas of the theory of computing where the ideas of intelligent men and intelligent machines merge. Such a focus could itself be a temporary phenomenon, however, reflecting the effects on homosexuals' imaginations of the stigmatisation they at present undergo. Within a generation or two, as this stigmatisation subsides, such effects could become increasingly vestigial, the cultures of hard science and technology proving to be what they seem: stamping grounds of the indelibly 'male' and indelibly heterosexual.

A master code-breaker at Bletchley Park during the war, and one of the nation's invisible war heroes, Turing was prosecuted at the age of forty on a charge of 'gross indecency with a male person'. It is eloquent of the homosexual's social and legal plight, at the margin of a heterosexual community, that he should commit suicide two years later, while still at the height of his powers. Even more eloquent is the claim that he did so by eating an apple which he had previously dipped in cyanide.

9 Jay (1988).

10 Van Hasbroeck (1983, 1989), Hicks (1984), Matanle (1986).

11 Schumann (1977), Bruton (1986). For an introduction to the history of jewellery as adornment, see Tait (1986). In all matters gemmological, we are grateful to Christopher Cavey for his guidance and advice.

12 Zucker (1984), p. 53. It is an intriguing footnote to the history of misogyny that Isaac Newton should have called his dog 'Diamond' (Balfour, 1987, p. 91).

13 We would also predict that men and women will respond dissimilarly both to retirement and to bereavement. Support for the first of these predictions comes from Matthews and Brown (1987). They found, rather remarkably, that the greater the number of antecedent life crises, the more likely a man was to respond badly to retirement from work; whereas, for a woman, the greater the number of antecedent life crises, the *better* she responded. These results suggest that men are cumulatively broken down by turbulent experience, whereas women gather strength from it. The literature on bereavement is one we have failed to penetrate. The indications are, though, that this prediction too will find support.

14 Schiebinger (1989). The Italians were in this respect atypical, the academies at Bologna, Padua and Rome regularly admitting women.

15 In science, most outstandingly successful practitioners, although often outsiders by background and temperament, have usually found their way to one of a handful of major institutions of scientific research by the time they are graduate students. This is certainly so for future Nobel Prize winners (Zuckerman, 1977; Hudson and Jacot, 1986). There is a strong tendency too, heightened no doubt by the mechanisms of patronage and nepotism, for Nobel Laureates to have been in a master/apprentice relation with one another. Although the academic records of the outstandingly successful often turn out to have been lacklustre, not only in science but in law and politics too (Hudson, 1958, 1976), most have a history of

working well when motivated, barely adequately when not (MacKinnon, 1962).

16 The avoidance of discovery may arise from a more basic alienation of perception from desire that the wound consolidates. Lacan (1977, p. 103) points to such an alienation, but does not explain how a minority of individuals might be equipped, however briefly, to escape from it: see Chapter 8 below.

17 Mitscherlich (1969), p. 232. Anthony Trollope showed the way, but an adequate psychopathology of institutional life remains to be written. In the case of modern science, it is sometimes proposed, its dominant themes will still be those of Barchester: vanity and revenge.

18 Mant (1983). Observation suggests that 'raiders' either have unusually efficient means of accommodating anxiety, or are largely impervious to it (and in that sense are psychopathic). We would predict, nevertheless, that once a 'raid' has been successfully made, a significant proportion of raiders will experience depression – which most control by mounting yet another raid.

19 This isomorphism presumably arises because modern institutions have been developed, in Keller's phrase, 'not by humankind but by men'. The extent to which science can accommodate modes of inquiry other than those which come naturally to the 'male' male remains to be established. If it fails to accommodate them, it may do so for reasons intrinsic to the tasks of science rather than from a conspiracy of insiders against the female, androgynous or homosexual.

The 'fit' between the character of an institution and the psychic needs of those who work inside it was first convincingly explored by Menzies (1961) in her study of nurses.

20 See, e.g., Harris (1978).

21 Arguably, Japanese culture embodies a pattern of attributes well suited to the demands high technology makes. The Japanese shun introspection, and find it natural to work in teams. Traditionally, it has been claimed, they regard the mind 'not as an engine of perception and cognition, but as the psycho-spiritual part of the person which seeks identification with ultimate reality' (Gregory, 1987).

22 Shilts (1987). Also at issue is the question of whether AIDS is a single disease with various manifestations, or a loose-knit cluster of mutually unrelated and opportunistic infections. Pertinent in this respect is the evidence of Beral et al. (1991). They show that, among AIDS patients, Kaposi's sarcoma is only transmitted sexually.

23 Hudson (1990a). This paper stresses the extent to which, despite conventional attitudes and beliefs, responses to AIDS are puzzling and paradoxical, on the parts of patients, relatives and professionals alike.

24 Sex- and gender-linked differences in accomplishment may still arise (Rhode, 1990) because ugly prejudices against women still abound; because, historically, women have subordinated their talents to those of men and many still feel constrained to do so; and because there is a tendency for a society run by men and masculinised women automatically to prize those forms of accomplishment which come more naturally to men than to women.

The difficulties facing emancipated women have a fine as well as a coarse grain: e.g., that of surnames – seemingly trivial, but none the less intractable. A girl takes her father's surname. If she takes her husband's surname on marriage, she loses the identity with which she grew up. If she keeps her maiden name, she preserves her identity, but does not shake herself free of the patriarchal pattern: what she is keeping is her father's name, or, if she takes her mother's, her grandfather's. She also runs into domestic inconvenience; and she loosens, too, the identity of the family unit within which her own children grow up. If she takes her husband's name at marriage, but continues to work under her maiden name, a woman signals a distinction between her working self and her domestic self in a way that men do not. If husband and wife join forces to create a double-barrelled name, the problem still remains for their daughters. Do they use the 'male' or the 'female' half of their double-barrelled surname when they themselves marry? If the husband takes his wife's name, the same problems are replicated but in reverse, the pattern becoming matrilineal not patrilineal. And so on.

These, in any case, are early days. In terms of our own biographies, it was less than ten years before we were born that the country in which we grew up gave women the vote. It was more than a decade after we graduated that one of us was excluded from evening meals at the Cambridge college where the other held a fellowship, on the grounds that, as a woman, her presence might give offence to the college's unmarried males.

25 Mackintosh and Mascie-Taylor (1986).

26 Altus (1966).

27 In a neat experiment Coltheart and his colleagues (1975) asked students of both sexes to picture the alphabet, and work their way through it twice, on one occasion counting those letters which are spoken with an 'ee' sound (like B, C, D, E and G, but not A, F and H), and on the other those which contained curved lines (like B, C, D and G, but not A, E, F and H). The first task is phonetic, the second visual. While women made rather more errors on the second task than the first, the men made many more errors on the first task than the second.

28 The evidence is by no means straightforward. See McGlone's (1980) review article and the responses to it.

29 Harris (1978).

30 Levy (1974) reports a strong verbal bias among left-handed students at the California Institute of Technology; meanwhile Critchley and Critchley (1978) were finding a high incidence of the land-handed among the dyslexic. Brown (1986) mentions the intriguing discovery that, among the deaf, sign language – though visual rather than verbal – is controlled by the left hemisphere, not the right.

It is widely assumed to be elitist, even fascist, to view such patterns of strength and weakness as 'wired in'; humane to treat them as the product of social learning. In practice, of course, there is nothing detectably humane about expecting a child with a poor verbal memory to learn poetry by heart, nor one who is tone-deaf to sing. Nor is it especially laudable to lure people into careers that they will eventually find disillusioning – the recruitment of women into engineering being, perhaps, a recently publicised instance. Far from assuming that everyone can do everything, an adequate pedagogy, whether at nursery school or in the postgraduate seminar, is the one that helps individuals to capitalise on their strengths and circumvent their weaknesses, occasionally turning those weaknesses into strengths.

31 See, e.g., Hudson (1983). Our interviews with designers were collected by the late Robert Wetmore, to whom we are indebted.

32 Geschwind and Galaburda (1987). Oliver Zangwill, a pioneer of studies of cerebral dominance, believed that confused patterns of dominance are associated with an oppositional temperament.

33 Witelson (1988) discusses the extent to which the anatomical variety observable among brains is sex-linked.

34 Benbow (1988).

35 The same holds for the relation of birth order to academic accomplishment. In

intellectual matters, the evidence suggests, first born and only sons tend to be conservative, younger sons more radical (Hudson, 1975b).

36 Nyborg (1983, 1988). He favours an explanation in terms of an androgen/oestrogen balance, deviations in either direction – both intrauterine and subsequent – having an adverse effect on spatial reasoning. Among adult women, it seems, the lowest levels of spatial ability correspond to the points in the menstrual cycle associated with highest oestrogen levels.

   Somewhat in the same vein, colleagues of ours in Edinburgh found that women tended to be classified as 'divergers' if tested in the week before ovulation, and as 'convergers' if tested in the fortnight after it (Cormack and Sheldrake, 1974). If originality depends on being subtly at odds with the prevailing wisdom of one's discipline, women may as a result be at their most creative in science in the week before ovulation; and at their most creative in the arts in the fortnight after it (Hudson, 1985b).

37 Girls who first menstruate early tend, it seems, to adopt conventional female roles (see Hudson, Jacot and Sheldrake, 1973). It is possible that they do so for biological reasons, but such patterns of personality can as easily be explained in terms that are psychological or social.

38 Harris (1978). The British chess master Alexander once claimed in conversation that players of the highest rank were distinguished by qualities that were not intellectual but 'moral'.

CHAPTER 6: PASSIONATE ABSTRACTION

1 Keynes (1951), p. 311.
2 Storr (1985a, 1988).
3 Christopher Zeeman has remarked on dissimilarities among mathematicians, and the different housing problems they have posed as visitors to his Warwick symposia. 'The geometers and the topologists generally all bring their families and have lots of parties and often stay longer than they intended. The algebraists are very precise, often come alone, without their families, on precisely the day they said they would three years previously. And the analysts are totally unreliable. They say they'll bring their families and then they turn up with their mistresses, and they never come on the days they said they would.' They are, he concludes, 'completely different psychological types' (Wolpert and Richards, 1988, p. 56).

   It is just such effects which a differential approach allows us to unpack, and which a correlative approach obscures. If individuals are drawn to a given discipline (like mathematics) by one psychological factor or set of factors (those associated, say, with the wound), one would expect them – once established within that discipline – subsequently to differentiate themselves in terms of other psychological factors (their obsessionality or bohemianism, say). It is for this reason that psychological differences are often more marked between specialities within a discipline than between one discipline and another.

4 Skinner (1976).
5 Ibid., pp. 241, 256.
6 Ibid., p. 288.
7 Skinner (1961), p. 420.
8 Skinner (1976), p. 42.
9 Ibid., p. 270.
10 Ibid., p. 269.

11 Ibid., p. 43.

12 Ibid., p. 47.

13 Skinner (1961).

14 Two years after becoming a graduate student at Harvard, Skinner had written an intriguing paper about the historical origins of the idea of the 'reflex' (Skinner, ibid., p. 319). He identifies Descartes as the first to 'propose a mechanism by which the characteristics of the living organism could plausibly be produced': not a 'mere activated doll' but *la bête machine*. In his *Traité de l'Homme*, Skinner claimed, Descartes treats animals for the first time as systems of reflexes activated by external stimuli. In man, however, Descartes reserved a role for the soul, the human body being a mechanism subject to the soul's intervention. Just as the automata then being created for the French royal fountains by men like Salomon de Caus could be switched on and off by the engineer in charge, so the action of the human machine could be switched on and off by the soul. If Skinner is right, Descartes' dualism of mind and body was in fact more subtle and more modern (though less Skinnerian) than is usually assumed.

15 Wittgenstein (1922, 1958). In isolation, and viewed from outside philosophy, the philosophical stance expressed in the *Tractatus* is philistine. (If all true statements are matters of fact, what becomes of the truths of art?) In contrast, the *Investigations* place the philosopher in the hands of the psychoanalyst and critic. (If meanings reside in uses, it requires the psychoanalyst and critic to establish what hidden freights of half-conscious and unconscious meanings the language, for instance, of the dream report or sonnet can in principle convey.)

16 Hugh-Jones (1989).

17 Hudson (1968).

18 Hugh-Jones (1989), p. 28.

19 Sulloway (1979), p. 181.

20 Wisdom (1953).

21 In Jean-Paul Sartre's thought, Stern (1966) points out, there is evidence of an abiding distaste for 'stickiness'; more generally a preoccupation with sensations of nausea and disgust. The antithesis between purity and dirt has in addition, of course, both social and cultural dimensions (Douglas, 1970).

22 In research on the heritability of intelligence, genetic explanations are at present inextricably confounded with environmental ones. Although identical twins are sometimes separated at birth and reared apart, the homes in which they are reared may in pertinent respects be alike. There are no short-cuts in resolving this problem, because, in advance, we have no means of knowing which environmental factors are pertinent, which not.

23 The term 'g' was originally coined by Spearman. Gould (1984) expounds the historical shift among psychologists from measuring brains and brain cases to measuring minds; spells out the assumptions implicit in the various forms of factor analysis; and distinguishes the attitudes towards 'g' which experts like Spearman, Thurstone, Guilford, Thomson and Burt held.

Unlike that of birth order, the predictive efficiency of tests high in 'g' drops off sharply as samples become more highly selected. In a roomful of able sixteen-year-olds, as a result, a knowledge of each individual's scores on tests high in 'g' is of little or no use in predicting what level of academic performance that individual will subsequently reach (Hudson, 1966).

24 Burt (1937), p. 10; Jensen (1969).

25 Jensen (1969). The illogicality of this argument was two-fold. (1) If consistent, it should have applied to all children of relatively low IQ, irrespective of race, not

to all black children irrespective of their IQs. (2) Nothing about the level of educational provision follows from the fact that (for whatever reason) some children have lower IQs than others. A prudent policy might well commit more resources to the education of children the lower the IQ scores they achieve.

The violence of the rows surrounding race and IQ was hard to picture for anyone not caught up in them. So too was the imperviousness of the protagonists to the ordinary processes of argument and inference (Hudson, 1970).

26 Serebriakoff (1965).

27 Argumentative technique plays a vital part in the maintenance of scientific visions. Burt relied on letters; courteous but of oppressive length and frequency. Skinner's method was particularly effective. If taken to task, he would repeat his original position until his interlocutor lost heart. In a lunch-time conversation, one of us once put it to Skinner that while his teaching machines were based on the principle of continuous reinforcement, he elsewhere advocated the principle of intermittent reinforcement. Patiently, he redescribed his teaching machines until silence ensued.

28 The debate about whether Burt wittingly cheated or was merely grossly careless rumbles on (Hearnshaw, 1979, Joynson, 1989).

29 Westfall (1973).

30 Koestler (1959), p. 225.

31 Ibid., pp. 225-38.

32 Ibid., p. 232.

33 Ibid., p. 247.

34 Ibid., p. 333. We have not tracked it to source, but rumour has it that Kepler, too, adjusted his observations to fit the solution he had reached.

35 Some of the more spectacular scientific frauds are documented by Broad and Wade (1985).

36 Morally, the position has a further layer of complexity. Many of science's prime movers are prime movers precisely because, in them, the usual 'male' ambivalences are heightened to an exceptional degree. (At root, what they seek is personal: not order but *their* order – order which has the stamp of their own identity upon it.) Their needs express themselves not only in luminous visions like Kepler's, but in rash loyalties, inexplicable lapses of judgement, tiresome personal quirks, and apparently pointless acts of public and private delinquency. Such people are not in the ordinary sense fraudulent or psychopathic. Their transgressions are less like forging cheques, more like writing on lavatory walls. Within the fabric of a scholarly discipline, such energies are none the less hard to contain.

37 Brown (1959, 1966), McClelland (1963). Drawing on Freud's later theorising, Brown concluded that science and technology are expressions of the death instinct; the impulse to return life to the peace of the grave.

38 Hudson and Jacot (1986). Latour and Woolgar (1979) demonstrate the steps whereby Guillemin and Schally's view about the chemical structure of TRF came to be accepted as correct. The idea that TRF was the peptide Pyro-Glu-His-Pro-NH_2 (as opposed to Pyro-Glu-His-Pro-OH, say, or Pyro-Glu-His-Pro-OMe) moved from being a claim to being the truth at the point at which Guillemin and Schally's competitors could find no other way of interpreting the experimental data then available. Accepted as crucial was the evidence of the mass spectrometer, in which TRF and a synthetic version of the peptide Pyro-Glu-His-Pro-NH_2 proved indistinguishable.

39 Latour and Woolgar (1979), p. 119.

40 Ibid., p. 118. It is hard to imagine women scientists of equal distinction - Dorothy Hodgkin, for example - speaking of their research in such terms. She describes the analogies between chemistry and crystallography and her childhood experience of archaeology in trans-Jordan with her parents: 'you're finding what's there and you aren't controlling your situation. You're finding what's there and then trying to make sense of what you find' (Wolpert and Richards, 1988, p. 79). As Keller (1985) suggests, this freedom – to find what's there and then make sense of it – may be one of the attitudes that gifted women bring to science. It is perhaps not coincidental that the recently emerging maps of the cosmos's sponge-like structure should also be the work of a woman, Margaret Geller. A woman's attention to 'what's there' – strangely lacking, in our experience, in many male engineers – could well have shortcircuited, too, the buffoonery which allowed NASA to put an incorrectly engineered mirror into space in the Hubble telescope.

41 Sampson (1977), p. 34.

42 Ibid., p. 35.

43 Jones (1974), Regis (1989). Our own observations and reflections as visitors to the Institute for Advanced Study in 1974-5 will, we hope, find their way into print in due course.

44 Regis (1989). There is a special place for the mysterious in mathematics, but only once formal mastery has been established beyond question, as the mystique attached to Gödel's incompleteness theorem shows. After an era of heroic experimentation, theoretical physics, too, seems to be moving in the direction of the fanciful, Murray Gell-Mann's 'quark' being a harbinger in this respect. Its name deriving from James Joyce's *Finnegans Wake*, the quark is an elementary particle of which experimenters have never found a trace.

45 Jones (1974), p. 42.

46 Regis (1989), p. 99.

CHAPTER 7: MALE VICES

1 Sexual intimacy, if we are right, offers the adult woman no equivalent fantasy of magic return. In comparison, she is freer to bend sexual experience to her own purposes. At one extreme, she can enjoy the *frisson* of being objectified – of being treated as an intensely sexually desirable object. At another, she can treat sex as a price she is willing to pay for physical comforts. There are dangers for the woman too, of course, but they are of a different order from those confronting the male. The most pressing is probably that she will commit herself to a relationship with someone who perceives her, apparently quite arbitrarily, as desirable and dangerous by turns.

2 Criminal Statistics, England and Wales (1990), p. 99. Here, as elsewhere, the official statistics are hard to interpret with any precision, 'sexual offences' being defined to include, for instance, abduction.

3 Bancroft (1983). While rape is a sexual act and constitutes a release of sexual energy, it characteristically serves non-sexual as well as sexual purposes. It can express dislike or hate; it can fulfil a controlling or 'policing' function; and, in the case of gang rapes, it can affirm a sense of camaraderie or of homosexual bonding. Even in coercive sexual intercourse (as opposed to forthright rape), the evidence suggests that the act rarely has voluptuous sexual pleasure as its goal.

4 Black and Kaplan (1988).

5 Criminal Statistics, p. 73. Regrettably, the data are not broken down in a way

that makes it possible to relate the sex of the victim to the sex of the killer. Hence one cannot tell how many of the male victims killed by 'spouse or lover' – in 1989, 10 per cent of a total of 342 – were in fact homosexual.

6 Mailer (1980). This book, like Capote's *In Cold Blood*, is an exercise in 'faction' – in the imaginative recreation of literal fact. As far as we know, no division of conceptual principle separates faction from biography, from the recreations of the skilled clinician or naturalistic novelist, or from the seemingly impersonal endeavours of the theoretician. All are (1) interpretative enterprises, in that they seek to impose order on otherwise chaotic human material, and thereby establish the truth; (2) susceptible to stereotyping and make-believe; and (3) invitations to the practitioner to explore his autobiography at one remove. In practice, the linkages between the worlds of fact, faction and fiction are sometimes close and disconcerting: for example, Ralph Greenson was Marilyn Monroe's psychoanalyst at the time of her death (Mailer, 1973).

7 Capote (1966).

8 Mailer (1980, p. 378) quotes part of a psychological assessment of Gilmore made after his arrest. This specifies a level of intelligence well above the threshold scientists must cross if they are to follow successful careers in research (Roe, 1953; MacKinnon, 1962). It speaks of a '35-year-old Caucasian single male . . . of superior intellect'. His 'vocabulary IQ' is given as 140, his 'abstraction IQ' as 120, and his 'full-scale IQ' as 129 – two standard deviations, that is to say, above the national average.

9 Ibid., p. 691.

10 Ibid., p. 405.

11 Ibid., p. 836.

12 Ibid., p. 488. All this is a far cry from the unguarded love Nicole offered in return: 'You have all my love. i believe that you know. And i know i have yours. if you die . . . so soon . . . i will know and feel your soul wrap around my thots and this soul who loves you so deeply. Goodbye now my love/Till then and forever/No matter where i walk/ill walk alone/Till again im by your side' (p. 848).

13 Kinsey et al. (1953), p. 683.

14 Brown (1986), p. 328.

15 Bell and Weinberg (1978).

16 Ibid., p. 308. Apparently objective, such survey data leave many methodological doubts unresolved, as the AIDS epidemic has recently made clear: see, e.g., Anderson and May (1988).

17 Bell and Weinberg (1978), p. 244. The driven nature of such behaviour is echoed in recent British evidence. Hunt et al. (1991) shows that rates of risk-taking among homosexual men, having dropped in response to the threat of AIDS, have once again risen. Both the proportion of men in their cohort having anal intercourse and the number of those men's partners increased significantly between 1988 and 1989.

18 Simenon (1958), Bresler (1983).

19 Simenon married twice and had four children. But, his biographer suggests, he had only two real relationships with members of the opposite sex, his mother and his daughter; both unsatisfactory. Simenon's daughter committed suicide in her twenties. Emotionally and also perhaps physically, their relationship was incestuous (Bresler, 1983, pp. 244-51).

20 Mailer (1973), p. 18.

21 Rosen (1979).

22 Bancroft (1983), p. 185.
23 Comfort (1990), p. 352. The semantics of terms like 'abnormality' and 'perversion' are complex, and the temptation is either to reject them altogether, or to give them a quasi-legal basis in the notion of consent. Following this second path, homosexuality can be seen as normal if it occurs between consenting adults; abnormal if it does not. Pedophilia, on the same argument, must always be seen as abnormal because children cannot properly be said to consent. Although helpful as a first approximation, this line of reasoning soon falters. It takes account neither of the driven (and in that sense involuntary) nature of much sexual behaviour, nor of the distorted states of mind that this behaviour often expresses. Just as there are depraved sexual acts between consenting adults, so there are innocent ones between adults and those regarded in English law as minors (between a Pakistani husband in his twenties, for example, and his wife still in her early teens). In the field of sexual behaviour, issues of motive cannot be avoided.
24 Rycroft (1972), p. 116.
25 Stoller (1975).
26 Stoller (1985b).
27 Khan (1979).
28 Grunberger (1989). Grunberger reports a homosexual male, the willing victim of a particularly disquieting perversion, as experiencing 'a deep, exhilarating sense of communion, a sort of complicity, filled with fervour and love'. The sinister concomitants of such 'highly spiritualised feeling' express themselves, Grunberger suggests, not in experiences of pain and disgust, but in subsequent impulses of disloyalty and betrayal.
29 Hopkins (1984). Many empirically-minded investigators, among them Kinsey (1953), assume that men condition more easily than women to the psychological stimuli associated with sexual pleasure. An adjacent line of argument claims that men are more perverse than women only in that they are more literal-minded than women, and more likely, therefore, to act their fantasies out. It is this literal-minded, objectifying tendency, allied to a sense of agency, which we see as the wound's legacy.

    The orthodox psychoanalytic view is that 'fetishism is clearly associated with a very severe castration complex' (Greenacre, 1979, p. 83). To our eyes implausibly, the penis is thought of as detached – whether from the female body or the male – and as serving in its detached state as model and precursor for any object (people, fetishes, works of art) which carry an intense erotic charge. The behavioural and the psychoanalytic views, it should be noted, are by no means mutually exclusive. Men may condition more easily to sexual stimuli than women precisely because they are vulnerable to the forms of anxiety associated with fantasies of castration.

    It is our impression, supported by the kind of clinical material revealed in Hopkins' study of Sylvia, and – altogether more obliquely, by experimental studies of cognition in infants (e.g. Bower, 1989) – that perversions can take their fully-fledged form in the imagination of quite small children. Subsequently repressed, it is these thought-formulae which resurface in adult life.
30 Stewart (1971), p. 25.
31 Far from being natural and unproblematic, the sequence which leads men and women from desire to seduction, from seduction to intercourse, and from intercourse to further desire, is one which admits complexity at every stage. The phenomenon is demonstrated in John DeLillo's *The Names* (1983). The narrator's

coercive intercourse with Janet Ruffing means nothing and leads to nothing: within DeLillo's text it serves as a microcosm of the tension between the over-civilised and the barbaric around which the book as a whole rotates. When inter-course finally takes place, in the dark, against a wall, each urges the other 'into a rhythm and a need'. DeLillo's words are as usual carefully chosen. This is not an instance of two cups of desire at last brimming over. After the overwrought toings and froings of its preliminaries, it is the act itself which creates desire. First the rhythm, then the need. Sexual intercourse is the only means available to either party of bringing an otherwise dangerously anomalous social episode to an end.

At present, psychology has no language with which to do such phenomena justice. In standard scientific parlance – though the idiom is more than usually comic – what is now needed is a reconciliation between the 'bottom-up' and 'top-down'. The 'bottom-up' view is that of the radical sociobiologists, who assume that any subtleties of experience individuals may associate with their sex-ual actions are epiphenomenal. Like marks on a sandy beach, they are swept away at the first contact with biology's incoming tide. The 'top-down' view is that of the poststructuralists and deconstructors. They hold that our experience only becomes available to us when constructed in the light of one of the dis-courses our culture provides for this purpose. In and of themselves, our bodies and their needs are meaningless. There can be no such thing as a body until a re-levant discourse provides us with the concept 'body'. No such thing as sex. No such thing as a person. There is nothing, in other words, 'outside the text' – apart, of course, from another text.

The 'top-down' language of the deconstructors is neatly caught, for those un-familiar with it, by the characters in David Lodge's *Nice Work* (1989). As Lodge has noticed, the exalted and the demotic here operate side by side. 'When I was younger', his heroine Robyn Penrose concedes, 'I allowed myself to be con-structed by the discourse of romantic love for a while, yes.' But 'that was just a fuck', she also informs her hapless middle-aged lover, 'nothing more or less' (pp. 293, 301). Sociobiology, poststructuralism and the demotic all have this in com-mon, then. Each is a polemic against the subject-matter of psychology as tradi-tionally understood: the belief, in this instance, that sex is a venue within which men and women, if they see fit, can exercise to the full their capacity for aesthetic and moral discrimination.

32 Bowie (1987), p. 118. 'There is no such thing', Lacan also declares, 'as a sexual relationship' (Bowie, 1991, p. 154). In doing so, he recognises the otherness to which sexual intercourse leaves its participants exposed.

33 Lucie-Smith (1970), p. 142.

34 Although we rely on it here, 'unacknowledged' is not quite the right word. Or, rather, it becomes so only when allowed wider connotations of otherness: those of difference; of the strange or alien; of the denied or repressed; and of the feral, barbarous or potentially engulfing.

35 Diagrams of a similar form are used in Hudson (1982, 1990b). The present one, it is worth noting, does not map neatly on to the Freudian distinctions between conscious, preconscious and unconscious. The most interesting phenomena of erotic life – shrouded in embarrassment, joked about obliquely, disowned in one context but boasted about in another – sprawl across all three.

Diagrams like ours create not only a traffic but also a *meta-traffic*. Consonances and dissonances arise not just between one self and another self, but between pairs of selves – that is to say, between relationships. Where the diagram permits six traffics between selves, it also permits meta-traffics between pairs (and trios) of selves. The patterns are those familiar from match-stick puzzles.

36 Stoller (1974).

37 Such discoveries are, we assume, 'couple-specific': they follow not from the qualities of either partner considered as an individual, but from the nature of their 'chemistry' when joined.

   The individuation of sexual experience has nothing to do with the bodily postures recommended in sex manuals. It relates, rather, to trust. Trust in turn depends, we believe, on the discovery of a symbiosis which echoes the individual's infantile experience, but is categorically segregated from that experience's more alarming reverberations. At the heart of sexual boredom and promiscuity in the male, in other words, is the fear of intimacy that is engulfing or incestuous.

CHAPTER 8: BEYOND DESIRE

1 Our assumption, to repeat the point made in Chapter 5, is not that men are necessarily better than women at musical composition, but that, in the hands of gifted women, musical composition may take distinctively new forms.

2 It has been said of Beethoven's *Grosse Fugue* that 'What grips the listener is the dramatic experience of forcing – for there is frequently a sense of violence in this mastery – two themes which have, by nature, nothing in common, to breed and produce a race of giants, episodes or variations that have no parallel in musical history' (Storr, 1985b, p. 56, quoting Martin Cooper).

3 Hudson (1990b). Male scientists not only describe work they find gratifying as 'beautiful', but also as 'sweet' or 'sexy'. They distinguish the beautiful from the merely 'pretty'; and dismiss as 'tarted-up' work that is empty or pretentious. The language could be that of a sculptor or an architect.

4 Our claim, in a nutshell, is that: (1) The creative arts explore and exploit ambiguity and have a living past; (2) the scholarly arts avoid ambiguity but, especially in the form of seminal texts, have a past that remains in significant respects alive; and (3) the sciences shun ambiguity and have pasts that are for all practical purposes of current research inert. If, for whatever reason, a discipline needs to shift its perceived position in this thought-landscape, it is with these two dimensions that play is made. So in the Oxford of the 1950s, both the psychologists and the philosophers were under urgent political pressure to appear rigorous; and their students were therefore required to make only sketchy contacts with historical sources (Hudson, 1972).

5 At the level of the metaphors that organise experience rather than of experience itself, what the successful artist exploits is a parallel between two sorts of imagined space: that in the sexual act within which erotic experience spontaneously individuates itself, and that in a work of art which enables ambiguities of perceived meaning to proliferate and resonate. Equally of course – at least by implication – there exists a parallel between the experience of the sexual act as driven and repetitive, and science's commitment to create symbolic formats in which ambiguities of meaning cannot arise.

   If science is conceived as an investigative engine which marches from hypothesis to prediction, from prediction to observation, and back again to further hypothesis, there is no opportunity for the natural world to 'answer back'. It is imagined space – the equivalent of Keats' 'negative capability' (Rycroft, 1979) – which allows the practitioner to 'find what's there'; and it is the dialectic between desire as structure-creating and desire as space-creating, we believe, which underlies feminist hopes for less driven and less colonial ways of doing science.

6 Freud (Standard Edition, 21), p. 177. Since his death, the relation of psychoanalytically inspired texts to works of art has undergone a shift (Wright, 1984). In some cases, still, the role of theory remains straightforwardly explanatory, as in natural science. In others – as with Lacan and Barthes – the text stands side by side with the work of art, each destablilising (and, in doing so, elucidating) the other. The 'best hope' that Lacan offers for this uneasy relation is that each should serve, not as an obliging mirror, but as 'an insistent and disobliging "other scene"' (Bowie, 1987, p. 163).

7 In preparing the book's illustrations, our roles have been reversed, BJ drawing and LH editing. As anyone who has collaborated knows, partnership in such ventures depends on the harnessing together of dissimilar and sometimes mutually antipathetic skills. Like marriage or charioteering, it has its dangerous moments; and, quite suddenly, can go irretrievably wrong.

8 Hudson (1982, 1990b). Each of the six traffics between Artist, Model, Image and Spectator are shown there to harbour surprises and, in some cases, paradox.

9 Hobhouse (1988), pp. 94 and 119. Earlier in his career, Matisse often depicted his models realistically and voluptuously; but, among the modernists, was relatively unusual in doing so. Picasso, in contrast, frequently appears to have distorted for distortion's sake; his painting, as he himself put it, 'a sum of destructions'.

10 Campbell (1981), p. 205. Although Brassai, a friend of Picasso and the surrealists, and a painter before he became a photographer, would have enjoyed a special status in Matisse's eyes, the relation of painter to photographer would have been reminiscent of those between a scientist and a laboratory technician, or between a statesman and a journalist. Those were the days when the photographer could expect to have his work published anonymously, a fate which men like Brassai bitterly resented. A Hungarian born in Transylvania at the turn of the century, Brassai lived in Paris from the mid-1920s. One of a series of portraits of famous arrtists in their studios, this photograph appears to have been taken on commission for *Harper's Bazaar*.

11 Viewed schematically, the ideas underpinning our argument about the wound and its sequelae arrange themselves into conjunctions; not neat and unequivocal arrangements, like pieces of machinery, but complex and indeterminate, the conceptual equivalent of personal relationships. (As people move from relationship to relationship, so too do ideas.) Two conjunctions have been especially influential. The first was shown in Chapter 3, note 30. There, the distinction between the perceptions of *difference-in-similarity* and of *similarity-in-difference* was set beside the distinction between two imaginative preoccupations, those with *things-as-people* and with *people-as-things*. The second conjunction, outlined here, places side by side cognate diagrams and the traffics they permit:

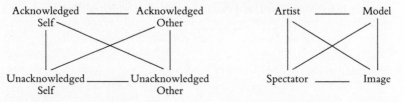

Far from being mutually insulated, the two conjunctions – the one shown in Chapter 3 and the one shown here – reverberate fruitfully upon one another.

As those who enjoy them already know, even the humblest of diagrams have their secret lives. When ours are set side by side as they are here, it is possible to see their elements as having undergone an interesting shift; one that helps illuminate what leads a man to paint or photograph the woman he desires as opposed to having sexual intercourse with her. It is possible to see the *Acknowledged* and *Unacknowledged Selves* of the left-hand diagram amalgamating to become the *Artist* in the right-hand one; and the *Acknowledged* and *Unacknowledged Other* of the left-hand diagram as amalgamating to become the *Model*. The position previous occupied by the *Unacknowledged Other* is now occupied by the *Image*, and that previously occupied by the *Unacknowledged Self* is now occupied by the *Spectator*. The last of these changes hints at a distinctive feature of the artist's (and especially the erotic artist's) psychological development: that in order to regulate the turmoil desire creates in him, he becomes the spectator of that desire. But, lingering close, he learns to execute the steps that turn eroticised being into spectator, and spectator back again into eroticised being. It is precisely the dissociations and objectifications implicit in manoeuvres of this kind that the wound equips him to perform.

12 In perhaps the most remarkable of his books, *Sexual Excitement*, Stoller describes and analyses just such a system of fantasy. It was reported to him by his patient 'Belle'. Twenty-four years old at the beinning of her analysis, 'quiet, intelligent, attractive, well-groomed, feminine', Belle conveyed 'a slightly addled yet refreshing innocence; soft, round, dreamy erotism; an unbounded focus on males, romance, silken garments, flowers and bees, bosoms, bare behinds, and babies'. This outward gentleness was sharply at odds, though, with the contents of her erotic imagination. A year or so into her analysis, her chief erotic reverie began to surface, and Stoller devotes much of his book to making sense of it. This reverie is dominated by 'The Director', a cruel, Nazi-like male. In it, Belle is raped by a stallion that has been roused to a frenzy by a mare placed at a safe distance. Arranged around in a circle, there stands an audience of men masturbating, ignoring as they do so one another, Director, Belle, stallion and mare. Aroused to a pitch of helpless sexual excitement, she is humiliated and made to seem ridiculous. What finally drives Belle's excitement out of control is the alteration of some crucially placed detail. The stallion is replaced, for example, by a dirty old man; or a spotlight plays on her own genitals (Stoller, 1979a, p. 59).

13 Bersani (1986). Bersani's elusiveness is intentional. In the modern manner, he wishes to elucidate rather than to be seen to make claims about causes.

14 Barthes (1979), p. 10.

15 Ibid., p. 48.

16 Ibid., p. 134.

17 Barthes (1984). Close attention is paid by literary specialists to the form of Barthes' texts. Little seems to have been made, in comparison, of Barthes' final choice: the photograph, the ground-rules of which are categorically different from those of the sentence (Hudson, 1990b).

18 Schopenhauer, as we have already seen, treated the will as sexual. Pertinent too is the discussion of 'The Line and Light' and 'What is a Picture?' in Lacan (1977). There, in what Bowie (1987, p. 125) aptly describes as 'Lacan's glamorous and conceited prose', the rudiments of a psychology of visual art are juggled before the reader's eyes. The most interesting of the claims Lacan makes there – '*what I look at is never what I wish to see*' – reflects, if we have read him correctly, an inescapable alienation of experience from desire (inescapable, because rooted in the infant's initial step from symbiotic intimacy into the 'Symbolic Order'). In dis-

tinguishing *punctum* from *studium*, Barthes suggests that this alienation is not inescapable after all.

19 Barthes (1984), p. 26.

20 Ibid., pp. 26-7.

21 Ibid., p. 59.

22 Ibid., p. 72.

23 Like certain of his French contemporaries, Derrida (1981) is a determined player of word-games. He distinguishes between *différence* spelt with an 'e' and *différance* spelt with an 'a' (pp. 25-8), the former seeming to mean roughly what one might expect it to mean, the latter signifying a more fundamental and philosophically inclusive 'process of differentation' (p. 101). Derrida puns, too, from the notion of a text to that of a textile. When we read, what we meet, he suggests, is a weaving that is itself continually interwoven with other weavings. Each consists of traces which are themselves both displaced and displacing. 'Dissemination', the 'seminal differance', is based on the 'fortuitous resemblance, the purely simulated common parentage of *seme* (i.e., sign, mark) and *semen*' (p. 45).

In making these puns and points about the process of differentiation, Derrida does not state the obvious: that the detection of differences is formally dependent upon the detection of similarities, and vice versa. Any discriminative system concerned exclusively with differences generates not fruitful diversity but a nominalist wilderness.

24 Gibson (1976).

25 Jeremiah 51:20. Bailey (1970, p. 421) also detects an echo here of God's promise to Noah after the Flood: 'While the earth remaineth, seedtime and harvest, and cold and heat, and summer and winter, and day and night shall not cease' (Genesis 8:22).

26 Hardy (1962), p. 378.

27 Millgate (1985), p. 128. The two sketches are reproduced in Gittings (1980).

28 Hudson (1982), pp. 70-83.

29 To say that a meaning-system like *In Time of 'The Breaking of Nations'* is ambiguous and unstable is to say neither that any one interpretation of it is as defensible as any other, nor that the greater its ambiguity or instability, the greater the work's potential aesthetic merit. Here as elsewhere, the principle of 'good Gestalt' seems to apply, the formal properties of many great works being relatively simple.

CHAPTER 9: A PHOTOGRAPHER, A POET, AND A PAINTER

1 Gass (1976), pp. 86-9. Two blemishes are detectable in Gass's otherwise formidably competent presentation. He fails to grasp that the photograph can contain consciousness in much the way that a sentence can. Likewise, he fails to make it adequately plain that our sexual acts themselves contain consciousness, erotic and non-erotic alike. It is part of the impoverishment of our time that the subtleties of this second phenomenon should be subsumed to adjectives like 'meaningful' and metaphors like 'turn-on'.

Stoller, one of the few psychiatrists and psychoanalysts interested in the relation of sex (as opposed to 'sexuality') to art, sees both as dependent on the search for 'controlled, managed ambiguity' (1975, p. 117).

2 Krauss and Livingston (1986).

3 Maddow (1977), p. 221.

4 Like Gass, Susan Sontag speaks of the camera as a piece of alien technology in-

truding itself upon states of mind properly human. 'To photograph someone is a sublimated murder', she says, 'a soft murder, appropriate to a sad, frightened time' (1979, p. 14). She does not explain why the camera should lie beyond the pale in this way, while the typewriter evidently lies within it. Our own view is that traditional crafts and skills (like those of oil painting), technologies (like the camera), and electronic aids (like the word processor) each crystallise modes of being and patterns of relationship that can otherwise exist only as potentials. The relevant distinctions are highly specific. In photography, a motorised 35mm camera and a 10″ × 8″ plate camera elicit quite different responses from photographer and model alike (Campbell, 1981). In sculpture, carving is both psychologically and aesthetically distinct from clay modelling (Stokes, 1967). In painting, water-colour is different from oils; and using a pallet knife with oil paint is different from using a brush.

The patterns of imaginative cost and benefit attached to specific technologies of representation are a strangely neglected topic. Would Hardy have written *In Time of 'The Breaking of Nations'* if he had had access to a word processor? Or would he too have fallen victim to 'Amstrad's palsy'?

5 Maddow (1977), p. 416.

6 'I was lost and have been ever since,' Weston wrote; but he also said, 'a new and important chapter in my life opened on Sunday afternoon.' In as much as it assumes a narrative divisible into episodes, this was an inauspicious turn of phrase (Wilson, 1977, p. 81).

7 Ibid., p. 13.

8 Sontag (1979), p. 96.

9 Wilson (1977), p. 115. Striking in this respect is the conjunction in Weston's mind of the technical and the intimately sexual. There is a well-known passage in his journal which describes his troubled relationship, a decade before he met Charis, with Tina Modotti, an actress who became a significant photographer in her own right, and also a Trotskyite revolutionary. The style is more than a shade embarrassing, but the implication is crystal clear: 'she leaned against a whitewashed wall – lips quivering – nostrils dilating – eyes heavy with the gloom of unspent rain clouds – I drew close to her – whispered something and kissed her – a tear rolled down her cheek – and then I captured forever the moment – let me see f.8-1/10 sec. K1 filter-panchromatic film – how brutally mechanical and calculated it sounds – yet really how spontaneous and genuine . . . the moment of our mutual emotion was recorded on the silver film – the release of those emotions followed – we passed from the glare of sun on white walls into Tina's darkened room – her olive skin and sombre nipples were revealed beneath a black mantilla – I drew the lace aside . . .' (Maddow, 1977, p. 419).

10 Dunlop (1979), p. 72.

11 Hudson (1982).

12 Farova (1986), pp. 33-4. These quotations from Drtikol's journal are in our translation from the French. Unsurprisingly, these and other entreaties failed. Quite soon thereafter, Drtikol met and married a modern dancer. They had a daughter, but his wife abandoned him for a life of adventure in the Soviet Union. The collapse of his marriage did not greatly distress him, but it proved a watershed of sorts. By then in his forties, it was in the four or five years after its failure that he was to enjoy his period of greatest imaginative vitality.

13 Ibid., p. 54. Evidently, his dismay was specifically sexual, for he goes on: 'For me, there is always something painful about having made love. It is like being a whipped dog but at the same time terribly comic. The woman always gets up

gratified, physically and psychologically. She's satisfied and she has satisfied him. The man on the contrary feels as though he has lost something.' Between writing this and rejecting photography altogether, Drtikol spent some time fashioning highly stylised models of women out of wood and taking photographs of these in place of the live model.

14 Stokes (1967), p. 36.

15 Gittings (1980), p. 203. Hardy has had two excellent recent biographers; Gittings (1978, 1980) the more outspoken, and Millgate (1985) the more comprehensive. While he records evidence damaging to Hardy, Millgate seems constrained to adopt a more balanced view of Hardy's motives than does Gittings.

16 Bailey (1970), p. 444.

17 Gittings (1978).

18 It is unclear whether or not, once he had established it, Hardy believed his own family myth (Byng-Hall, 1979). Also puzzling, especially in the lives of creators of fiction like Hardy and Simenon, is the question of what purposes such obfuscations serve.

19 Stewart (1971), p. 6.

20 Millgate (1985), p. 488.

21 Fermigier (n.d.), p. 9, and Gilot and Lake (1966), p. 263.

22 Hobhouse (1988) says that the couple first met in 1894, when Marthe was sixteen. Heilbrun and Neagu (1987) say that they met in 1893, and give her date of birth as 1869. Nothing is more elusive in the world of art history and criticism, you discover, than hard facts.

23 Heilbrun and Neagu (1987). Until 1906, Bonnard used a pocket Kodak, and only subsequently moved to a larger format. The images of Marthe he used in his graphic work – to illustrate Verlaine, for example – were based, Heilbrun and Neagu indicate, not on enlargements, but on tiny, jewel-like prints, measuring little more than 35mm × 50mm.

24 Hobhouse (1988), p. 38.

25 Ibid., p. 36.

26 This painting is now in Pittsburgh, and Bonnard is said to have spent five years at work on it. Like Hardy, an inveterate tinkerer, Bonnard even altered his paintings furtively as they hung in museums, carrying a miniature paint box around with him for this purpose, and was once arrested in the Musée du Luxembourg as a result.

27 Weston had four children by an earlier marriage, and Wilson two by a subsequent one. The Hardys were childless; and so too, as far as we have been able to discover, were Bonnard and Marthe. One possibility is that these were unconsummated relationships, and were aesthetically productive for this reason.

28 Wilson (1977), pp. 8-11.

29 Ibid., p. 10.

30 Gittings (1980), p. 200.

31 Clark (1966), p. 130. Clark distinguishes between Catholic and Protestant portraiture. Titian, he believes, 'saw each sitter as a type to be enhanced till it reached its perfect state, rather as our bodies will be (the theologians tells us) on the Day of Judgement'. Rembrandt, in contrast, 'saw each sitter as an individual soul whose weaknesses and imperfections must not be disguised' – these weaknesses and imperfections being 'the raw material of grace'.

32 Pafford (1990). Greene's Pandosto, the Triumph of Time was published 1588; The Winter's Tale, one of Shakespeare's last plays, appears to have been written in 1610-11. In 1592, the year of his death, Greene had published an autobiograph-

ical tract, *A Groatsworth of Wit bought with a Million of Repentance*, in which he attacked Shakespeare – the 'upstart Crow, beautified with our Feathers' – on the grounds that he habitually borrowed his fellow playwrights' ideas. Despite this evidence of animosity, Shakespeare follows Greene's version of the plot quite closely. In *Pandosto*, though, the queen dies. It is Shakespeare's invention that re-unites her with her grieving and remorseful husband.

33 *The Winter's Tale*, IV.iv. 140-3.

Allen, I., *Doctors and their Careers*, Policy Studies Institute, 1988.

Altus, W.D., Birth order and its sequelae, *Science*, 151, 44, 1966.

Anderson, R.M. and May, R.M., Epidemiological parameters of HIV transmission, *Nature*, 333, 514, 1988.

Andreas-Salomé, L., *The Freud Journal*, Hogarth, 1965.

Aries, E.J. and Olver, R.R., Sex differences in the development of a separate sense of self during infancy, *Psychology of Women Quarterly*, 9, 515, 1985.

Bailey, J.O., *The Poetry of Thomas Hardy*, University of North Carolina Press, 1970.

Baker, C., *Ernest Hemingway*, Collins, 1969.

Baker, C., *Hemingway, Selected Letters 1917-1961*, Granada, 1981.

Balfour, I., *Famous Diamonds*, Collins, 1987.

Bancroft, J., *Human Sexuality and its Problems*, Churchill Livingstone, 1983.

Barthes, R., *A Lover's Discourse*, Cape, 1979.

Barthes, R., *Camera Lucida*, Fontana, 1984.

Bateson, P., Biological approaches to the study of behavioural development, *International Journal of Behavioural Development*, 10, 1, 1987.

Bateson, P. and Hinde, R.A., Developmental changes in sensitivity to experience, in *Sensitive Periods in Development*, ed. M.M. Bornstein, Erlbaum, 1987.

Battersby, C., *Gender and Genius*, Women's Press, 1989.

Beardslee, D.C. and O'Dowd, D.D., Students and the occupational world, in *The American College*, ed. N. Sanford, Wiley, 1962.

Bell, A.P. and Weinberg, M.S., *Homosexualities*, Simon & Schuster, 1978.

Bem, S.L., Probing the promise of androgyny, in *Beyond Sex-Role Stereotypes*, ed. A.G. Kaplan and J.P. Bean, Little, Brown, 1976.

Benbow, C.P., Sex differences in mathematical reasoning ability in intellectually talented preadolescents, *Behavioral and Brain Sciences*, 11, 169, 1988.

Beral, V. et al., Is risk of Kaposi's sarcoma in AIDS patients in Britain increased if sexual partners came from United States or Africa?, *British Medical Journal*, 302, 624, 1991.

Bersani, L., *The Freudian Body*, Columbia University Press, 1986.

Black, D. and Kaplan, T., Father kills mother, *British Journal of Psychiatry*, 153, 624, 1988.

Bloom, B.S., *Stability and Change in Human Characteristics*, Wiley, 1964.

Bower, T.G.R., *The Rational Infant*, Freeman, 1989.

Bowie, M., *Freud, Proust and Lacan*, Cambridge University Press, 1987.

Bowie, M., *Lacan*, Fontana, 1991.

Bowlby, J., *The Making and Breaking of Affectional Bonds*, Tavistock, 1979.

Bresler, F., *The Mystery of Georges Simenon*, Heinemann/Quixote, 1983.

Broad, W. and Wade, N., *Betrayers of the Truth*, Oxford University Press, 1985.

Bronfenbrenner, U., *Two Worlds of Childhood*, Russell Sage, 1970.

Brown, N.O., *Life Against Death*, Wesleyan University Press, 1959.

Brown, N.O., *Love's Body*, Random House, 1966.

Brown, R., *Social Psychology*, Free Press, 1965.

Brown, R., *Social Psychology, The Second Edition*, Free Press, 1986.

Bruton, E., *Legendary Gems*, NAG Press, 1986.

Building Industry Council, *Educational Futures for the Construction Industry*, Proceedings of the first heads of courses meeting, 24 May 1989.

Burt, C., *The Backward Child*, University of London Press, 1937.

Butler, J., *Gender Trouble*, Routledge, 1990.

Byng-Hall, J., Re-editing family mythology during family therapy, *Journal of Family Therapy*, 1, 103-16, 1979.

Campbell, B., *World Photography*, Hamlyn, 1981.

Capote, T., *In Cold Blood*, Penguin, 1966.

Carlsmith, L., Effect of early father-absence on scholastic aptitude, *Harvard Educational Review*, 34, 3, 1964.

Chodorow, N.J., *The Reproduction of Mothering*, University of California Press, 1978.

Chodorow, N.J., What is the relation between psychoanalytic feminism and the psychoanalytic psychology of women?, in *Theoretical Perspectives on Sexual Difference*, ed. D.L. Rhode, Yale University Press, 1990.

Clark, K., *The Nude*, Penguin, 1960.

Clark, K., *Rembrandt and the Italian Renaissance*, Murray, 1966.

Coltheart, M., Hull, E. and Slater, D., Sex differences in imagery and reading, *Nature*, 253, 438, 1975.

Comfort, A., Has sexual behaviour really changed with time? *Journal of Obstetrics and Gynaecology*, 10, 351, 1990.

Cormack, M. and Sheldrake, P.F., *Cognitive Bias and Patterns in Dream Recall*, Occasional Paper 18, Centre for Research in the Educational Sciences, Edinburgh University, 1974.

Crick, F.H.C. and Mitchison, G., The function of dream sleep, *Nature*, 304, 111, 1983.

Criminal Statistics, England and Wales (1989), HMSO, 1990.

Critchley, M. and Critchley, E.A., *Dyslexia Defined*, Heinemann, 1978.

D'Andrade, R., Sex differences and cultural institutions, in *The Development of Sex Differences*, ed. E.E. Maccoby, Tavistock, 1967.

Darwin, C., *The Descent of Man*, Murray, 1887.

DeLillo, D., *The Names*, Vintage, 1983.

Derrida, J., *Positions*, trans. A. Bass, Athlone, 1981.

Douglas, M., *Purity and Danger*, Penguin, 1970.

Dunlop, I., *Degas*, Thames & Hudson, 1979.

Ellmann, R., Freud and literary biography, in *Freud and the Humanities*, ed. P. Horden, Duckworth, 1985.

Erikson, E., *Childhood and Society*, Norton, 1963.

Erikson, E., *Identity*, Faber, 1968.

Farova, A., *Frantisek Drtikol*, Schirmer/Mosel, 1986.

Fermigier, A., *Bonnard*, Thames & Hudson, n.d.

Feyerabend, P., *Against Method*, Verso, 1975.

Freud, S., *The Interpretation of Dreams*, Standard Edition, ed. J. Strachey, Hogarth, 4-5, 1953-74.

Freud, S., *'Civilised' Sexual Morality and Modern Nervous Illness*, Standard Edition, 9.

Freud, S., *Leonardo da Vinci and a Memory of his Childhood*, Standard Edition, 11.

Freud, S., *A Child is Being Beaten*, Standard Edition, 17.

Freud, S., *Dostoevsky and Parricide*, Standard Edition, 21.

Gass, W., *On Being Blue*, Godine, 1976.

Geschwind, N. and Galaburda, A.M., *Cerebral Dominance*, Harvard University Press, 1987.

Gibson, J. (ed.), *The Complete Poems of Thomas Hardy*, Macmillan, 1976.

Gilot, F. and Lake, C., *Life with Picasso*, Penguin, 1966.

Gilvarry, E., Selection changes to be urged, *Law Society's Gazette*, 6, 20 February, 1991.

Gittings, R., *Young Thomas Hardy*, Penguin, 1978.

Gittings, R., *The Older Hardy*, Penguin, 1980.

Goffman, E., *The Presentation of Self in Everyday Life*, Doubleday, 1959.

Gould, S.J., *The Mismeasurement of Man*, Penguin, 1984.

Greenacre, P., *Trauma, Growth and Personality*, International Universities Press, 1952.

Greenacre, P., Fetishism, in *Sexual Deviation*, ed., I. Rosen, Oxford University Press, 1979.

Greenson, R.R., Dis-identifying from mother: its special importance for the boy, *International Journal of Psycho-Analysis*, 49, 370, 1968.

Gregory, R.L. (ed.), Japanese concept of mind, *The Oxford Companion to the Mind*, Oxford University Press, 1987.

Grunberger, B., *New Essays on Narcissism*, Free Association Books, 1989.

Guilford, J.P., Creativity, *American Psychologist*, 5, 444, 1950.

Hall, R., *Dear Dr Stopes*, Deutsch, 1978.

Hardy, F.E., *Life of Thomas Hardy*, Macmillan, 1962.

Hare-Mustin, R.T. and Maracek, J., *Making a Difference*, Yale University Press, 1990.

Harlow, H.F. and Harlow, M.K., The affectional systems, in *Behaviour of*

Non-human Primates, ed. A.M. Schrier, H.F. Harlow and F. Stollnitz, Academic Press, 1965.

Harris, L.J., Sex differences in spatial ability, in *Asymmetrical Function of the Brain*, ed. M. Kinsbourne, Cambridge University Press, 1978.

Hearnshaw, L.S., *Cyril Burt: Psychologist*, Hodder & Stoughton, 1979.

Heilbrun, F. and Neagu, P., *Pierre Bonnard, Photographe*, Réunion des Musées Nationaux, 1987.

Held, R., Perception and its neuronal mechanisms, *Cognition*, 33, 139, 1989.

Henry, J., *Culture Against Man*, Tavistock, 1966.

Hibbard, H., *Masterpieces of Western Sculpture*, Chartwell, n.d.

Hicks, R., *A History of the 35mm Still Camera*, Focal Press, 1984.

Hinde, R.A., *Individuals, Relationships and Culture*, Cambridge University Press, 1987.

Hinde, R.A. and Stevenson-Hinde, J., Implications of a relationships approach for the study of gender differences, *Infant Mental Health Journal*, 8, 221, 1987.

Hirschman, A., *Shifting Involvements*, Princeton University Press, 1982.

Hobhouse, J., *The Bride Stripped Bare*, Cape, 1988.

Hodges, A., *Alan Turing: the Enigma*, Burnett, 1983.

Hopkins, J., The probable role of trauma in a case of foot and shoe fetishism, *International Review of Psychoanalysis*, 11, 79, 1984.

Hudson, L., The undergraduate academic record of Fellows of the Royal Society, *Nature*, 182, 1326, 1958.

Hudson, L., A differential test of arts/science aptitude, *Nature*, 186, 413, 1960.

Hudson, L., *Contrary Imaginations*, Methuen, 1966.

Hudson, L., The stereotypical scientist, *Nature*, 213, 228, 1967(a).

Hudson, L., Arts and sciences: the influence of stereotypes on language, *Nature*, 214, 968, 1967(b).

Hudson, L., *Frames of Mind*, Methuen, 1968.

Hudson, L., Intelligence, race, and selective attention to data, *Race*, 12, 283, 1970.

Hudson, L., *The Cult of the Fact*, Cape, 1972.

Hudson, L., Fertility in the arts and sciences, *Science Studies*, 3, 305, 1973.

Hudson, L., *Human Beings*, Cape, 1975.

Hudson, L., The singularity of talent, in *Individuality in Learning*, ed. S. Messick, Jossey-Bass, 1976.

Hudson, L., Picking winners; a case study in the recruitment of research students, *New Universities Quarterly*, 88, Winter, 1977.

Hudson, L., *Bodies of Knowledge*, Weidenfeld & Nicolson, 1982.

Hudson, L., *The Great Miscegenation*, Society of Industrial Artists and Designers, 1983.

Hudson, L., Psychology, in *Social Sciences Encyclopaedia*, ed. A. Kuper and J. Kuper, Routledge, 1985(a).

Hudson, L., *Night Life*, Weidenfeld & Nicolson, 1985(b).

Hudson, L., Review of Joynson's *'The Burt Affair'*, *Times Literary Supple-*

ment, 3 November 1989.

Hudson, L., *AIDS, Paradoxical Attitudes, and Professional Education,* paper given to the conference on Supervision as a Way of Learning, Tavistock Clinic, London, 2 August 1990(a).

Hudson, L., The photographic image, in *Imagery; Current Developments,* ed. P.J. Hampson, D.F. Marks and J.T.E. Richardson, Routledge, 1990(b).

Hudson, L. and Jacot, B., Marriage and fertility in academic life, *Nature,* 229, 531, 1971.

Hudson, L. and Jacot, B., The outsider in science, in *Personality, Cognition and Values,* ed. C. Bagley and G.K. Verma, Macmillan, 1986.

Hudson, L., Johnston, J. and Jacot, B., *Perception and Communication in Academic Life,* Occasional Paper 8, Centre for Research in the Educational Sciences, Edinburgh University, 1972.

Hudson, L., Jacot, B. and Sheldrake, P., *Lieben und Arbeiten; Patterns of Work and Patterns of Marriage,* Occasional Paper 12, Centre for Research in the Educational Sciences, Edinburgh University, 1973.

Hugh-Jones, S., *Edmund Leach 1910-1989,* King's College, Cambridge, 1989.

Hunt, A.J. et al., Changes in sexual behaviour in a large cohort of homosexual men in England and Wales, 1988-9, *British Medical Journal,* 302, 505, 1991.

Jay, B., Portfolio, *Photography,* October 1988.

Jensen, A.R., How much can we boost IQ and scholastic achievement? *Harvard Educational Review,* 39, 32, 1969.

Jones, L.Y., Bad days on Mount Olympus, *The Atlantic,* 37, February 1974.

Joynson, R.B., *The Burt Affair,* Routledge, 1989.

Jung, C.G., *Memories, Dreams, Reflections,* Routledge, 1963.

Kagan, J. and Moss, H.A., *Birth to Maturity,* Wiley, 1962.

Keller, E.F., *Reflections on Gender and Science,* Yale University Press, 1985.

Keynes, J.M., *Essays in Biography,* Hart-Davis, 1951.

Khan, M., *Alienation in Perversions,* Hogarth, 1979.

Kinsey, A.C., Pomeroy, W.B. and Martin, C.E., *Sexual Behavior in the Human Male,* Saunders, 1948.

Kinsey, A.C., Pomeroy, W.B., Martin, C.E. and Gebhard, P.H., *Sexual Behavior in the Human Female,* Saunders, 1953.

Kirschenbaum, H. and Henderson, V.L., *The Carl Rogers Reader,* Constable, 1990.

Koestler, A., *The Sleepwalkers,* Hutchinson, 1959.

Krauss, R. and Livingston, J., *L'Amour Fou,* Arts Council of Great Britain, 1986.

Kuhn, T.S., *The Structure of Scientific Revolutions,* Chicago University Press, 1962.

Kuper, A. and Stone, A., The dream of Irma's injection, *American Journal of Psychiatry,* 139, 1225, 1982.

Lacan, J., *The Four Fundamental Concepts of Psychoanalysis,* ed. J-A. Miller, Hogarth, 1977.

Latour, B. and Woolgar, S., *Laboratory Life*, Sage, 1979.

Leavy, S.A., Introduction to *The Freud Journal of Lou Andreas-Salomé*, Hogarth, 1965.

Leishman, J.B., Introduction to *Rilke, Selected Poems*, Penguin, 1964.

Levenson, R., Intimacy, autonomy and gender, *Journal of the American Academy of Psychoanalysis*, 12, 529, 1984.

Levy, J., Psychobiological implications of bilateral asymmetry, in *Hemisphere Function in the Human Brain*, ed. S.J. Dimond and J.G. Beaumont, Elek, 1974.

Lodge, D., *Nice Work*, Penguin, 1989.

Lucie-Smith, E., *British Poetry Since 1945*, Penguin, 1970.

MacKinnon, D.W., The nature and nurture of creative talent, *American Psychologist*, 17, 484, 1962.

Mackintosh, N.J. and Mascie-Taylor, C.G.N., The IQ question, in *Personality, Cognition and Values*, ed. C. Bagley and G.K. Verma, Macmillan, 1986.

McClelland, D.C., On the dynamics of creative physical scientists, in *Contemporary Approaches to Creative Thinking*, ed. H.E. Gruber, G. Terrell and M. Wertheimer, Atherton, 1962.

McClelland, D.C., The calculated risk, in *Scientific Creativity*, ed. C.W. Taylor, and F. Barron, Wiley, 1963.

McGlone, J., Sex differences in human brain asymmetry: a critical survey, *Behavioral and Brain Sciences*, 3, 215, 1980.

Maddow, B., *Faces*, Chanticleer, 1977.

Magee, B., *The Philosophy of Schopenhauer*, Oxford University Press, 1983.

Mailer, N., *Marilyn*, Grosset & Dunlap, 1973.

Mailer, N., *The Executioner's Song*, Arrow, 1980.

Mant, A., *Leaders We Deserve*, Martin Robertson, 1983.

Marcus, S., *The Other Victorians*, Weidenfeld & Nicolson, 1966.

Marcuse, H., *Eros and Civilization*, Beacon, 1955.

Matanle, I., *Classic Cameras*, Thames & Hudson, 1986.

Matthews, A.M. and Brown, K.H., Retirement as a critical life event, *Research on Aging*, 9, 548, 1987.

Mead, M., *Sex and Temperament*, Morrow, 1935.

Mead, M., *Male and Female*, Morrow, 1949.

Menzies, I.E.P., *The Functioning of Social Systems as a Defence Against Anxiety*, Tavistock Pamphlet 3, Tavistock, 1961.

Millgate, M., *Thomas Hardy*, Oxford University Press, 1985.

Mitchell, J., *Psychoanalysis and Feminism*, Allen Lane, 1974.

Mitscherlich, A., *Society Without Father*, Tavistock, 1969.

Money, J., Two cytogenetic syndromes, *Journal of Psychiatric Research*, 2, 223, 1964.

Money, J. and Ehrhardt, A.A., *Man and Woman; Boy and Girl*, Johns Hopkins University Press, 1972.

Morris, P., Holloway, J. and Noble, J., Research report: gender representation within the British Psychological Society, *The Psychologist*, 3,

408, 1990.

Nyborg, H., Spatial ability in men and women: review and new theory, *Advances in Behaviour Research and Therapy*, 5, 89, 1983.

Nyborg, H., Mathematics, sex hormones, and brain function, *Behavioral and Brain Sciences*, 11, 206, 1988.

Osten, G. von der and Vey, H., *Painting and Sculpture in Germany and the Netherlands, 1500-1600*, Penguin, 1969.

Pafford, J.H.P. (ed.), *The Winter's Tale*, The Arden Edition of the Works of William Shakespeare, Routledge, 1990.

Painter, G.D., *Marcel Proust*, Penguin, 1983.

Regis, E., *Who Got Einstein's Office?*, Penguin, 1989

Rhode, D.L., *Theoretical Perspectives on Sexual Difference*, Yale University Press, 1990.

Roazen, P., *Freud and his Followers*, Knopf, 1975.

Robinson, P.A., *The Sexual Radicals*, Paladin, 1969.

Robinson, P.A., *The Modernization of Sex*, Elek, 1976.

Roe, A., A psychological study of eminent biologists, *Psychological Monographs*, 65, No. 14, 1951.

Roe, A., A psychological study of eminent psychologists and anthropologists and a comparison with biological and physical scientists, *Psychological Monographs*, 67, No. 352, 1953.

Rose, S., Kamin, L. and Lewontin, R.C., *Not in our Genes*, Penguin, 1984.

Rosen, I., Exhibitionism, scopophilia and voyeurism, in *Sexual Deviation*, ed. I. Rosen, Oxford University Press, 1979.

Rosenberg, J.D., *The Darkening Glass*, Routledge, 1963.

Rosenthal, M.K., Sex differences in mother–infant interaction during breast feeding in the neonatal period, *Southern Psychologist*, 2, 3, 1984.

Royal Horticultural Society, *The Rhododendron Handbook*, 1980.

Rutter, M., *Maternal Deprivation Reassessed*, Penguin, 1981.

Rycroft, C., *A Critical Dictionary of Psychoanalysis*, Penguin, 1972.

Rycroft, C., *The Innocence of Dreams*, Hogarth, 1979.

Sampson, A., *The Arms Bazaar*, Hodder & Stoughton, 1977.

Schiebinger, L., *The Mind Has No Sex?* Harvard University Press, 1989.

Schumann, W., *Gemstones of the World*, NAG Press, 1977.

Sears, R.R., Maccoby, E.E. and Levin, H., *Patterns of Child Rearing*, Row, Peterson, 1957.

Serebriakoff, V., *A Mensa Analysis and History*, Hutchinson, 1965.

Shilts, R., *And The Band Played On*, Penguin, 1987.

Simenon, G., in *Writers at Work*, ed. M. Cowley, Secker & Warburg, 1958.

Skinner, B.F., *Walden Two*, Macmillan, 1948.

Skinner, B.F., *Cumulative Record*, Methuen, 1961.

Skinner, B.F., *Particulars of My Life*, Cape, 1976.

Skinner, Q. (ed.), *The Return of Grand Theory in the Human Sciences*, Cambridge University Press, 1985.

Snow, E., Introduction to *Rainer Maria Rilke, New Poems (1908)*, North Point, 1987.

Sontag, S., *On Photography*, Penguin, 1979.
Steiner, G., Review of Hodges' *Alan Turing*, *Sunday Times*, 23 October 1983.
Stern, D., *The Interpersonal World of the Infant*, Basic Books, 1985.
Stern, K., *The Flight from Women*, Allen & Unwin, 1966.
Stewart, J.I.M., *Thomas Hardy*, Longman, 1971.
Stokes, A., *Reflections on the Nude*, Tavistock, 1967.
Stoller, R.J., *Sex and Gender*, Aronson, 1968.
Stoller, R.J., Symbiosis anxiety and the development of masculinity, *Archives of General Psychiatry*, 30, 164, 1974.
Stoller, R.J., *Perversion*, Pantheon, 1975.
Stoller, R.J., *Sexual Excitement*, Pantheon, 1979(a).
Stoller, R.J., The gender disorders, in *Sexual Deviation*, ed. I. Rosen, Oxford University Press, 1979(b).
Stoller, R.J., *Presentations of Gender*, Yale University Press, 1985(a).
Stoller, R.J., *Observing the Erotic Imagination*, Yale University Press, 1985(b).
Storr, A., Isaac Newton, *British Medical Journal*, 291, 1779, 1985(a).
Storr, A., Psychoanalysis and creativity, in *Freud and the Humanities*, ed. P. Horden, Duckworth, 1985(b).
Storr, A., *Solitude*, Collins, 1988.
Sulloway, F.J., *Freud, Biologist of the Mind*, Basic Books, 1979.
Tait, H. (ed.), *Seven Thousand Years of Jewellery*, British Museum, 1986.
Tajfel, H., *Human Groups and Social Categories*, Cambridge University Press, 1981.
Tanner, J.M. *Foetus into Man*, Open Books, 1978.
Van Hasbroeck, P.-H., *Leica*, Sotheby, 1983.
Van Hasbroeck, P.-H., *150 Classic Cameras*, Sotheby, 1989.
Weinberg, M.S., *Sex Research*, Oxford University Press, 1976.
Westfall, R.S., Newton and the fudge factor, *Science*, 179, 751, 1973.
Whiting, J.W.M., Kluckhohn, R. and Anthony, A., The function of male initiation ceremonies at puberty, in *Readings in Social Psychology*, ed. E.E. Maccoby, T.M. Newcomb and E.L. Hartley, Methuen, 1966.
Wilson, C., *Edward Weston Nudes*, Aperture, 1977.
Wilson, G., *The Great Sex Divide*, Peter Owen, 1989.
Winnicott, D.W., *Playing and Reality*, Tavistock, 1971.
Wisdom, J.O., *The Unconscious Origin of Berkeley's Philosophy*, Hogarth, 1953.
Witelson, S.F., Neuroanatomical sex differences, *Behavioral and Brain Sciences*, 11, 215, 1988.
Wittgenstein, L., *Tractatus Logico-Philosophicus*, Routledge & Kegan Paul, 1922.
Wittgenstein, L., *Philosophical Investigations*, trans. G.E.M. Anscombe, Blackwell, 1958.
Wolpert, L. and Richards, A., *A Passion for Science*, Oxford University Press, 1988.

Woodcock, A. and Davis, M., *Catastrophe Theory*, Penguin, 1980.
Wright, E., *Psychoanalytic Criticism*, Methuen, 1984.
Zucker, B., *Gems and Jewels*, Thames & Hudson, 1984.
Zuckerman, H., *Scientific Elite*, Free Press, 1977.